# F R A U D

*Books by E. J. Kahn, Jr.*

Fraud

The Boston Underground Gourmet (with Joseph P. Kahn)

The First Decade

Harvard: Through Change and Through Storm

The Separated People

A Reporter in Micronesia

The World of Swope

The Stragglers

A Reporter Here and There

The Big Drink

The Merry Partners

The Peculiar War

Who, Me?

The Voice

McNair: Educator of an Army

G.I. Jungle

The Army Life

# FRAUD

*The United States Postal Inspection Service and some of the fools and knaves it has known*

by E. J. KAHN, JR.



HARPER & ROW, PUBLISHERS

1817

NEW YORK EVANSTON SAN FRANCISCO
LONDON

Chapters 6, 8, and 16 originally appeared, in slightly different form, in *The New Yorker.*

 For information address Harper & Row, Publishers, Inc., 10 East 53rd Street, New York, N.Y. 10022. Published simultaneously in Canada by Fitzhenry & Whiteside Limited, Toronto.

FIRST EDITION

*Designed by Sidney Feinberg*

Library of Congress Cataloging in Publication Data

Kahn, Ely Jacques, 1916–

Fraud: the United States Postal Inspection Service and some of the fools and knaves it has known.

1. United States. Postal Inspection Service.
2. Fraud--United States. I. Title.

HE6457.K3 364.1'32 72–9757

ISBN 0–06–012242–0

For David and Lexy

# Contents

# Introduction

In the long two-hundred-year history of the United States Postal Service, there have been, up to this time, only two comprehensive accounts in book form of the history and function of the Postal Inspection Service—the law-enforcement, internal audit, and security arm of the Postal Service. It was therefore with pleasure that we recently agreed to make available to E. J. Kahn, Jr., historical data and hundreds of reports and case histories of concluded investigations, so that he might chronicle, without restriction, something of the history and work of this Service. Particularly do we feel that the public interest is served through gaining a greater awareness of the infinite number of fraudulent schemes practiced through criminal misuse of the postal system. We are grateful that an author of Mr. Kahn's stature conceived the thought of writing such a book and undertook to do so.

The book thus written represents the author's own evaluation and independent assessment of our procedures and work performance. The characterizations, comparisons, and conclusions are his own. On his request, he was put in touch with many of the Postal Inspectors who investigated the cases which Mr. Kahn chose to include in his book, in order that he might obtain details not normally reflected in official reports.

While only a relatively few examples of the work product of this

Service are included, they are fully representative of the thousands of investigations made annually, and in my opinion reflect accurately the dedication, integrity, and professionalism of the men and women of the Postal Inspection Service, past and present, whose labors have earned it the proud reputation it enjoys today.

The Postal Inspection Service is dedicated to serving the Postmaster General of the United States in carrying out his responsibility to maintain the integrity and security of the United States Postal Service—the greatest communication and transportation system the world has yet known—and to enforcing the laws which protect its facilities and employees and the American public it daily serves.

In discharging our responsibility to maintain the inviolability of the United States Mails and the postal system, we daily receive the unstinting cooperation and assistance of the total law-enforcement community, including all other federal agencies and local law-enforcement groups. Additionally, the results of the evidence developed by Postal Inspectors in their investigations would mean little in terms of effective law enforcement if it were not for the highly professional prosecutive efforts of United States Attorneys and their Assistants throughout the United States and its possessions. I welcome, therefore, the opportunity this book presents to gratefully acknowledge the assistance the Postal Inspection Service receives from the law-enforcement community throughout the United States.

—William J. Cotter
Chief Postal Inspector

# Author's Note

Not long ago, at the age of seven, the youngest of five boys in whose upbringing I have been privileged to share wrote a letter to the President of the United States. The lad had sent part of his easy-earned allowance, it seemed, to a mail-order mountebank peddling gold bricks or something of the sort, and now he was grumbling to the White House that inasmuch as he had never received his forty-seven-jewel wrist alarm clock or whatever he had lavished a dollar on, somebody—very probably a postal clerk—must have stolen his money from the mails. Within a fortnight or so, the boy's mother received a visit from a clean-cut, polite, and businesslike man who identified himself as a Postal Inspector and said he was investigating a complaint from our household.

My wife was surprised that a busy federal agency should take the time to check up on what was obviously kids' stuff. I was not surprised. For some two decades I had followed, from a respectful distance, the multiple activities of the Postal Inspection Service, and I knew with what diligence its operatives pursue any inquiry, however innocent at first look, that seems to come within their purview. Since there are few aspects of contemporary American life that do not at least peripherally involve the use—honest or dishonest—of the mails, the purview is almost limitless. My introduction to this relatively little-known fraternity of law-enforcement officers came about accidentally. An upstate New York woman who had read some articles of mine in *The New Yorker* suggested that I might be interested in doing a piece for that magazine's "Annals of Crime" department about a Rochester chap who had been convicted of mail fraud. The idea sounded good, and I went up to Rochester on my investigative own. Thus I came to know Charles A. Miller, the Postal Inspector who handled that particular case.

Like quite a few Inspectors with twenty or more years in the Service, Miller comes from a postal family. His father was superintendent of mails at Johnstown, Pennsylvania. The senior Miller would regularly bring visiting Inspectors home to dinner, and the son would listen bug-eyed to their tales—often understandably embellished—of deception and derring-do. He decided while still in his teens to join their rakish ranks. At that time, all Inspectors were recruited from the postal service; and they were supposed to have had enough experience at mail-handling and other postal work—three years at the minimum—to be able to cope with mishandling when it occurred. Miller got his start as a substitute clerk in Johnstown during summer vacations from college.

It is indicative of how much the Postal Inspection Service, the nation's oldest law-enforcement agency, has changed in the last quarter of a century—reflecting, no doubt, the changing impact of violence on the American scene—that nowadays most Inspectors carry guns at all times. When Miller was starting in at Rochester, he generally left his weapon at his office over weekends. One of the few occasions when he felt in need of it was so unusual that he remembered it in sharp detail years afterward. He was at home on a Sunday afternoon when he got a call from a bartender at a downtown hotel. The bartender thought he might have just served drinks to a fellow who will here be known as Joe Esposito, and he thought the Inspector might like to know about it.

Miller was interested indeed. Esposito was a patriarch among convicted forgers, a veritable paradigm of recidivism; in addition to various apprehensions by state and municipal policemen and other federal agents, Postal Inspectors alone had arrested him no less than three times for mail theft. Recently out of prison, he was wanted again, and Miller had sent photographs of him to the security officers of the banks and hotels in his bailiwick. On learning from the bartender that someone resembling Esposito was in town, Miller decided to move fast. The man did not live in Rochester, and it was hard to believe he had come there to visit the museum or hear the symphony; he was more probably engaged in the hit-and-run business for which he was celebrated. Esposito had many unattractive habits, some verging on the homicidal, so on his way to the hotel Miller prudently stopped off at his office and buckled on his gun. When he arrived, he learned that his quarry had not only left the bar but, perhaps disconcerted by the intensity of the bartender's glances at him, had also checked out. There was a Greyhound bus terminal just across a park from the hotel. The Inspector hustled over there and spotted his man, waiting in a long line to board a bus to Albany. Miller queued up behind him, wondering if he had the right person. "It's hard to identify a guy from a two- or three-year-old photo to the point of being certain enough to touch him on the shoulder in a crowd on a Sunday afternoon and haul him in for questioning," Miller said later. "Before I pick up anybody, I like to have it nailed. I would hate to accuse somebody falsely. But the fellow was getting close to the door of the bus, and I knew I had to do something. So I touched him on the shoulder, showed him my badge, and said, 'Joe, come over to the post office. I want to talk to you.' He asked me who I thought he was, and I said Joe Esposito, which was who he turned out to be, all right, and he said he wasn't Joe anybody and told me to shove off. So I had to pull my gun out. I felt embarrassed. I felt like everybody in Rochester was looking at me, playing cops and robbers like that."

The increase in violence notwithstanding, Postal Inspectors are not often involved in shootouts, though they are all proficient in the use of firearms. Miller has never fired a gun at any human target. Rochester saw its last of him, on a permanent basis, when he moved to Washington in 1961, to become a fraud specialist in the Service, and subsequently the head of its criminal investigation branch. If Charles Miller, who has just retired, seems to figure in a disproportionate number of the fraud cases recounted in this book, the explanation is simple: He was the first Postal Inspector I ever met, the one I know best, and one whose long government career happened to be spent mainly in the investigation of the kinds of cases that I seem to find most fascinating. But—in large part through Chief Inspector William J. Cotter's genial intercession—I have also become acquainted with quite a few of Miller's colleagues. Among them, they have figured in literally thousands of criminal investigations. The files of the Inspection Service contained at last report more than 27,000 cubic feet of paper, and while talking to Inspectors about their work one gets the impression that they have committed most of this to their retentive memories. Among the Inspectors I should particularly like to thank for their patience and cooperation while I was compiling this book—and should like at the same time to absolve of any responsibility for whatever inadvertent errors of fact may have crept into it—are Chief Inspector Cotter and Inspectors Charles C. Cheezum, Karl Fein, Kenneth H. Fletcher, Elbridge M. Hamm, Jr., Elmer L. Jacobson, Charles J. Lerable, Frank J. Nemic, Jr., John D. Tarpey, and Leslie G. Turner. And an especially grateful touch on the shoulder to my friend Charlie Miller.

—E. J. K.

*New York, N.Y.*
July 1, 1973

# 1. Ben Franklin's Boys

The Postal Inspection Service is the oldest law-enforcement agency in the United States and an organization unique on earth; but few people who have had no direct experience with it are even aware that it exists. In parts of the underworld it is extremely well known, mainly because of its consistent effectiveness; year in and out, 98 per cent of the criminal cases it brings to trial result in convictions. (A comparable recent figure for the Federal Bureau of Investigation was 95.4 per cent.) The thus understandable reluctance of many crooks to have a showdown with the Inspection Service was illustrated by an incident that occurred not long ago in a small rural establishment that was part general store, part post office. Some burglars broke into it. They were not particularly worried about the local police, but the Postal Inspection Service was something else again. So they were careful to touch nothing in the postal section of the place, and on their way out they drew a line across the floor in chalk and scribbled on the postal side of it, "Inspectors, we didn't cross this line."

Like authors who particularly relish plugs from professionals in their field, Postal Inspectors are pleased by accolades from pros in *theirs;* a favorite one is a statement attributed to the late Dutch Schultz, a criminal of solid standing who once declared that "anybody who robs a post office is an idiot, and I don't want idiots working for me." (The confidence that crooks have in the mails, though perhaps exaggerated, is touching: One bank robber mailed $8,930 in loot to his wife and was so certain it would arrive safely that he insured the package for a mere $100.) Some criminals seem more familiar with the work of the Inspection Service than do other criminal investigators. The present Postal Inspector in Charge of the New York City field office, Elbridge M. Hamm, Jr., comes from Maine. His father, now retired, had always wanted to be an Inspector himself but settled for being Supervisor of Mails at Bangor. The son, who had accordingly known about the Service most of his life, was working his way through the University of Maine as a part-time policeman when he overheard his chief one day wondering how he was going to handle a case that had come up involving someone's trying to extort money through the mails. When the rookie cop suggested that his chief consult the Postal Inspection Service, it turned out that his boss had no idea what it was.

There are more than eighty federal crimes called "postal offenses." Beyond that, Postal Inspectors, because postal operations and mail deliveries cover so much ground, often find themselves in a position to obtain and pass along information useful to other federal, and to local, law-enforcement agents. Inspectors came up with some of the evidence that was instrumental in establishing the identity of the assassins of President Kennedy and of Martin Luther King. One reason for the general lack of knowledge about what the Service does, though, is that until fairly recently, unlike some other law-enforcement agencies, it traditionally shunned public notice. Its operatives were often called the Silent Investigators, and when they helped solve an attention-getting crime—they were largely responsible for the convictions of, among others, Charles Ponzi and Jimmy Hoffa; and they conducted interrogations of both Billy the Kid and Billy Sol Estes—they didn't expect to receive any personal, or even institutional, credit. In the late 1930s, when the F.B.I. was a household word, a fledgling Postal Inspector was assigned to his first case, the pursuit of a man widely wanted for selling forged Social Security cards. When the young Inspector succeeded, just about single-handedly, in apprehending the culprit, there was a good deal about this in the press. To his dismay, however, he was mentioned simply as "a federal agent with a passion for anonymity." It was a passion he had not realized until then he was expected to embrace. The Postal Inspection Service no longer covets anonymity, but its employees cannot escape their agency's long tradition of reticence. Recently, an Inspector in Oklahoma City worked almost full-time for eighteen months helping the Securities and Exchange Commission expose a $200 million stock fraud, but when the news of this particular defalcation was made public, nowhere in it was there a mention of his role in the investigation.

Criminals are often known by their *modus operandi.* So are criminal investigators. Postal Inspectors differ from F.B.I. agents in a number of respects. The Inspectors, by and large, have more latitude and independence. The F.B.I. generally espouses what is called a lead-system approach to most cases; an agent here will dig into one aspect of it, an agent there into another. The Inspection Service prefers, on the whole, what is called an X-case approach; a single Inspector is assigned principal responsibility for an investigation and (with assistance from his colleagues as requested) may travel to other parts of the country, or in major cases even out of it, until he has completed his mission. The F.B.I. has operatives stationed all over the world—some of them assigned to American embassies under bland titles like "legal attaché"—but the Postal Inspection Service has no personnel permanently assigned to foreign posts. However, its operatives get around. Inspector Charles Miller once enjoyed a stimulating few days in Copenhagen while working on a pornography case with widespread international ramifications. Inspector John Davis found himself in the town of Saint Peter Port on the Isle of Guernsey, in the English Channel. He was looking into the Bank of Sark, a gossamer institution that a group of Florida men had dreamed up as the ostensible source of $150 million worth of loan commitments, all actually worthless, that they made to hundreds of corporations and individuals, who permitted themselves en masse to be fleeced of millions out of blind faith in the Bank of Sark's existence. (The promoters of this scheme would deposit alleged drafts on that bank in other banks, as proof of their financial stability.) Davis discovered the Bank of Sark to be nothing more than a one-room mail drop with a single employee—a seventeen-year-old Guernsey girl, a retired barmaid, who had no idea that the outfit whose mail she was circuitously forwarding, en route to a Florida bank, purported to have assets of $72.5 million. The scheme rolled along merrily for more than two years, coming to an abrupt halt early in 1972 when twenty-two individuals and a solid-sounding corporation they had set up in the Bahamas, the Trans-Continental Casualty Insurance Company, Ltd., were indicted on seventy-six counts of fraud and conspiracy.

Inspector Charles J. Lerable, for his peripatetic part, traveled to Germany and Italy to obtain vital evidence against the proprietor of a California gun shop whose eyebrow-raising activities earned him an appearance before a Congressional Committee conducting hearings on firearms legislation and who had advertised widely in publications like *Shotgun News* that he had great buys to offer in Colt 1860 .44-caliber cap-and-ball percussion revolvers and "rare S.S. Walther P-38 pistols with a small S.S. death's head stamped on the pistols in red blood." The gun man's thousands of bargain-hunters ended up with nothing to show for their patronage save canceled checks, which of course constituted useful evidence when their deceiver was finally centered in Lerable's sights.

By the standards of federal bureaucracies, the Postal Inspection Service is quite small. Altogether, there are fewer than 1,600 Inspectors, scattered from Puerto Rico to Hawaii. (The F.B.I. has more than a thousand agents in New York City and Long Island alone.) But in their silent way they get a good deal done. In 1972, for example, they undertook over 90,000 criminal investigations and recorded 18,972 arrests, with 16,316 ensuing convictions. Their principal function is to protect and enhance the integrity of the United States Postal Service and the mail it transports, a formidable task; the Postal Service now handles nearly 90 billion pieces of mail a year, just about as much as the rest of the world combined. That is a lot of mail, but at the same time it should perhaps be noted that much mail-order fraud results from the fact that most Americans, for all their gripes about junk mail, actually receive far less mail of any sort than they would apparently like to have and thus welcome mail from any source; the average American gets only one first-class letter every day. Postal Inspectors, it should also be noted, are not permitted to open anybody else's first-class mail, whatever the circumstances, unless they have a court order authorizing them to do so. This worthy libertarian restriction has been imposed on them throughout their more than two hundred years of existence, under a variety of names—Postal Agents, Post Office Inspectors, and, since 1954, Postal Inspectors. Because of their seniority in the federal investigative area, Inspectors have been transferred over the years to get other investigative agencies under way—the Intelligence Division of the Internal Revenue Service, for one, as well as the Investigative and Security Branch of the State Department and the Investigative Branch of the Civil Aeronautics Board. During the Second World War, Postal Inspectors further set up the armed forces' postal services, and 240 Inspectors were shifted to the military services to supervise their worldwide operations.

In a sense, one can trace the history of the Service all the way back to 1737, when the British colonial authorities designated Benjamin Franklin postmaster at Philadelphia and enjoined him with "regulating the several post offices and bringing the postmasters to account." Franklin was concerned, as his successors are today, with maintaining the security of the mails and keeping tabs on individuals entrusted with postal funds. (It was easier then; there were seventy-five Postmasters in America, as opposed to 1972's thirty-five thousand.) He was a conscientious administrator. In 1753, he visited every post office in the country except the one at Charleston, South Carolina. That same year, Franklin was promoted to Deputy Postmaster General, a post he kept until the eve of the Revolution. He was fired in 1774, while he was in England protesting, of all things, the Stamp Act. The following year, though, the Continental Congress appointed Franklin *its* Postmaster General, and he named William Goddard "Surveyor of the Post Office." Goddard's Surveyors (among them the literate Noah Webster, who was assigned in 1793 to apprehend the villain robbing the posts in Connecticut) became Special Agents in 1801, and in 1830 the Post Office Department established an Office of Instructions and Rail Depredations, whose director, according to *his* instructions, "communicates the decisions of the Postmaster General on questions referred to him by postmasters and others, concerning the construction of post office laws and regulations; directs under his order, prosecutions for their violation and mail robberies; attends to all cases of mail losses and depredations, and the tracing of lost letters. Connected with this duty is that of corresponding with the agents of the Department, making out their instructions, and examining their reports, etc."

So finally there was an office through which all the agents functioned. And they functioned in singular fashion. A striking aspect of their role was, and is, that, unlike postal investigators in other countries, those in the United States have full powers of arrest. In Great Britain, postal investigators have Scotland Yard men attached to them, to whom they must defer when actually apprehending a suspect; the United States stands alone among nations in that its postal investigative agency is a full-fledged law-enforcement body. In the nineteenth century, there were plenty of depredations for the Inspectors to busy themselves with, and as they roamed the West, tilting with mail-train robbers (and sometimes fighting Indians), they became ubiquitous figures. (Until 1973, a Pony Express rider was romantically and sentimentally used to decorate the badges they all carry as credentials; then, in a somewhat prosaic gesture of modernization, an eagle was substituted.) The Inspectors fell short, though, of being universally beloved. Some got deeply involved in partisan politics; one old-time Inspector engaged in a battle at a polling place of such egregious savagery that for a while all Postal Inspectors were known as "ear-biters." The Tombstone, Arizona, *Epitaph* saw fit to observe in 1888 that "The special inspector of the postal service has been visiting Tombstone and Bisbee during the past week, making himself obnoxious to everybody with whom he came in contact." And at about the same time an anonymous critic of the Service declared, with heavy-handed humor, "A typical Post Office Inspector is a man past middle age—spare, wrinkled, intelligent, cold, passive, non-committal; with eyes like a codfish, polite in contact but at the same time unresponsive; calm, and as damnably composed as a concrete post or a plaster of Paris cast; a petrification with a beard of feldspar and without charm or the friendly germ; minus passion or a sense of humor. Happily they never reproduce and all of them finally go to Hell."

Among less jaundiced observers of their work, Postal Inspectors have been considered a valuable national asset because they can be called in to tackle almost any kind of crime. Their versatility derives from legislation passed by Congress in 1872—Section 1341 of Title 18 of the United States Code. Designed originally to frustrate a rash of swindles that erupted after the Civil War (one of its Congressional sponsors declared: "Thus all through the country thousands of innocent and unsophisticated people, knowing nothing about the ways of these city thieves and robbers, are continually fleeced and robbed, and the mails are made use of for the purpose of aiding them in their nefarious designs"), the statute has been but slightly revised over the years. It has read substantially as follows:

**Section 1341: Frauds and Swindles**

Whoever, having devised or intending to devise any scheme or artifice to defraud, or for obtaining money or property by means of false or fraudulent pretenses, representations, or promises, or to sell, dispose of, loan, exchange, alter, give away, distribute, supply, or furnish or procure for unlawful use any counterfeit or spurious coin, obligation,

> security, or other article, or anything represented to be or intimated or held out to be such counterfeit or spurious article, for the purpose of executing such scheme or artifice or attempting so to do, places in any post office or authorized depository for mail matter, any matter or thing whatever to be sent or delivered by the Post Office Department, or takes or receives therefrom, any such matter or thing, or knowingly causes to be delivered by mail according to the direction thereon, or at the place at which it is directed to be delivered by the person to whom it is addressed, any such matter or thing, shall be fined not more than $1,000 or imprisoned not more than five years, or both.

A companion statute, Section 3005 of Title 39, U.S. Code, provides no criminal sanctions but does permit the Postmaster General to withhold mail deliveries to any firm or individual soliciting money by mail on the basis of false representations. These actions are prosecuted by attorneys in the Law Department of the Postal Service, on the basis of evidence gathered by Inspectors.

Considering that there are many counts in some mail-fraud indictments (there can be one for every single piece of mail involved in a scheme), Section 1341 is a law not to be taken lightly. The government has found this umbrellalike statute useful in widely varying circumstances. It proved serviceable for the apprehension and prosecution, for instance, of a Saint Louis man who, with nefarious designs on the locker room of a men's club in that city, worked out a scheme for obtaining a master list of the combinations of the locks. Rightly wary about using the mails, he ordered the list by phone and asked to have it delivered by United Parcel Service, but he slipped up and had it sent to a post office box, and that was enough to get him on mail-fraud charges. Section 1341 proved equally useful when it came to halting the much larger-scale activities of, to cite just another of many examples, the Black Hand gangs that flourished ruthlessly just after the turn of the century. They extorted money from the European immigrants who settled in industrial communities like Chicago and Gary, Indiana; the Black Handers practically ran some of the towns they terrorized. They would send their victims threatening letters decorated with such ornaments of their trade as skulls and crossbones. When people neglected to pay up for the "protection" their oppressors were supposed to furnish them, they were often tortured, or had their homes bombed. Local police officials were ill equipped to curb them (and were sometimes in cahoots with them), but because they often used the mails Postal Inspectors could go after them, and between 1910 and 1921 they arrested hundreds of Black Handers, on the grounds of false representation. Numerous convictions were obtained, but then the Supreme Court brought the campaign against the extortionists to a temporary halt. It ruled that if you told a shopkeeper you'd blow up his shop unless he gave you some money, you were not making a false representation provided you really *intended* to blow it up—and the Black Handers had been demonstrably not fooling. It was a Supreme Court of strict constructionists. The upshot of that decree was the passage by Congress of a new law to plug the loophole; it is now a federal crime to send a threatening letter demanding money or other things of value in any circumstances. The Mafia has lately been finding the mail-fraud statute an equally annoying snag to smooth operations. Postal Inspectors work with all of the Organized Crime Strike Force groups established in 1972 by the Department of Justice, and in the fiscal year of 1972, more than one hundred indictments obtained against organized crime figures involved charges of mail fraud. When Salvatore ("Bill") Bonanno, the son of Joseph ("Joe Bananas") Bonanno and the leading character in Gay Talese's *Honor Thy Father*, went to prison in 1971, it was not because he had been caught in the front lines of a gang war, but because Postal Inspectors had caught him misusing somebody else's credit card.

The United States Postal Service is a huge operation, with about 680,000 employees and a gross annual business of $7,884,188,000. From the very inception of the Inspection Service, it has been one of its duties to conduct operational and financial audits of all post offices. The Service now numbers among its people nearly two hundred highly trained Inspector-Auditors, many of whom are

C.P.A.s. In a spot check not long ago of one area where some new mail-sorting machines had been installed, the Service discovered that initially 8.9 per cent of the mail thus being sorted was being missorted. Audits carried out at large post offices during just one year resulted in modifications of procedures that all at once were supposed to improve postal service and to reduce operating costs by $25.5 million. In the 1972 fiscal year, the Service conducted 17,868 audits of post offices, and in 2,151 instances it found some deficiencies in revenue.

Alas, not all these were inadvertent. Eighty-seven postal employees were arrested for embezzlement that year. Even though there had been a 17.1 per cent drop in the number of arrests of postal employees for theft, rifling, or other criminal mistreatment of the mails, the total number of arrests for such crimes nonetheless stood at a robust 1,396. Among the culprits were a New Jersey Star Route driver caught with nearly a truckload of tape recorders and stereo equipment that he had elected to deliver not to the proper addressees but to himself; and a Mississippi postmaster who'd been using the mails to submit $32,000 worth of false claims for Blue Shield and Blue Cross benefits.

The temptation to steal from the mails is strong, and postal employees have been known to commit such dastardly deeds as to filch funds addressed to charitable organizations and to take unto themselves such items of inestimable value as tickets to Michigan–Northwestern football games. It somewhat cheers the Inspectors who uncover distressing mischief of this sort to be able to reflect that, considering the vast numbers of postal employees who lay hands upon the mails, only a comparative few succumb to such temptation; and that about one-third of all internal crimes they deal with are committed by postal employees with less than six months on the job—men and women conceivably too new to have become imbued with the old team spirit. Resignedly, the Inspectors have come up with special devices for keeping tabs on their own people. One is a tiny beeper that can transmit radio signals for miles. If a truck driver is suspected of dumping off packages along his route—for a confederate to retrieve and dispose of—a beeper can be put in a test package enclosed in his load; and if radio-equipped Inspectors stationed along his route fail to hear the reassuring beep as he rolls past, they can be fairly certain he is up to some shenanigans.

Much of the internal policing of post office functions is handled by a group, now over two hundred strong, once known as Depredation Details but now as Special Investigators. These agents are not technically Postal Inspectors, but they come under the jurisdiction of the Service, and in the last few years they have had their hands full, inasmuch as they deal not merely with rascally postal clerks but also with the far larger number of folk who rob mailmen or pilfer mail from postboxes and residences. The federal courts have long ruled that it is a federal crime to steal mail even after it is thus delivered, so the Inspection Service must be concerned with *that.* For one thing, there is a question of pride involved: People are always claiming that checks due them have been lost while in postal custody, and the Inspection Service likes to have it made clear, by apprehending the individuals who actually rifle the boxes, that it was outsiders who caused the trouble. This can be a tedious process; more than 700 million United States Treasury checks and state and local welfare checks are distributed annually through the mails, and the Inspection Service gets more than 200,000 complaints a year about missing ones.

About 13 per cent of the time and effort of the Inspection Service, however, is now devoted to mail fraud, because of which the trusting American public is now the poorer by close to $500 million a year (though devious segments of it are by the same token the richer). In the 1972 fiscal year, the Service investigated 9,922 reported frauds, and Inspectors either recovered or prevented the additional squandering of what they have reckoned at $73 million. There are infinite varieties of mail-fraud schemes. A not necessarily complete list of categories drawn up a while ago by the Service included advance fees, check kiting, unordered C.O.D. parcels, falsified contest entries, phony coupon redemption plans, credit-card frauds, delinquent debtor schemes, fictitious classified directories, endless chain-referral selling plans, alleged business opportunities, chain letters, missing-heir swindles, false financial statements, numbers rackets and lucky charms, home-improvement frauds, investments, supposed job opportunities, mortgage-loan and debt-consolidation schemes, phony manuscript- and song-publishing companies, matrimonial swindles, numismatic and philatelic swindles, real estate (improved and unimproved), shady correspondence schools and diploma mills, fake charity solicitations, and dubious work-at-home schemes.

Postal Inspectors sometimes say jokingly nowadays, among themselves, that because of inflation no mail-fraud case in which less than a million dollars has changed hands can be prosecuted; but in practice many of the matters to which they address themselves seem quite petty from a fiscal standpoint—the case of one man, for instance, who received not a cent for his underhanded efforts. He merely tried to kill his mother-in-law, in whose will he did not figure, by mailing her a poisoned pecan pie. Then there was a chap who got his kicks from applying for jobs under false names and with false credentials. What he said about himself in his imaginative résumés sounded so impressive that companies regularly paid his expenses to travel around the country for employment interviews. Some frauds are not only petty but uncommonly mean. There are people who cull obituary pages and send trashy C.O.D. packages to survivors of the deceased, accurately figuring that the next of kin will assume that their departed loved ones had ordered the merchandise before they died and will unquestioningly pay for it. This is a nasty variation of an old fraud scheme: A criminal representing himself as, say, the Bureau of Unclaimed Merchandise will send out thousands of letters at a clip informing the recipients that by filling out an enclosed card and remitting, say, $4.60, they will be shipped forthwith "Parcel No. 391," which is awaiting their claim. Sometimes crime is compounded upon crime. A man was not long ago convicted of mail fraud for obtaining merchandise with worthless checks at the very time he was in an Alabama prison serving a fifteen-year sentence for forgery.

Mail frauds run the gamut from innocence to sophistication. No one can even begin to guess how many Americans have fallen for modest advertisements that say something like "Earn up to $1.68 an hour sewing baby shoes in your home." That particular come-on drew 200,000 responses. There was a catch, of course: At the same time that a nonreturnable registration fee of six dollars was sent in by 60,000 baby-shoe prospects, every one of them also had to submit a trial pair of shoes. Precious few registrants met the standards retroactively prescribed. Over the years, sewing- and knitting-machine frauds have been legion. The victim signs a contract agreeing to buy a machine, and expects to pay for it by creating men's shorts, or whatever, which the promoters have sort of agreed to purchase. By the time the shorts are sewn, the promoters have long since taken their money and run—like as not by paying $50 for a machine that normally retails at $80, getting the victim to buy it for $380 on a time-payment basis, and then selling the sales contract to a loan company for $290. That gives the promoters a cash profit of $240 per machine and leaves it up to the victims and the loan company to argue over who owes whom what. The loan company usually has more muscle and better lawyers.

There is a cyclical aspect to postal-fraud crimes, as though everybody gets the same wicked idea at the same time. One year there will be a great flurry of scurrilous work-at-home schemes, another year of some other monkey business. Criminals are sensitive to the society they live in. With the general public keenly interested in the environment, a man in California made out nicely by selling a phony directory of businesses and other organizations specializing in ecology. Directories are a perennial source of illegal funds, and so are other special-interest publications. One man made half a million dollars in nine years by persuading businesses to take advertising space in a magazine that was supposed to circulate among police officers; the gimmick here was that the advertisers would receive handsome-looking but worthless wallet cards that would theoretically keep them from getting a summons if they were stopped for speeding.

Chain letters are mysteriously cyclical. They flourish in abundance every three or four years. The last big year was 1970. In August, 1969, the Inspection Service had only 97 chain-letter frauds under investigation, but by January, 1970, there were 559. Nobody knows why. All chain-letter frauds are variations of the same theme: You put your name at the bottom of a list and when it reaches the top you'll be rich. One trouble is that all the names above your own, and those of your concurrent victims, may belong to the original forgers of the chain. Several New England Postal Inspectors were especially outraged to discover that the man behind one chain-letter fraud was a rural mail carrier who used only one real name—his own. All the other names on his list were those of people on his route who had died and to whom there was no danger of his having to hand over any letters. One chain-letter crook, posing as a grieving father of a Vietnam casualty, tried to entice into his web names he got from the *Army Times*—the next of kin of authentic Vietnam casualties. All the names above theirs on his chain letters were aliases of his own.

Chain letters are closely related, as far as the Inspection Service is concerned, to lotteries, which though condoned and even encouraged by several states are illegal under the postal law; that is why the states that have them cannot sell chances through the mails (although early in 1973 the Congress had some bills up for consideration that would permit the use of the mails in state lotteries). Not long ago, a postal clerk in Montgomery, Alabama, was puzzled when a man who had never been known to exchange letters at a rate much higher than the one-a-day national average began turning up with hundreds of thousands of them for mailing. The clerk jotted down the license number of his car and turned it over to the nearest Postal Inspector; in due course customs officials seized a converted Air Force bomber that was smuggling 125,000 West Indies Hospital Sweepstakes letters in from Haiti and Jamaica. On another occasion, when Postal Inspectors seized about 100,000 pieces of lottery mail, they disposed of it by selling the stuff to a paper-processing company for $23.04. Then they dutifully remitted the proceeds to the only American recipient of a windfall from that particular gamble—the United States Treasury.

In 1873, a few years after the postal obscenity law was passed, the Postmaster General, under Congressional pressure, took on, as an honorary, unpaid Inspector, a dry-goods salesman from Connecticut named Anthony Comstock, who soon became a zealous crusader against vice, so eager to make his own standards of propriety universal that he was something of an embarrassment to the Service. Nearly everybody wanted to get rid of him, but since he had never been on the payroll he couldn't be removed from it, and he wore his badge proudly until his death in 1915, all the while flailing away against sin. Despite its misgivings about Comstock's activities, the Service has inherited some of his gung-ho righteousness, and it still serves as a national watchdog against mail-order obscenity and pornography. This is a confused area at best, since few people agree on what is obscene and what is not. Some admirers of the Service, for instance, deplore its having been involved in the investigation that led to Ralph Ginzburg's prosecution for peddling an erotic magazine that was tame by comparison to many publications being openly circulated at the time, in 1971, that he went to prison. By then, there had been a notable drop in complaints by his fellow citizens about receiving unsolicited and allegedly obscene material—from 284,766 in the fiscal year of 1970 to 73,003 in 1971. The diminution was in part attributable to a law enacted by Congress on February 1, 1971, under the terms of which people have the right to have their names put on a list of individuals who don't want to get any such mail; distributors of it can incur severe criminal and civil penalties for ignoring the list. There are now more than 600,000 names on it. The largest number live in California, with Ohio and Pennsylvania next in order and New York only fifth. New Yorkers are apparently broader-minded than many of their fellow citizens.

In 1971, also, no less than 436 Americans were convicted of taking part in credit-card frauds. As the use of such cards has multiplied, so has the misuse of them, and this now occupies a considerable amount of Inspection Service time, not to mention even more of the time of the private security forces now perforce maintained by the credit-card companies themselves—investigators who often work closely with the Inspectors, who come into the picture, of course, because the mails are used for both sending out the cards and sending out the bills for purchases charged to them. It is as often from these private investigators as from the victims themselves that the Inspection Service first learns about credit-card crimes. Some of these crimes are comparatively innocuous: A man who was angry at a policeman who had twice stopped him for speeding avenged himself by using phony credit cards to order all sorts of things in his tormentor's name, and the puzzled cop found himself in receipt of, among other unsolicited gifts, an Iranian rug, sixteen Maine lobsters, the deeds to two lots in Honolulu, and twenty-five poplar trees. Some credit-card crimes are on a larger scale. A federal judge in Los Angeles sentenced an Alhambra, California, man named James L. Stockwell to three years in prison as penance for a two-year spree in the course of which he defrauded twenty-five credit-card companies of $175,000. Stockwell had been only a minor hoodlum until be became aware of the magic properties of credit cards; enriched through them, he achieved high entrepreneurial status among the topless and bottomless bars of Southern California, and at the time of his arrest he was trying to organize a trade union among some fourteen hundred exposed young women who worked in them. One credit-card case that took months to unravel involved a ring of long-haul trucking companies and their drivers, who traveled from coast to coast paying for their fuel, food, and lodging with stolen cards. They also stole license plates, which made them harder to catch.

Credit-card crimes, however reprehensible, rarely result in injuries or deaths. Bombs are something else again, and the flurry of letter-bomb scares (and explosions) in 1972 proved to be one of the Service's most critical and exasperating problems. Even in an ordinary year, it conducts close to a thousand investigations of postal-related bomb incidents, real or threatened. When their fabricators are caught, it is sometimes due to pure luck. Two Inspectors on the West Coast were poring over some known handwriting specimens in a run-of-the-mill stock-fraud case when one of them spotted a sample remarkably similar to the handwriting of an unknown person who'd been sending letters to a department store threatening to blow it up. A man who telephoned the New York Police Department, warning it that a bomb was going to be detonated in a Queens post office, was almost as quickly identified. The police record all such calls, and a Postal Inspector took their tapes over to the post office, where its supervisor recognized the voice as that of a former temporary clerk who had a grudge against the place.

The most serious bomb cases, and the hardest to solve, have been those involving the small but diabolically potent bombs, enclosed in envelopes, that have been sent to prominent Jews—presumably from Arab terrorists—throughout the world. Within a few weeks in the late summer and early fall of 1972, more than 150 of these turned up in the mails somewhere around the world; Chief Inspector Cotter kept a defused one in his desk, and for a short while a sizable crew of Inspectors were working full-time trying to identify both the senders of these lethal missives and, so they could be warned not to open suspicious mail, the likely recipients. If every Postal Inspector did nothing but look for letter bombs, it would still be physically impossible to screen all the mail coming into the country, but the Service—working with the F.B.I., the State Department, Interpol, and postal officials in countries whence letter bombs were known to have been mailed (Holland, Malaysia, Singapore, and India among them)—managed to intercept a good many of these devices. It also spent $400,000 developing an x-ray machine that can rapidly scan large quantities of mail, and one of these was installed at the postal station in New York that handles all mail addressed to the United Nations and the various missions attached to it. Certain Postal Inspectors, moreover, were given an intensive refresher course in bomb-investigation techniques.

The study of bombs has always been part of the training curriculum for new Postal Inspectors. Much of their instruction, too, has consisted of on-the-job training. ("You'd go out with an old guy for a few months," one veteran of the Service recalls, "and whatever he happened to know was what you learned.") The more formal training takes place at the Service's academy for recruits, now located at Bethesda, Maryland. The newcomers are put through a demanding twelve-week course, under the tutelage of veteran Inspectors who lecture them on and drill them in basic criminal law, search-and-seizure, auditing, firearms, hand-to-hand combat, and, inevitably, filling out forms. The academy has a small post office of its own. It is burgled for each class of trainees, so they can learn how to look for clues. They represent, for the Service, a new breed. Up to 1969, all Inspectors were drawn from the regular postal service. A college degree was not required, and openings were few.

Early in 1970, a lot of Inspectors took advantage of a new retirement plan for federal employees, and there were three hundred openings in the force. With the blessing of the then Postmaster General, Winton Blount, Chief Inspector Cotter decided to try to fill these with college graduates (preferably ones with prior postal experience or some investigative background), and he persuaded the White House to exempt Inspectors from certain inhibiting Civil Service requirements. Then the Inspection Service sent recruiters to campuses all over the country. To its delight and astonishment, the Inspection Service came up with thirteen thousand applicants for its three hundred jobs. Now nearly half of the fifteen hundred and fifty Inspectors on duty are of post-1969 vintage, 90 per cent are college graduates, and their average age on starting in has dropped from thirty-four to twenty-seven.

A new training program was put into effect by Cotter, who became Chief Postal Inspector in the spring of 1969. He was the first holder of that position who had not come up through the ranks. Cotter had spent twenty-two years in law enforcement, four with the F.B.I. and eighteen with the C.I.A., but like most Americans knew practically nothing about the Inspection Service. One of the first things he learned about it was that every Postal Inspector had an "R" or a "D," for "Republican" or "Democrat," alongside his name in his personal file; this stemmed from an executive order issued by President Woodrow Wilson in 1917. Hoping to make the Service reflect the nation, Wilson had decreed that it should try to be representational in terms of both geography and politics—so many from each state, according to the population figures of the preceding decennial census, and so many Republicans or Democrats, according to the voting in the preceding presidential election. Moreover, it had become the frequent practice for the Inspectors in charge of each of the fifteen field divisions into which the Service then divided the country administratively to be shuffled around every time a new party took over the White House. Cotter had the party designations purged from his men's dossiers, and when he summoned his fifteen regional supervisors to his first meeting with them, thirteen of them who happened to be Democrats at the time that the Nixon administration took over were astounded to learn that their status was not to be summarily altered.

Under Cotter, there were other innovations. There was a lot of publicity when the F.B.I. announced in mid-1972 that it was planning to augment its G-men with G-women; by then there already were a dozen female Postal Inspectors, who had established themselves as highly effective operatives in stakeout and surveillance situations where an unaccompanied man might have aroused suspicions. (In a training film produced at the Bethesda school, a young man and a young woman, both of them incipient Postal Inspectors, were shown tossing a frisbee back and forth while waiting for an extortionist to materialize in a park; this was a disguise unavailable to the Inspection Service during the first 234 years of its existence.) There was early in 1973 one black woman

Postal Inspector, and under Chief Cotter's stewardship the number of black Inspectors rose from eight to fifty—only a 3 per cent representation if you look at the figures one way, but a 300 per cent increase in three years, if you look differently.

When Cotter took over, furthermore, he began a program of updating and expanding the Service's scientific and technological facilities in certain areas; its document-examination and chemical-analysis laboratories were already recognized as among the best—as well as oldest—in the law-enforcement field. Inspectors were supplied with first-rate photographic equipment (including surveillance cameras that could take close-ups from more than a block away), and its crime laboratories and field investigative units were equipped with the most modern technical aids—silent burglar alarms for post offices, for instance, broadcasting stations that fit into a suitcase that fits under an airplane seat, and other sophisticated devices. In 1972, the Service hired twenty-four electronic technicians to assist in field and laboratory work. Postal Inspectors have been pioneers in the use of neutron activation analysis, a relatively new and extremely helpful method of unearthing evidence. By this means, it became possible not long ago to make incriminating evidence of some rope by comparing it with microscopic fibers found on the clothing of some men who'd been tied up during a robbery.

Basically, however, the work of the Service boils down to human ingenuity and persistence. In 1972, three men were convicted of a million-dollar fraud that involved the purported selling by mail of merchandise that was rarely delivered. During the trial, thirty-five angry customers rounded up by Postal Inspectors took the stand as prosecution witnesses. After they had had their say, the defense counsel tried to pooh-pooh their testimony by asserting that thirty-five griping customers were just about what anybody might expect to find in the operations of a business with an annual sales volume of $7 million. The Postal Inspector who investigated the fraud was prepared to counter that argument. He appeared in court himself the next day with a box containing 3,825 letters of complaint that he had painstakingly accumulated from other customers. The defendants, one of whom had earlier written a book entitled *How to Retire Without Money,* were swiftly retired (in this instance not without a large sum of unrecovered money) from the fraud business and into jail.

# 2. The Investigation

On July 7, 1972, Frank J. Nemic, Jr., a Postal Inspector assigned to the New York Divisional Office of the Inspection Service, at the main post office across Eighth Avenue from Madison Square Garden, made out a final report on an investigation of which he was by then nominally in charge. In keeping with the Service's standard procedure, Nemic was supposed to answer the question "Did Inspection Service effort cause scheme to be stopped?" In keeping with the Service's tradition of laconism, he wrote, "Yes." It was routine also for Inspectors supervising cases to fill out a printed form designed originally for use in connection with business swindles. In the space following "Dealer's Gross Annual Receipts," Nemic wrote, "$750,000." The dealer in this instance was Clifford Irving, and the receipts were what he had obtained from McGraw-Hill, Inc., for himself and, ostensibly, for Howard Hughes.

Had Clifford Irving known much about the Service's 98 per cent ratio between trials and convictions, Postal Inspectors might never have been able to contribute as much as they did to his downfall. For it was he, through his attorney of the moment, who first invited them to examine his peculiar relationship—or nonrelationship—with Hughes. Postal Inspectors read the papers and watch television like everybody else, so they were as familiar as any other Americans with Irving's bizarre history as its chapters unfolded, but until late January, 1972, they were, like most other people, merely fascinated onlookers. On January 7, Hughes held his celebrated disembodied press conference, during which, by telephone, he ridiculed Irving's claims about their literary collaboration. Just two weeks after that, on January 21, there was another telephone call—this one to Charles Miller, then the director of the Office of Criminal Investigation of the Service, whose office in Washington, D.C., adjoined that of Chief Inspector Cotter. The caller was William Lambert, an investigative reporter for *Life,* which had paid McGraw-Hill $100,000 for the first serial rights to Irving's book on Hughes, and which was casting about desperately for some way of determining whether or not it had bought a pig in a poke.

Here was the situation, Lambert told Miller: Irving, in a January 18 affidavit notarized by his attorney, Martin S. Ackerman, had said that one of his furtive meetings with Hughes—the one when Irving had supposedly been blindfolded at the Miami airport and driven to a rendezvous about an hour and a half distant—had been arranged by a Hughes emissary named George Gordon Holmes. Now *Life,* anxious to get through to Hughes, if possible, for some clarification of Irving's story, had learned that the author had written a letter from his home in Ibiza, in the Balearic Islands, to Holmes, in care of general delivery at the main Miami post office. What Lambert hoped was that the Service could delve into the mystery, and as a start find out who picked up the letter to Holmes.

Miller listened with interest. As Lambert knew, he replied, if the letter could be traced the Service could not open it without a court order—and there was no ascertainable reason to ask for one—to see what it said; if a Postal Inspector opened anybody else's mail without such authorization, he would himself be committing a felony. But Inspectors can and do put "hold orders" on mail, requiring identification of the person to whom it is delivered, and this Miller would undertake to do at once in the case of the letter from Irving to Holmes. (The letter was already in Miami, Miller learned soon afterward, and arrangements were made whereby anybody who came around asking for it would have to identify himself to Inspector John Brady, stationed in Miami, before he could get it. Of course, inasmuch as Holmes did not exist, that was the end of that.) But as far as an investigation of any other aspect of the case was concerned, Miller advised Lambert, there wasn't really anything the Service could do just then, for nobody had informed it that any crime involving the mails had been committed or was in process; before the Inspection Service could even think about acting, it would need a direct request from some party that had reason to believe there were reasonable grounds for its acting.

Lambert replied that he had been in touch with Ackerman, who was then still serving as Irving's lawyer, and he thought Ackerman might make an acceptable request; on the basis of what his client had told him, Ackerman believed that if Hughes hadn't authorized Irving to write about him, Irving had probably been the victim of a fraud. Ackerman had been trustingly representing Irving for a year or so, in a lawsuit stemming from the writer's book *Fake*, about an art forger; the lawyer and his client had become quite friendly, and when Irving was in New York he would sometimes stay at Ackerman's town house. Earlier, in letters to Ackerman from Ibiza, Irving had denounced the lawyers lined up against him in the *Fake* case as "out and out liars" (he would break their jaws if he ever got close enough to them, he said), and had also denounced Hughes for taking a disproportionate share of the funds McGraw-Hill had advanced toward their joint project. "In effect, the richest man in America deftly scooped a potential quarter of a million bucks from my pocket to his," Irving had written Ackerman in October, 1971. "Now I know why he's that rich." Touched by such laments from a writer, Ackerman, who had not long before scuttled the *Saturday Evening Post*, had declined to charge Irving any fee for his services.

On January 22, the day after Lambert talked to Miller, Ackerman wrote the Postal Inspector a letter to the effect that, as Irving's attorney, he was investigating the possibility that mail fraud might have occurred in connection with his client's book on Hughes; and wondering if the Service could find out what had happened to letters ostensibly sent by Irving to Hughes. Ackerman, who is not a criminal lawyer, stopped representing Irving only a few days later, when it became evident that the whole business might have criminal connotations; but it was this letter, written at a time when he *was* representing the writer, that precipitated a sweeping and incriminating investigation that must have given Irving some fresh insights into the efficacy of mass trained research.

Several hours after Ackerman wrote privately to Miller, the Swiss governmental authorities in the canton of Zurich made an electrifying public disclosure: the "H. R. Hughes" who had been depositing McGraw-Hill checks in a bank there was a woman, identity so far unknown. By the time Miller got Ackerman's letter, accordingly, it seemed clear that something strange, if not fishy, was going on. Miller conferred with his boss, Chief Inspector Cotter, and with one of their principal assistants, John D. Tarpey, another veteran of the Service. Tarpey had worked as a part-time postal clerk, in 1941, to put himself through Rutgers; by 1972, he was stationed at the Service's headquarters in Washington, and soon took charge of its field office there. The Chief Inspector agreed that, despite the murky aspects of the matter, or perhaps because of them, the Service had a responsibility to start an investigation; mail fraud might be involved. On January 25, Cotter notified *his* superior, Postmaster General Elmer T. Klassen, that the Service, which in its early days had guarded the Pony Express, was, in effect, saddling up; Cotter added to Klassen, "We do not know at his point whether a swindle has been perpetrated."

When the Postal Inspection Service sets forth on an investigation, it does so by, in the jargon of criminology, "jacketing" a case. This simply means that the pursuit is on, and that somebody is responsible for calling the signals. Inasmuch as the only hard fact the Service had on January 25 was that an undelivered letter from Clifford Irving to George Gordon Holmes was in its custody at

Miami, the case was initially jacketed there, to J. Alexis Callahan, the Inspector in charge of the Service's southeast area. From his headquarters in Atlanta, Callahan was dispatched to Miami and was asked to begin corroborating, or disproving, Irving's sworn account of his movements in that area. Not long afterward, though, the news from Switzerland of the female H. R. Hughes persuaded Cotter and Miller that if anybody had been defrauded it was less likely to be Clifford Irving than McGraw-Hill, and that the case should be rejacketed to New York, where the publishing house wrote out and mailed its handsome checks. And these checks might be crucial, for the mail-fraud statutes are so broad that to indict anyone for that crime merely required evidence that he used the mails in connection with the commission, or attempted commission, of *any* scheme to defraud. If, then, there was a fraudulent scheme attempted here—and if there wasn't, why would H. R. Hughes be a woman?—and if it could be established that a McGraw-Hill check to Hughes had been deposited in Switzerland and returned by mail for clearance in New York, why, that would constitute mail fraud quite apart from whatever other mischief might come to light.

On the night of January 25, Cotter and Miller decided that in the light of the international aspects of the investigation Tarpey should go to New York and take charge in the field. Tarpey seemed especially well suited for the assignment because there had been all sorts of alleged letters from Howard Hughes and endorsements by him of checks. Tarpey had concentrated in Accounting at Rutgers, and on becoming a Postal Inspector in 1946, after four and a half years in the Army, he had worked extensively on forgery cases. He was very good with slants and squiggles. Miller called Tarpey at his home in Potomac, Maryland, twenty miles outside Washington, and relayed Cotter's request that he go to New York and supervise the investigation. Tarpey said he'd be on the seven o'clock shuttle the following morning. At breakfast, he told his wife he'd probably be back in a couple of days. He didn't return home for six weeks.

The Postal Inspection Service, like the F.B.I., is strictly an investigative agency. All federal prosecutions are conducted by the Department of Justice, through its scattered United States Attorneys. The first thing Tarpey did on reaching New York, then, was to get in touch with Whitney North Seymour, Jr., the U.S. Attorney, and advise him that the Service had had a complaint from Clifford Irving—or, at any rate, from Irving's lawyer—and was in the process of following it up. "You came a day too late," Seymour replied. "*We* got a complaint *against* Irving yesterday from McGraw-Hill, and we've assigned the case to the F.B.I. We've turned over to them all the documents we have." Seemingly off the case even before he'd got onto it, Tarpey said he'd nonetheless like to discuss the whole matter further with Seymour. They made an appointment for four o'clock that afternoon at the U.S. Attorney's office at the Federal Courthouse Building on Foley Square.

The delay gave Tarpey time to reflect how he would proceed if he ever got to carry out his mission. Assuming for the moment —and there had to be such an assumption—that a fraud had been committed, he believed it would make sense to focus on two areas. First, there was the obvious question of handwriting identification. McGraw-Hill and *Life* already had the opinion of the private firm of Osborn Associates that the evidence that Howard Hughes had actually written the documents Irving had attributed to him was "overwhelming." Tarpey had been around too long to be overwhelmed by anything; he wanted samples of the bona-fide handwriting of all the principals in the case to be subjected to the scrutiny of Robert A. Cabanne, the Postal Inspection Service's own expert, who in a twenty-year career had earned high marks for accuracy. A second consequential factor, Tarpey thought to himself, was the probable necessity of amassing so vast an amount of evidence that whoever was eventually accused of a crime would, on being confronted with the facts, be prompted to confess without standing trial. Tarpey had previously talked to friends of his in the Justice Department about Hughes, and they had said that on the basis of what they knew about him, no one would ever get him into a courtroom; failing that, Tarpey suspected, a smart attorney representing someone with interests at variance with Hughes's could simply keep demanding during a trial, "But where is Mr. Hughes?" and would erode the prosecution's case with each iteration.

Meanwhile, Tarpey figured, he might as well get acquainted with some of the available dramatis personae in the scenario. So he went over to *Life* to call on Ralph Graves, its managing editor; and over to McGraw-Hill to talk to several of its executives. "I'm glad the professionals have arrived," Tarpey was told by Harold McGraw, the harassed chairman of the publishing house. "Everybody around here has been trying too hard to play detective." He himself, McGraw told Tarpey glumly, had just received some information that further dissipated his already fast-ebbing confidence in Irving's probity: When the writer was supposed to have been in Mexico alone, interviewing Hughes, it now seemed that he might have been accompanied by a woman named Nina.

Who was Nina? Tarpey had never heard of her, but Beverly Jane Loo, Irving's closest associate at McGraw-Hill, had met her in London once, and although she couldn't remember her surname, she had a phone number for her somewhere that Irving had given her, although she couldn't remember right off where it was. But she promised Tarpey to look for it. Miss Loo had a footnote to that Mexican trip to recount. Clifford Irving, she said, had told her on February 10, 1971, that Hughes had instructed him to check in that day at the Hotel Buckingham in New York, and await orders; Irving had duly received a message there to go at once to the American Express office at 374 Park Avenue and pick up some plane tickets. Miss Loo had accompanied him, though Irving had had her wait outside, in case Hughes had the place under surveillance; and after Irving had emerged from American Express he had said to her, affecting great surprise, "Guess what! I'm going to Mexico!" Before Tarpey completed his rounds that day, he realized he might be too pressed for time to initiate talks with the U.S. Attorney's office, so he had phoned Seymour and put off their meeting until the following morning. He also phoned Inspector Bill W. Mason of the New York regional staff, and asked him to visit the American Express place the next day and find out what he could about Irving's visit there just over a year earlier.

At the morning conference on January 27, Seymour introduced Tarpey to a number of his assistants who had been detailed to the Hughes–Irving–*Life*–McGraw-Hill puzzle—Robert A. Morvillo, Henry Putzell III, and John T. Tigue, Jr. Tigue said that from what little he knew about the case thus far, the simplest way for the federal government to get an indictment—whatever charges any state or county or foreign authorities might also lodge—would be under the mail-fraud statutes. Accordingly, Seymour's office was transferring the case from the F.B.I. to the Postal Inspection Service, now the responsible investigating agency. From that morning until March 3, when Irving acknowledged his hoax, it was Tigue and Tarpey who masterminded the inquiry, and when it was all over Tigue graciously told the *Wall Street Journal,* "The Inspectors did a sensational job. The whole Postal Inspection Service deserves a lot more credit than it gets."

Tarpey set up task force headquarters at 90 Church Street, on the premises of Earl J. Ingebright, the Regional Chief Inspector for the New York Metropolitan Region, which embraces the city and its environs. Inspector William J. O'Keefe, Ingebright's senior fraud man, was assigned to Tarpey, as were eight agents from the New York office—which covers Manhattan, the Bronx, and some suburbs, not to mention Puerto Rico and the Virgin Islands—with Frank Nemic as their crew chief. On making them available, their supervisor, Elbridge M. Hamm, Jr., sent Tarpey a note couched in the best stagecoach-and-outrider tradition. "Good hunting!" it said. Tarpey realized that his targets were far-flung. Clifford and Edith Irving and Richard Suskind were off the coast of Spain—the Irvings at Ibiza and Suskind on Mallorca. A Spanish-speaking Inspector from New York, Augusto L. Vazquez, was at once sent in their direction. Another bilingual Inspector, Rae Fernandez, was told to proceed from Fort Worth, Texas, to Mexico, to see what light he could throw on Irving's—and the still enigmatic Nina's—movements in that country. Frank Nemic was dispatched to the West Indies, to learn what he could about Irving's supposed rendezvous with Hughes in Puerto Rico and the Virgin Islands. Because the matter of the checks and the Swiss banks was so potentially crucial, an Inspector with a fiscal background, Donald I. Hunter, was dispatched from Washington to Zurich, where the female H. R. Hughes had executed most of her transactions. Callahan of Atlanta was already in Florida. Dozens of other Inspectors were available elsewhere for special assignments, and many of them would ultimately be called on; before the case was solved, although in total man-hours expended it fell far short of many other cases the Service has worked on, leads would be pursued and interviews conducted by Postal Inspectors in, among other areas, Arizona, California, Connecticut, Georgia, Illinois, New Jersey, New Mexico, North Carolina, Wisconsin, and Washington, D.C.

Tarpey had barely set up shop when he heard from Inspector Mason, who'd gone to the American Express office. Mason had examined its records for February 10, 1971, and what had he found but a request for hotel reservations, in Mexico City and Oaxaca, for a Mr. and Mrs. Clifford Irving, with, beneath the "Mrs.," the notation "Baroness Nina van Pallandt." The clerk who'd written that remembered the occasion; a tall and handsome man had come in and explained he had only just got married, which was why his wife was still using a passport with her maiden name on it. So now the Postal Inspectors appeared to have Nina's identity. But she wasn't listed in the London telephone directory, and Beverly Jane Loo hadn't yet unearthed her number there. No matter; it was now merely a question of time, Tarpey was sure, before his men tracked the woman down. Meanwhile, there were other things to think about. With Inspector Vazquez heading toward Spain, Tarpey phoned Richard Suskind in Mallorca, on January 29, and inquired whether he would return to the United States voluntarily to answer some questions. Suskind said he didn't think he would. Tarpey had a subpoena drawn up for him and flown to

Vazquez in care of the American consulate at Barcelona. At just about the same moment, Inspector Nemic's heart was breaking. Everybody had been looking for a woman who resembled Edith Irving and might be the female H. R. Hughes, and he had gone to the Virgin Islands carrying the only photograph of Edith he could get in a hurry—one clipped from the New York *Daily News*. Following Irving's earlier movements at Saint Croix, Nemic had dropped in at the King Christian Hotel at Christiansted, where Irving had been well remembered, largely for the reason that he and the young woman accompanying him had requested separate bedrooms and—clearly a novelty in that area—had slept in separate beds. Nemic had shown his picture of Edith Irving to several hotel employees, and they had said, yes, she was the woman in Room 303; but Nemic had ascertained that she wasn't at all; the person was the scuba-diving instructor Anne Baxter, whom Irving had met in Florida at the Newport Beach Hotel. So Anne Baxter, Nemic concluded triumphantly, had to be Helga Hughes! He had cracked the case! He was reaching for a telephone to convey the exciting news to his superiors in New York when he paused to listen to a news bulletin on the radio: Irving's brand-new lawyer, Maurice Nessen, had just announced that Helga Hughes was Edith Irving.

On Monday morning, January 31, Miss Loo reported triumphantly to Tarpey that she had found Nina's number. Tarpey at once rang it. There was no answer. He called William Lambert, at *Life*, and through him soon learned from an editor who'd worked in London that Nina van Pallandt was a fairly well-known entertainer there. Tarpey put in another call to London, this one to its Celebrity Service, and not only did it know about the titled singer but it thought it knew where she was—on holiday, in the Bahamas, with her manager, John Marshall, and his wife, Elizabeth. Now, if the Baroness was not an American citizen and was sojourning on British soil, there was no way the Postal Inspection Service could compel her to come to the States and speak her piece. Persuasiveness and tact seemed to be in order. Inspector

Brady, a man believed to be endowed with both traits, as well as —and this was nearly more important—enjoying a close relationship with law-enforcement officials in the Bahamas, was ordered to the islands. Brady's instructions were to advise the Baroness, if he could find her, that if she'd come to New York, the Service would do its best to shield her from the publicity she was certain to generate; it would arrange for her to be flown to some place like Philadelphia, to be driven unobtrusively to New York, and to be slipped through the side door of the federal courthouse into the chamber where a grand jury was conducting secret hearings.

On February 1, with Brady en route to Nassau, the task force received the first of a series of unsolicited tips—many of these vague and most of them worthless—that were to plague it for the next month. One of the Service's regular informants called to suggest that Postal Inspectors look into a Mafia angle; the informant had heard that Irving had borrowed $50,000 from Carlo Gambino, and although $40,000 of it had been repaid, there was still—such is the arithmetic of loan-sharking—an outstanding indebtedness of $65,000. There was never any further indication from any source that Irving, with all his real financial problems, also had that particular one to fret about. By February 2, Inspector Hunter had established himself in Zurich, where it quickly became clear that his relations with Dr. Peter Veleff, the chief investigating authority of the canton of Zurich, were going to be stiff. Dr. Veleff had professed surprise on learning from Hunter that the Irvings had not yet been arrested, and he had reminded the Inspector, who hoped to recruit Swiss witnesses for a grand jury hearing or subsequent trial, that in Switzerland all foreigners, whatever their credentials or motives, are liable to arrest and imprisonment for questioning or seeking affidavits from Swiss citizens. Hunter had sought to explain that in the operation of the American system of criminal justice there were safeguards that sometimes precluded summary action, but Dr. Veleff had been unimpressed; the Inspector could—through him exclusively—obtain copies of bank records, he had said, but he couldn't talk directly with any bank employees. "I hope you have a pleasant trip home," Dr. Veleff said to Hunter, who hadn't even unpacked.

When Hunter transmitted that discouraging intelligence to New York, Tarpey told him to keep cool, hang around Zurich, await developments, and accomplish whatever he could without being jailed. Hunter said that at least he was registered at the Hotel Glärnischhof, where Edith Irving had once put up as Helga Hughes, and that he thought he could get a sample of her handwriting from its records without ending up in solitary. As it turned out, he remained in Switzerland for a month, serving as liaison man between the American and Swiss authorities and even as an errand boy—meeting Swissair flights, for instance, to receive communications from the U.S. Attorney's office that were hand carried by pilots, and rushing these over to Dr. Veleff. Haste, Hunter soon learned, was unnecessary during weekends; for from Friday evening to Monday morning all Swiss officials, no matter what the exigencies of an investigation, were totally inaccessible.

Hunter's news on February 2 was dampening, but as dusk fell in New York the whole day brightened, for now Brady was on the phone from the Bahamas. He had found Nina van Pallandt, sunning herself on the beach at Treasure Key, and she had been most cooperative, telling him, as the whole world would shortly also know, that Clifford Irving couldn't have interviewed Howard Hughes or anybody else in Mexico, because he had scarcely left her sleek side there. Nina had been taken aback when Brady had walked down the beach in a business suit and accosted her; just the evening before, she told him, she'd been talking things over with her manager and his wife and they'd agreed there was "no way" —provided Irving didn't blab—for anyone ever to determine that she'd been in Mexico with him. Brady spent five hours talking to the Baroness, whose age he gallantly estimated in his ensuing report as between thirty-five and thirty-eight (she was thirty-nine); and she freely recounted everything she could recall of her Mexican fling. When she agreed to testify voluntarily before a grand jury, Brady, mindful of his injunction from Tarpey, brought up the logistics of spiriting her unnoticed into the courthouse. She seemed grateful for this concern about her privacy. An hour later, though, at just about the time that Brady was calling New York, she herself called a press conference to reveal all. "We are sometimes a little bit naïve about show business," Tarpey said afterward. "Still, Nina was lovely. She had a kind of inner-glow gentility that real beauties have."

On February 4, Inspector Vazquez, in the company of the American consul from Barcelona, Russell M. Winge, served the subpoena on Suskind at Mallorca, thus ensuring (unless he wanted to face contempt charges) his appearance in court. Suspecting that Suskind might plead that he couldn't afford a trip to New York, Vazquez had brought along a government check for $639, to cover his expenses, and he served that, too. Suskind was being evicted, Vazquez also reported, not for nonpayment of rent but for notoriety; his landlady had had it with all the journalists hiding behind her hedges. Vazquez left them lurking there and took off for Ibiza, where, he had already learned from Spanish authorities, the local police were planning to search Irving's home. He wanted to be in on that hunt.

That same day, February 4, Tarpey's dispersed troops were busy on the home front. In Chicago, Inspector D. E. Keefer was calling on the editors of *Hobbies* magazine; it was a long shot he was tracking down, but could there have been any connection between Clifford Irving and a classified ad that had run in three recent issues of that publication: "Wanted: Original autographs of industrialist Howard Hughes—Box 6294, Burbank, Calif. 91505"? That one was easy; the ad had been placed, at eight dollars the insertion, by an unconnected ex-police sergeant who collected celebrities' signatures and lacked a Hughes. In New York, that same day, Beverly Jane Loo delivered to Tarpey all the telephonic records she could lay her hands on—a listing of every long-distance call charged to McGraw-Hill for the previous year. Dealing with Irving was never cheap. From August 24 to August 26, 1971, there had been three calls between McGraw-Hill and Ibiza, which cost the publishers a total of $162.20, not counting tax.

Miss Loo, while she was at it, had an odd incident to report to Tarpey. Earlier that day, a young man had turned up at McGraw-Hill with a check in his hand from Merrill Lynch, Pierce, Fenner & Smith in the amount of $650,000. He had said he was representing a Mr. Katz of Nassau (Howard Hughes territory, as the world well knew), whom the bearer had met in 1968. Mr. Katz had told him then to incorporate himself in New York as a tennis club. More than two years later, Mr. Katz had reappeared, with the Merrill Lynch check, made out to the tennis club; its incorporator (who by then, it developed, had a one-room office on Fifth Avenue, but no courts) was to present himself at McGraw-Hill and tender the check in return for all its rights to the Hughes manuscript.

Miss Loo had brushed aside the offer (which in any event was $100,000 short of what her firm had already laid out to Irving) and thought it almost too frivolous to mention, but she did have the young man's name and address. Within a couple of hours, he was being questioned by Inspectors Nemic and James J. Boyle. So were some of his relatives, one of whom said he had mental difficulties. The big check, which the Inspectors took away with them for further scrutiny, turned out to have been kited; it had been made out by Merrill Lynch, all right, but in the amount, originally, of $1.50. Tarpey passed that side issue along to Inspectors who weren't in on the Irving case, and dismissed it from his mind.

In the days that followed, there were numerous similar occurrences that began practically anywhere and ended nowhere: A brief encounter, for instance, with a factory foreman whose hobby it was to pretend to be a buddy of Hughes's and a courier for correspondence with him; the man had got so far as to persuade a celebrated motion picture actress to send the industrialist a note offering to meet him at any time, at any place, for any purpose. Then there was a phone call that Tarpey took early one morning from a man who said he was a lawyer and was at the John F. Kennedy Airport, about to fly to Europe; out of public-spiritedness, he wanted the Service to know that the key person in the

Irving case was a disaffected accountant who had once worked for Hughes and who had very likely been the source of whatever biographical information Irving might have about him. Inspectors Nemic and O'Keefe went around to see the accountant; he denied everything, and was not judged a likely enough source of hard facts, or even soft rumors, to waste any more time on. Nobody yet knows who made the call that purportedly came from the airport.

By this time, the task force had assembled enough hard facts, and had enough more almost within its grasp, to be reasonably certain that Irving was culpable of mail fraud. Tarpey, however, still held to the view that, barring an appearance by Hughes on a witness stand, a confession would be essential to make a charge stick, and that to get a confession Irving would have to be confronted with so enormous a pile of evidence that its weight would stagger him. Postal Inspectors, accordingly, continued to check out every detail of every one of his alleged meetings with Hughes, the dates and places of which Irving had spelled out in his self-serving affidavit; and also to check out all his other ascertainable movements. Beverly Jane Loo, for instance, knew that Irving, just before his jaunt to Mexico with Nina van Pallandt, had stayed in New York first at the Buckingham and then at the Hotel Elysée. Inspectors pored over the registries, room charges, and telephone bills of both establishments for the relevant periods, and it became clear why Irving had moved from a $21-a-night room at the modest Buckingham to a $42 one at the fancier Elysée: He had phoned Nina, in London, from the first hotel, and after she had flown over to join him there (they were registered as "Mr. and Mrs. I. Clifford") he had concluded that it was an inadequate setting for such a jewel and had engaged in what the demographers call upward mobility.

Irving was no piker, the task force observed with grudging admiration, and perhaps even envy. They had long since learned from a study of his travel habits that a credit card he was partial to was (how appropriate!) that of Carte Blanche; and on the two days he was entertaining the Baroness in New York, pre-Mexico, he had twice used Carte Blanche to buy flowers for her at Irene Hayes Wadley & Smythe—the first time, a dozen roses at $19.08, the second time, mixed roses and chrysanthemums at $21.20. Concurrently, Inspector F. E. Klein, raking some embers in Houston, Texas, where Irving and Suskind had gone early in their venture to peruse the daily *Chronicle*'s morgue on their subject—Klein sent Tarpey a copy of an order Irving had placed for photostats of twenty-six items the paper had carried about Hughes—was able to report, not that it made much difference, that Irving had used his Carte Blanche card to buy a suit and four shirts at the Norton Ditto store. The suit, Klein said, "has a belt in the back only and has 'bat-wings' on each side of the back from the belt to the shoulder." Throwing details like that at a man might make him confess to anything. Wherever it became known that Irving had paused in his flight of fancy, Inspectors pounced, obtaining records of credit-card companies, banks, hotels, and motels, and, as these last two disclosed the numbers to which Irving or Suskind had placed toll calls, telephone companies. Clifford Irving did not yet know it, but his entire real life for a year was being methodically reconstituted, down to the last phone call, while at the same time his pseudo life was being just as methodically torn apart.

By February 5, less than a fortnight after Tarpey had reached New York, the unauthorized biography of Irving being compiled by the Postal task force—unauthorized by Irving, that is—was taking shape nicely. That day, Inspector Frank Orr, out in California, interviewed Irving's Aunt Hannah and her husband, Michael Hamilberg; it was they who had introduced Irving to Stanley Meyer, from whom he borrowed (and hastily photographed) the Noah Dietrich–James Phelan manuscript on Hughes, which in turn he borrowed from so liberally. While Orr was busy at Paradise Cove, Inspectors Leslie G. Turner and Barry L. Smith were getting set to call on still another author of Hughesiana, a Tucson woman named Marjel DeLaur, who was writing a book under the name of Becky St. John. All she had to contribute to the quest was her unsubstantiated belief that Howard Hughes was dead and that his business interests had been taken over—here came the Mafia again—by Meyer Lansky.

She proved to be of not much more value to the investigation than a young man in Menasha, Wisconsin, who had written to McGraw-Hill in the early stages of the proceedings that he had positive proof that Hughes had authorized Irving to write about him. Inspector J. H. Hallberg was asked by Tarpey to call on him. The Menasha man admitted right off that his allegation had been purely a stunt, pulled in the hope of getting some publicity for a book he'd written covering, in eighty pages, the disintegration of civilization from Genesis to the present, which up to then had been little noticed except by President Nixon and Billy Graham.

At around the same time, Inspector Charles C. Cheezum, then with the Washington field office and now in Pittsburgh, was digging into a five-day trip Irving and his wife—this time it was actually his wife—had made to the national capital in the spring of 1971, the purpose being not so much to look at cherry blossoms as to steal Hughes material from the Library of Congress. And Callahan, in Florida, was concurrently and painstakingly comparing Irving's affidavit about his activities there in December, 1971, with his establishable activities. There was the story, for one thing, about renting a car at the Miami airport on December 3, leaving it in a parking lot, and going off blindfolded with George Gordon Holmes, at eighty miles an hour, to a rendezvous ninety minutes off. Well, now, reported Callahan: Irving, using his reliable old Carte Blanche card, had rented a National car at Eastern Airlines Counter No. 1 at 2:34 P.M. on the third and had checked in at the Newport Beach Hotel at 4:51 P.M. Irving had had no reservation, and Callahan wondered why not, if his business there was so important; the Inspector guessed that it wasn't important and that Irving had driven around from motel to motel until he found one with a vacancy. And why would a man, Callahan wondered further, have rented a poolside deck chair at the Newport Beach Hotel (Anne Baxter's place), and have incurred two restaurant charges, at the very time he was supposed to be gabbing with Howard Hughes?

Moreover, where could anyone have driven in that part of the world at that time of the year at that time of day at eighty miles an hour? Only on the turnpike north toward Palm Beach, Callahan had ascertained, and surely a toll-taker would have noticed a blindfolded man in the front seat. Callahan hadn't been able to find a toll-taker who'd seen anything like that.

Callahan is a man totally unimpressed by anything that is not logical. "Travel from Miami to West Palm Beach, since it is implied that's where he [Irving] was meeting Mr. Hughes, by any road other than the turnpike would be practically out of the question because the traffic is so slow and crowded," he reported to Tarpey, in a statement characteristic of Inspectorial thoroughness. "Furthermore, anyone knowing his way in the Miami area would use the turnpike for a trip from Miami to West Palm Beach or to any point an hour and a half away from the city. It would be possible for a person to drive from Miami Airport to West Palm Beach in an hour and a half. He probably could drive it in about an hour and fifteen minutes. The exit from the turnpike is six miles from downtown West Palm Beach and one must go through West Palm Beach to get over to Palm Beach. Wealthy persons staying in the area stay at Palm Beach and not West Palm Beach.

"The Newport Hotel is twenty miles from the Miami Airport. Driving time is thirty-nine minutes. Had the trip been made as outlined in the Irving Affidavit, at least ten minutes would have been lost from the time the vehicle was rented until Mr. Irving claimed his automobile and drove to a point where he could have been picked up by Mr. Holmes. Taking the one hour and a half to the point where Mr. Hughes allegedly was met and one hour and a half, plus forty-five minutes' interview with Mr. Hughes, plus ten minutes from car rental time to meeting with Holmes and changing automobiles now totalling three hours and fifty-five minutes, plus at least thirty minutes to the Newport Hotel, brings the elapsed time to four hours and twenty-five minutes; this is compared with the two hours and nineteen minutes between car rental time and check-in time at the hotel."

Satisfied that if anybody tried to make Irving's December 3 yarn stand up he could knock it down, Callahan moved along to the Beachcomber Lodge at Pompano Beach, where Irving and Suskind had stayed in late August and early September, 1971, while —again according to Irving's affidavit—Hughes had posted a guard carrying a cane in front of a shell shop, to watch their motel room and make sure they weren't running off with any of the tapes on which conversations with him had been recorded. (Irving's invention of the distinctive sentinel inspired a false tip from an informant in Europe, who said he thought he knew the man with the cane. It was probably a sword cane, the informant asserted, and this dangerous character whom the guardians of the law might find it necessary to shoot in self-defense was a fellow who'd been having an affair with the informant's wife.) Callahan discovered at Pompano Beach that the quarters Irving and Suskind had occupied adjoined a parking lot; that there were guards hired by the motel to patrol the lot; that if any outside watchman, with or without a cane, had tried to intrude upon their territory they'd have shooed him off, but they hadn't had to because there wasn't any such person; that the door to the Irving-Suskind room wasn't visible, by day or by night, from the entrance to the shell shop; and that the shop's proprietor, who lived on the premises and was a light sleeper, was always wandering around in the middle of the night and had never seen any stranger lounging around his portals. Callahan was ready to testify—with toll-takers, poolsiders, shell-sellers, and a sheaf of documentation to back him up—that whatever Irving had been doing on those two Florida excursions, he hadn't been doing what he'd said he'd done.

On February 8, Inspector Vazquez phoned Tarpey from Ibiza. The search of Irving's home there had not produced anything breathtaking, but the raiders had come upon two cablegrams from Clifford to Edith that were suggestive of equivocation: "DO NOT TALK TO NEWSMEN" and "DO NOT LET YOURSELF BE PHOTOGRAPHED." Back in New York, that same day, Inspector Nemic and Inspector Harvey Kaudule made an unrewarding trip to the home of another writer, Stephen Birmingham, who they'd heard had himself once contemplated doing a book on Hughes. The subject had come up, Birmingham told them, but he had never taken it very seriously. Nor, it appeared, did he take Irving very seriously as a fellow professional; Birmingham said that Irving was considered a fourth-class writer by his peers.

While Nemic and Kaudule were thus engaged in literary palaver in Westchester County, back in New York City things were humming. Tarpey, it will be remembered, wanted from the outset to let Robert Cabanne, the Service's handwriting expert in New York, have a go at the documents that Osborn Associates had authenticated as Hughesian; and to analyze them alongside the Irvings' handwriting. Cabanne had met with U.S. Assistant Attorney Tigue and had suggested fairly foolproof ways of obtaining serviceable specimens. Both Irvings, he advised, should write the same start of a communication on ten different sheets of paper, so there could be no question of copying one performance from another. But by now the Irvings were volunteering nothing, and when they appeared before the grand jury sifting their affairs they took the Fifth Amendment rather than furnish any handwriting samples.

Tigue thereupon asked Federal District Judge Morris E. Lasker, who was presiding over the grand jury, to order the Irvings to comply. The Judge did, and on the morning of February 8 the couple reappeared in court to oblige. Soon afterward, the precious samples in tow, Tigue went to lunch in nearby Chinatown with Tarpey and Inspector O'Keefe, who was resting up after an epic interview with Miss Loo, the transcript of whose recapitulation of her role in the episode ran almost as long as a novella. Returning to the courthouse, Tarpey asked Tigue if he could borrow the samples. He took them to a room upstairs and laid them out alongside copies of the "Hughes" communications to Irving.

Tarpey's mind clicked back to the time he had worked on the Service's Check Squad in Baltimore, examining forged checks. "In that line of work," he has subsequently said, "you always had to satisfy yourself that you accused the right guy, so that at the very least you didn't make a fool of yourself." Now, squinting at the papers before him, Tarpey's eye once or twice lit up. On the face of it, Clifford Irving's handwriting was quite dissimilar to Hughes's. But there were beguiling analogies between what Irving had definitely written in court that morning and what he claimed Hughes had written earlier: a dash instead of a comma after the salutation in a letter, the method of dotting an *i* and of crossing a *t*, and so forth. Up to then, nearly everyone working on the case had presumed that Irving had a conspirator who'd done his forgeries, very likely some acquaintance from his *Fake* days. Now Tarpey thought otherwise. He rushed to find Tigue and, brandishing the papers, said, "I think old Irving could have written these himself."

Tigue was skeptical.

Tarpey sent everything over to Cabanne, and while awaiting word from the handwriting laboratory, began digesting other reports. ("We had some beautiful breaks in the case," Inspector Nemic said afterward. "Almost every day something new came up, and that's what made it interesting.") Inspector Hunter had been on the phone from Zurich just about daily. On February 9, Tigue and Morvillo flew over there, arriving in the morning of the tenth and going straight to Hunter's room at the Glärnischhof. They had a hunch they could get Irving and Suskind to plead guilty if Edith could escape imprisonment, and the Americans were leaning toward leniency provided the Swiss would go along. The arrangement would be for Edith to be charged with—but not imprisoned for—every crime that a Swiss indictment could conceivably cover, and the Swiss could satisfy themselves that international justice had thus been done. But this would depend on the cooperation of Dr. Veleff and of his immediate superior, Dr. Gerold Luthy, the chief prosecuting attorney for the Zurich canton. Meanwhile, Tarpey had a report of an interview conducted with Stanley Meyer at Encino, California, by Inspectors Kenneth M. Hearst and James K. Jones. After some difficulty gaining admittance to Meyer's estate, which was guarded by electric gates and watchdogs, they got to him and got from him a statement that he couldn't remember giving any manuscript to Clifford Irving. (After Meyer was subpoenaed, he said that he had. Inspector Hearst, by that time, had been to the Beverly Hills Camera Shop, where Irving had processed fourteen rolls of thirty-five-millimeter film, containing photographs of the Dietrich-Phelan opus.) Inspector Brady, in the meantime, had gone back to the Bahamas, on this occasion to check up on trips Irving had made there in April and September, 1971, purportedly to talk to Hughes. Even the earlier date was subsequent to Irving's supposed meetings with Hughes in Mexico; yet Brady had no trouble finding people—among them Connie Jo Justice, a local journalist whose brains Irving had assiduously tried to pick—who recalled that Irving (very peculiar, Brady reckoned, for a man who had already met Hughes four times) wanted them to tell him what Hughes looked like.

Promising as all this intelligence was to Tarpey, what was needed most was Cabanne's handwriting analysis. From Postal Inspectors in California and Nevada, Cabanne had procured the few generally accepted specimens of Hughes's writing: a signature on an arrest report in Los Angeles, deriving from an automobile accident some thirty years back; another signature on a document on file at the Nevada Gaming Control Board in Carson City; an autograph scribbled in an uncharacteristically unguarded mood on a Las Vegas waitress's order pad. Cabanne and his associates had studied these, and the Irvings' samples, and the news they had for Tarpey on February 11 was, from his viewpoint, exceedingly good. For Cabanne now declared unqualifiedly that Hughes had not written any of Irving's Hughes documents. As the expert would state it in a more formal report a couple of days later, "Although there is a pictorial resemblance between Hughes's handwriting and the questioned material . . . significant characteristic differences are also present which unequivocally eliminate him as the writer."

Cabanne did not stop there. If the withdrawal slips from the Swiss Credit Bank in Zurich signed "H. R. Hughes"—copies of which Inspector Hunter had by then managed to pass along—had in fact been written by Edith Irving (and Irving's lawyer had already said she was Helga Hughes), then Edith was also unequivocally the forger of the "H. R. Hughes" endorsements on several of McGraw-Hill's checks. Cabanne explained further that as a rule it is possible to detect a forgery without detecting the forger. But when it came to the stuff Hughes had allegedly sent to Irving and to McGraw-Hill, inasmuch as "many of the unconscious habits or traits of Clifford Irving have been injected into the questioned handwriting," the expert had arrived at a "definite conclusion" that the various Hughes documents produced through Irving had been written by Irving.

So much, then, for Howard Hughes; there was ample evidence that he had neither met with Irving nor communicated with him. But what of the biography of him, or autobiography, that Irving and Suskind had assembled? James Phelan, Noah Dietrich's ghost writer, arrived in New York on February 13. Like many others before and after him who have been involved in criminal investigations, he was booked into the Hotel New Yorker; it is only a block from the General Post Office, and an easy walk away for Inspectors and their interviewees. Phelan got into town that evening, and by the time Tarpey, with Callahan accompanying him, arrived at the hotel, it was ten-thirty at night. The two Inspectors talked to him for three hours and then made another date for the following morning. Phelan apologized then for having been tired the night before and thus unable to remember much of what he'd recounted. But he remembered certain things sharply, and he kept stressing them in further interviews he had with Postal Inspectors and with editors from *Life* and McGraw-Hill: There were parts of Irving's manuscript that had surely been filched from his. One example that stuck in Tarpey's memory was this: Noah Dietrich had told Phelan offhandedly, and Phelan had tossed the fact into his manuscript without verifying it, that a certain scientist was the president of the California Institute of Technology at a certain phase of Hughes's life. Phelan had subsequently learned that this was inaccurate. And yet the exact same inaccuracy appeared in Irving's manuscript. *Very* peculiar coincidence.

On February 14, after that first late session with Phelan, Tarpey was tired, too, when he turned up at his office, but his spirits were fast lifted. Inspector Fernandez was finally reporting in from Mexico, where, since Irving had covered a lot of ground, he had had to cover a lot, too. He was able to state emphatically that when Irving and his lady had arrived at the Hotel Victoria in Oaxaca they had been lodged in a bungalow called "Julia," and that during one sultry evening there—and there were duplicates of signed bar chits to corroborate it—they had between them consumed six Margaritas. One should never try to lead a double life while committing mail fraud. On February 15, 1971, Fernandez went on, Nina van Pallandt had rented a 1970 Volkswagen, and when it was turned in its speedometer indicated it had traveled 630 kilometers. Registering at the Camino Real Hotel in Mexico City, moreover, Irving had somewhat roguishly described himself as a McGraw-Hill editor. The road from Oaxaca to Monte Albán was winding, steep, and narrow, and it took . . .

But enough, Tarpey thought. He was ready to take the next step. On the afternoon of February 14, Inspectors Tarpey, O'Keefe, and Callahan conferred with Tigue and Morvillo, just back from the frustrating Alps. Cabanne, the handwriting man, joined them and reprised his findings. The Irvings' and Suskind's attorneys were invited to still another session of the group that evening. The investigators briefly summarized what they knew, and that was sufficient for the lawyers to agree that they should try to convince their clients to plead guilty. If there was to be no trial, though, Tarpey proposed, the Irvings and Suskind should be required to make a full confession for the public record. The lawyers agreed.

Back in Switzerland, however, Inspector Hunter was traveling a rougher road. On February 16, the Zurich authorities, deciding not to make any deal with the New York authorities, issued a warrant for Edith Irving's arrest. Dr. Veleff had been to Spain himself, Hunter reported just after that, and the Swiss prosecutor had been persuaded by his sources of information there that no matter what anyone else thought or said, Edith Irving was the dominant member of her household and the chief villain in the piece. Veleff wanted a set of her palm prints sent over on the double, and had been undeterred by Hunter's mild response that he wasn't sure anyone in the United States *had* her palm prints. In fact, Hunter was trying to wangle from Veleff's custody a copy of a single smudged palm print that Edith might have deposited on a Swiss Credit Bank withdrawal slip.

By February 16, Tigue and Morvillo felt confident enough to start, with Tarpey's collaboration, drafting an indictment that they hoped the grand jury would return against the three conspirators, so they would have something to plead guilty to if they elected to take that course. But there was no assurance yet that they would, so the hunt for evidence pressed on. In Switzerland, Hunter somehow came up with a Swiss Credit Bank man who was prepared to testify that in the normal course of business in Zurich, McGraw-Hill checks banked there would be returned for collection in the United States by mail. Inspectors Mason and Kaudule of the New York crew were, more mundanely, out in the Westchester suburbs talking to another aunt of Irving's. She said stoutly that if anybody had been duped in this whole queer business it had surely been her nephew who'd been duped by Hughes; why, Clifford had never lied to her in his entire life.

That happened on March 2. The next day, Irving appeared at Morvillo's office and, with Tigue and Tarpey and half a dozen government officials and lawyers as an enchanted audience, acknowledged that just about his entire life for the previous year had been a lie. "Listening to him talk for hours and hours," Tarpey said later, "the thing I was proudest of was that there were no real surprises. We knew every material point he mentioned by then except one—that it was Suskind who had mailed one Hughes letter from the Bahamas to McGraw-Hill. All we'd known about that one was that Clifford and Edith weren't in the Bahamas when it was mailed. I felt after listening to Irving that we had done a good investigation." So did Whitney North Seymour, who stated not long afterward, "In all respects Mr. Tarpey did a superb job which was a credit to him as well as to the Postal Inspection Service. Without his skill, knowledge, and dedication to duty it is unlikely the investigation would have been brought to a conclusion as quickly and successfully as it was."

Irving pleaded guilty, and was sentenced on July 16, 1972. Shortly before that, Tarpey, back in Washington, got a phone call from U.S. Attorney Putzell in New York. "Say, there's an old friend of yours here who wants to know something," Putzell said.

"Who is it?" asked Tarpey.

"It's Clifford Irving," Putzell said. "He's writing a book about what happened to him, and he doesn't want to speculate about anything, because he doesn't want to make any mistakes. So could you tell him how you found out about Nina?"

# 3. All in the Family

Human beings, like Clifford Irving's aunt, are understandably defensive about their kin, but in that they are fairly rare among living creatures. Nobody, for instance, expects a frog, which can lay hundreds of eggs at a clip, to leap to the protection of every member of each of its litters. Considering, then, that about ninety billion pieces of mail are spawned annually in the United States, it is astonishing to what lengths Postal Inspectors will go to carry out their long-standing responsibility to protect them. On Labor Day in 1970, an Inspector in Texas, using his automobile as an anchor, lowered himself by rope halfway down a sheer cliff to retrieve merely a few stolen stamps that were stuck to it. After an Alaska Airlines crash on a mountainside a year later, four Inspectors rushed to the scene and, although they were untrained as mountaineers, lashed themselves together and recovered, from icy crevices and other uninviting spots, 380 of the 1,658 pounds of mail that had been aboard.

Policemen are notoriously persistent at tracking down and punishing cop-killers. So it is with Postal Inspectors when anyone in their family—a very large family—is assaulted. In criminal circles, it is widely known that Postmasters may not keep more than a trickle of cash on their premises overnight; they are supposed to bank their money at the end of every day. Thus the minutes immediately before closing time are the most promising in which to stage a holdup. At a post office in Inkster, Michigan, a suburb of Detroit, just before 5 P.M. on October 4, 1972, a young man walked in, brandished a gun, and, when a clerk made a move he didn't like, shot and killed another clerk with twenty-one years of postal service. Forty-five Inspectors converged on the scene and worked on the case around the clock until (with the help of an F.B.I. informant) they'd caught the killer eight days later.

Nowadays, such crimes are becoming more and more frequent. It used to be that the sanctity of the U.S. mails was almost universally accepted. The ordinary mail carrier was thought of as a jolly, Norman Rockwellish character susceptible to attack only from dogs. No longer. Carriers are considered fair game for street prowlers, like any other pedestrians, and inasmuch as their sacks are apt to contain negotiable checks and other valuables, they make especially inviting targets. Their potential assailants do not pause to reflect—particularly when they are narcotics addicts not much given to the rational appraisal of alternatives—that armed robbery of the mails is a federal crime carrying on conviction a mandatory penalty of twenty-five years' imprisonment. It is not only people in need of a fix, though, who prey these days on mailmen. On March 17, 1972, in Atmore, Alabama, a carrier was shot to death because he didn't have in his bag a magazine that a subscriber felt was intolerably overdue. Neither the killer nor his victim, alas, was aware that help was on the way; at the time of the incident, the Postal Inspection Service, at the request of Postmaster General Blount, an Alabaman who'd received a number of complaints from his hometown neighbors about delays in second-class mail deliveries, was investigating the matter, and not long afterward magazine deliveries in the area were speeded up by as much as twenty-four hours. Postal employees, whatever their rank, do not expect much public thanks for their labors; when Blount ran for the Senate that same fall, his fellow Alabamans turned him down.

There are more than 200,000 mail carriers in the country, and with only 1,550 Postal Inspectors, it is manifestly impossible to guarantee all the carriers immunity from assault. In San Francisco, lately, the Service has been experimenting with a pocket-size alarm that an endangered mailman can set off by squeezing; it makes a hideous screech that can be heard several blocks away. Some such sort of deterrent would seem to be useful: In the 1970 fiscal year there were 36 crimes committed against postmen on the streets; in 1971, 148; in 1972, 274. The 40,000 post offices and postal stations scattered around the country have fared somewhat better, owing largely to a number of precautionary steps that have been taken to protect them. Under the jurisdiction of the Chief Postal Inspector, there now exists a special security force, nearly two thousand strong, to patrol post offices, some of which, like banks, are also now fitted out with closed-circuit television. Brighter lights and bulletproof glass have been installed in many spots, and since 1967, 13,000 post offices have been rigged out with new burglar alarms, mostly of the silent variety.

Moreover, the Inspection Service's engineers have developed a new kind of safe, supposedly almost impossible to break into and undamageable by unsuccessful attempts to crack it open; 28,000 of these are now in place. In 1972, there were sixty-three vain efforts to loot such fortresses; had they succeeded, the losses would have amounted to $786,541 in stamps and cash, plus 21,496 blank money orders, each of which could have been passed for $100. On January 31, 1972, thanks to a silent alarm, four men were caught inside the post office at Robinson, Pennsylvania, hammering away at a safe that was frustratingly impregnable. Between 1970 and 1972, burglary losses in post offices dropped from more than three million dollars annually to less than half a million. "I think the hoods are finally beginning to get the idea that it's easier to hit a supermarket than to hit us," Chief Inspector Cotter said not long ago.

For all the efficiency and derring-do of the Inspection Service, not every postal crime gets solved. The Plymouth, Massachusetts, robbery of August 14, 1962, in which $1,500,000 in cash being transported by an armored mail truck from Hyannis to Boston was stolen, remains unpunished, and the statute of limitations for prosecutions in connection with it has now expired. The biggest robbery in the history of the Service *was* solved, but ruefully. This involved the removal of $2,050,611 from the mail car of a train at Rondout, Illinois, on June 12, 1924. All but $264,861 of the money was recovered, and eight perpetrators were duly apprehended and convicted; but the identity of one of them was acutely embarrassing to the Service, for he turned out to be the Postal Inspector in charge of security for all mail trains to and from Chicago during the lawless 1920s. "We don't talk about that one too much," says Inspector Charles Miller, "though we take a certain satisfaction from the Service's having solved the case and from the renegade Inspector's having received a twenty-five-year sentence." Still, Miller has a sense of history, and when somebody found in a postal archive the very blasting machine used in the crime and the shovel used to dig up some of the loot, Miller put these relics on exhibit in his office, thus neatly combining memorialization and mortification.

A lot of money travels through the mails. Between 1967 and 1970, some $70 million in stocks, bonds, and other securities, being shipped by registered airmail, disappeared from, largely, the John F. Kennedy Airport at New York. Postal Inspectors determined that most of it was being filched by former airlines employees who knew their way around the area and, wearing their old uniforms, simply strolled onto the landing field and walked off with the gilded pouches as they were being moved by authentic airline employees. Now, armed postal guards monitor all such transfers, and losses from this kind of depredation have dropped to zero. En route to its destination, this sort of mail is further carried in special armored trucks, with two-way radios and sophisticated electronic controls. If a truck deviates by more than a few feet from its prescribed route, this becomes instantly known at its dispatching point, and a posse can be sent out after it. Despite such deterrents, however, crooks are aware how many valuables the mails contain, and are forever trying to obtain a share of them. One man who took part in the hijacking of a mail truck in Florida in 1971 was quickly brought to bay; he made the mistake of trying to sell some of the securities he had stolen to a Postal Inspector.

Other cases have proved more complicated to pursue. A fairly recent one, to which, at one time or another, one hundred Inspectors were assigned, began quietly enough at 12:01 A.M. on December 23, 1969, when an airmail pouch arrived at the registry section of the main post office at Washington, D.C. It was opened by a clerk on night duty, David W. Rice, Jr. In it he found a carton from Frankfort, Germany, twenty inches by fourteen by twelve, addressed to the Treasury Department and bearing the legend "Armed Escort Required." Rice knew what that meant. A great deal of currency is shipped by mail from the armed forces in Europe to the States—$81,410,274 of it between July and December of that year alone. (An impressive sum to most mortals, but not necessarily to Postal Inspectors. In the 1930s they safeguarded the transfer by registered mail, from New York to Fort Knox, of gold worth $15.5 billion.) Whenever a package contained as much as $250,000, which was frequently the case, the "Armed Escort Required" notice was affixed to it. In this instance, the parcel had in it $381,000, in bills of denominations ranging from one dollar to one thousand. The money was being sent by the Army's Finance Section to the Treasury to be removed from circulation because it was somewhat frayed. But it was not sufficiently mutilated—no more than two-fifths of any single bill was missing—to be nonnegotiable. In other words, it was real money.

Rice locked the package in a safe; the first truck to be used for local deliveries was not scheduled to arrive until 6 A.M. When it showed up, with Andrew Arnold at the wheel, it was a U-Haul vehicle that the Post Office had leased to augment its regular trucks during the Christmas rush. Rice decided to go along himself as the armed escort. He removed the parcel from the safe and stowed it with other mail in the back of the truck, which Arnold then locked. The two men set off at daybreak; the first stop on their route was the Home Loan Bank Board building on Indiana Avenue. When they got there, Arnold stepped out to unlock the rear compartment, and he was jumped by a masked man with a gun, who'd been lying in wait behind a parked milk wagon. Two other masked men, one in an old mail carrier's uniform, got the draw on Rice before he could reach his weapon. The two postal employees were ordered into the back of their truck, and two of the robbers got in with them, while the third took the wheel. The three robbers, like the two postal employees, were black, and the intruders evidently thought of themselves as contemporary Robin Hoods; while they were riding through the nearly deserted streets of the capital, one of them told Rice and Arnold that when they were questioned about the crime they should say it had been committed by white men, and the other one said, "This money will feed a lot of black kids for Christmas, from here to New York."

It is possible that some of the $381,000 was used for that. Only $62,286.76 of it was ever recovered. The Black Panthers were then making a big thing of providing meals for needy children, and two of the three robbers, Robert L. Johnson and Calvin S. Jones, then both twenty-three, had been active in the Panther movement. Jones claimed when he was finally caught that out of his share of the take he had bought a lot of toys for children and had stuffed a five-dollar bill into each one before presenting it. He also claimed that he had given a lot of the stolen money to six orphanages. The gleam of his philanthropy was a bit tarnished when he didn't seem to be able to recall the names of any of the orphanages. What *was* known about his disbursements was that he spent $17,000 on a romp through Hawaii and California. On being arrested in a Berkeley hotel, after having made the error of leaving a fingerprint in a second rented truck to which the robbers had switched in a parking lot not far from the scene of the crime, Jones had with him a goodly amount of cocaine, two rifles, a revolver, 750 rounds of ammunition, several bankbooks and savings bonds, and $10,358 in cash. He also had a twenty-one-year-old woman who was the ex-common-law wife of his confederate Johnson; Jones said he had run into her, by chance, out on the West Coast.

The fingerprint Jones had left behind proved handy as evidence, but it was not the cause of his arrest. Many law-enforcement agencies rely heavily on tips to solve crimes, and in this instance, the Postal Inspection Service was considerably helped by an undercover informant who suggested that it look into a Washington bar called the African Hut, a popular Panther hangout where Johnson had worked for a while as a bartender and in which a third member of the gang, a one-time substitute post office clerk named Haywood T. Kirkland, had a proprietary interest. The holdup, in fact, had been planned there, and had initially been set for December 22; but when the robbers had watched the truck on the Treasury Department run early that morning, they had noticed that the driver had no accompanying guard, and had knowledgeably deduced that there was less than a quarter of a million dollars aboard. The African Hut was not an easy place to get into. Like post offices, it had its own security guards, and they scrutinized strangers at the entrance. But a couple of black Postal Inspectors breached the portals, and it didn't take them long to learn about Johnson, Jones, Kirkland, and two further accomplices named John H. Bowman and Arthur B. Knight.

In all, by the time the investigation was concluded, the Service paid out $5,000 in rewards to four informants. One of these was a bank employee, whose suspicions were aroused when, on January 12, 1970, a man named Linwood Chatham asked to be issued a cashier's check in return for a wad of fifty- and one-hundred-dollar bills, most of them somewhat scuffed. Chatham was a crony of Kirkland's and one of a number of outlets through whom the stolen money flowed. When Postal Inspectors went around to see Chatham on January 12, they found $19,850 in cash on him; he said some strangers had donated it—here was the Robin Hood theme again—to help out a community group with which he was associated. Unimpressed by this story, the Inspectors arrested him. They picked up Kirkland, with $5,000 on him, when he came to call on Chatham four days later to see how he was making out with the law. Another $1,550 was discovered under a rug at the home of one of Kirkland's brothers. In due course, the implacable federal government got back some more of the haul by demanding restitution of $365.23 from a Sears, Roebuck store in Oakland, California, which had the bad luck to accept that amount in stolen funds from the high-living Jones in exchange for a color television set. A somewhat more substantial sum was recovered the following September, after a man named Kyle H. Price walked into a Washington bank and requested change for a couple of hundred-dollar bills. He was one of six individuals—among them a minister of sorts—who were picked up for receiving and possessing stolen goods. The minister drew attention to himself by trying to change a five-hundred-dollar bill at still another bank.

Price had been a handyman at a Ford dealer's, and in January, 1970, shortly after the big theft, he had attracted attention to *himself* by buying a used Thunderbird from his employer and paying for it with eighteen hundred-dollar bills. The following June, he had deposited $47,800 in a bank, ostensibly to start a used-car business of his own. By that time, he may have thought that the heat was off. All the principals in the crime had long since been arrested—Johnson in Montreal, where he was registered at a hotel under an African name, with a loaded M-1 rifle among his belongings—and perhaps Price believed that the investigation had concluded. It hadn't. Postal Inspectors knew that Price was living with Johnson's mother, and his strange affluence led them to apply for a warrant to search his residence. They found $1,700 in twenty-dollar bills stashed in an old boot. To this day, though, they haven't yet found $318,713.24 of the worn money that was taken from the rented truck. One would like to hope that some of it at least did ultimately go into ghetto lunch programs; but the only people whose standard of living is known to have been markedly altered by any of it are now in prison, and it will be quite a while before the sincerity of their charitable motives becomes determinable.

That particular mail-truck holdup was a one-shot job, fairly amateurishly conceived and conducted. By and large, the Inspectors are much more concerned with those individuals—professionals in a sense—who make a full-time living by stealing from post offices, and in pursuit of whom the man-hours racked up by the Service (7,875 of these were attributed to the Washington truck hijack) have been of epic proportions. Among all the burglaries of post offices in 1970 and 1971, for instance, perhaps 80 or 85 per cent were committed by a small handful of gangs whose professional members had no other known occupations. There was a Saint Louis group, headed by Michael Wayne Cool, that was credited with twenty-five post office break-ins and a total take of $800,000 in stamps alone. When Cool was released from prison after a brief stay there, Postal Inspection Service headquarters—which wished he had stayed longer and which knows that anticipation can often lead to apprehension—sent a tight-lipped memorandum to its field divisions reporting the news and adding, "It is reasonable to expect that Cool will resume his post office burglary activities." There is no known cure for recidivism.

Circumventing the thieves, if only temporarily, is a big help. What matters even more to the Inspectors is putting their stamp-dealer confederates out of business. A burglar with, say, eight thousand dollars' worth of eight-cent stamps in his possession—one hundred thousand of them—is likely to sell them, for somewhere around $4,800, or 60 per cent of their face value, to a fence, who in turn peddles them to a shady stamp dealer for $6,400, who in turn disposes of them to a customer for $7,200. And who trades in cut-rate postage stamps? Lots of people, most of them perfectly law-abiding. The sellers may be stamp dealers who have gambled heavily, as if they were investing in pork-belly futures, that this or that commemorative issue will be much coveted by collectors and will fetch a premium. Then the commemoratives flop, and rather than be saddled with an excess inventory, the dealer gets rid of them at 90 or 95 per cent of their face value. And whom does he sell to? Not to the Postal Service itself; stamps are never redeemed for cash unless it can be shown that they were damaged when originally bought. The bargain-hunters are apt to be the operators of vending machines in drugstores and motels.

Postal Inspectors, accordingly, are always glad to clamp down on unscrupulous stamp dealers. (One of these people, a diversified crook, was additionally discovered not long ago to be fencing hot ski boots.) Without such dealers to get rid of stolen stamps, there is little incentive for thieves to take the risk of stealing them. It is hard, though, to obtain ironclad evidence to convict underhanded dealers. As a rule, there are no identifying serial numbers on rolls or sheets of stamps, and thus no way of tracing a particular batch of them to a particular source—a requisite, normally, for successful prosecution. There are rare exceptions: After the burglary, in 1972 of the Walland, Texas, post office, some stamps were found in an automobile from which the driver had fled following an accident. There happened to be a fingerprint on one sheet of stamps, and the print turned out to be that of the Walland postmaster. It was only a matter of time before the crime was pinned on the driver of the abandoned car.

Most stamp thieves like to get rid of their loot fast; it is hard for a non-Postal employee or non-stamp dealer to come up with a plausible explanation for having several thousand dollars' worth of postage in his possession. As soon as the Inspection Service learns of a burglary, accordingly, it quickly notifies its operatives in the region to cover the nearby airports, and inasmuch as most such burglaries take place at night, Postal Inspectors are as regularly routed from their beds as volunteer firemen. No blackguards have given Postal Inspectors more sleepless nights than a gang headed by two professionals, Jimmy Jack Holmes and William Stafford Allison. Between February 8, 1968, at Augusta, Georgia, and March 8, 1970, at Indianapolis, this fast-moving pair, sometimes with accomplices, accounted for forty-five attempted post office burglaries in nine states. Twelve of these were unrewarding; either the thieves got scared off or they couldn't open the strongboxes they were aiming at. But the remaining thirty-three produced in cash and stamps a total of $1,311,821—not bad for a couple of years' work, even when the stamps netted Holmes and Allison only about half their face value.

For a while, their principal fences were a Miami pair named John Clarence Cook and Herman Hy Gordon, who also handled jewels. Cook and Gordon were not altogether satisfactory fences. They only gave about 40 per cent of face value on stamps; in the underworld, it was considered inauspicious to argue with them about terms, because they were thought to have excellent organized-crime connections. When Cook was convicted in the spring of 1971 of conspiracy and of possessing stolen stamps and was sentenced to twelve years in prison and a $30,000 fine (Gordon died while awaiting trial), there was jubilation among law-enforcement agencies everywhere, because he had been a hard man to prove anything against. He had an arrest record going back to 1948—vagrancy, petty theft, fraud, armed robbery, disorderly conduct, assault and battery, and so forth—but he had few consequential convictions, and for good reason: A woman who had been expected to be the prime witness against him in a murder case had simply disappeared. He was also notably unflappable. A fellow like that is periodically under the surveillance of one law-enforcement agency or another; returning from a trip to Europe, Cook was naturally suspected of being a smuggler, and the Customs men who greeted him were not surprised to find some zircons under his tongue. His explanation surprised them, though. "I always carry zircons under my tongue," he had said.

Cook was under Dade County police surveillance one night when Holmes and Allison drove up to his house on Biscayne Bay with a footlocker containing $38,000 in stamps that they had removed from an Orlando post office a few hours earlier. As Cook and Holmes were carrying the loot into the front entrance, two cruising Dade County detectives happened to drive along, and they slowed down to see if anybody was being garroted on the premises. Cook and Holmes, without breaking stride, carried the locker straight through the house and out the back door and flung it into the bay. When the gang fished it out later, they discovered that many of the stamps in it had lost their mucilage, and as a result Holmes and Allison got a paltry $12,000 for the job.

Even under bone-dry conditions, Holmes and Allison felt that Cook was an illiberal associate, and they were glad in 1969 to be able to switch to the proprietor of a Tampa stamp-and-coin emporium named Otto Powers, who was usually good for 60 per cent of the face value of what they didn't throw away. (For they were cullers; they would normally not bother with postage-dues and precanceleds and migratory birds and other kinds of stamps that are not widely used.) Powers, moreover, liked to travel; he was always good for a trip to New York, where the big dealers were, and also the big money. His cut would usually run from 5 to 10 per cent of the face value of a theft. But his participation was not without its own tribulations; at the end of 1969, he flew some stolen stamps to New York, expecting to leave them with a downtown dealer who not long before had paid $20,000 for the proceeds of an Allison-Holmes raid upon the Tucker, Georgia, post office; and to Powers' dismay the dealer turned pious on him, saying he would no longer traffic in stolen stamps. He had made a compact with his son to stop selling the stuff if the son would stop smoking pot.

The Postal Inspection Service was on to Holmes, Allison, and Powers. Inspectors on an airport alert at Atlanta had seen the thieves pass a valise to the middleman that almost certainly contained the take from a Tulsa, Oklahoma, burglary, and the Inspectors boarded the same plane that Powers was taking to New York, hoping to be led to his collaborator there. But they lost him in traffic when he left a downtown hotel. That was on January 15, 1970. A couple of weeks later, without being observed, Allison and Holmes struck again. On the afternoon of Sunday, February 1, they stormed the West End Classified Branch of the post office at Richmond, Virginia. This time, Holmes had a double purpose; not only did he want to take away the contents of the safes there, but he wanted to remove the safes themselves so he could study their mechanisms at leisure and expedite future peculations. So Allison and he rented a truck and carted off three strongboxes. Their contents were a highly satisfactory $27,000 worth of stamps and money, and these were delivered to Powers at a rendezvous in a motel near the National Airport at Washington. Powers rented a car and drove with the loot to New York. That day, the airport alert system did not work, and Powers was not followed.

The system worked better the following month. When the Broad Ripple Station in Indianapolis was rifled on March 8, Inspector George A. Freeman at once sounded the alarm; the break-in, he said, had all the earmarks of a Holmes-Allison job. As soon as the news reached Tampa, Inspector R. M. Kelso concentrated on Powers; he learned that the fence had a reservation on a flight to Louisville, where he was due to arrive at 5:05 A.M. the following morning. Two Inspectors were on the plane with him. Meanwhile, Holmes and Allison had driven to Louisville and holed up in a motel near the airport, where they were soon under nonstop observation. Holmes drove to the airport at four-fifteen to meet Powers' flight. Powers debarked with two feather-light suitcases and accompanied Holmes to the motel. When the two of them returned to the airport an hour or so later, to put Powers on a plane to New York, the luggage was perceptibly heavier. As they were checking the bags in, the Inspectors lying in wait for them decided to arrest them; better to capture three birds in hand, the agents reasoned, than take a chance of being once more thwarted by New York traffic. The two suitcases contained $17,000 in postage stamps. In Holmes's automobile—a stolen one—the Inspectors found a handsome set of burglar tools and a lock cylinder that proved to have been removed from the Tulsa post office when it had been ransacked earlier. Holmes, a meticulous researcher, had apparently been studying *that.*

While awaiting trial, Holmes, presumably hoping to get some leniency, decided to talk, and on August 20 he had a revealing meeting with Inspector Freeman. His most telling disclosure was the name of a New York stamp dealer whose office on Nassau Street had been Powers' recent destination—Jacob Habib. At 10:30 A.M. on September 1, armed with a search warrant, eight Inspectors, Freeman among them, descended on a startled Habib. They found, among other things, a big batch of six-cent coils with burn marks on them—just the kind of marks that could have resulted from opening a safe with a blowtorch. When Habib was asked where they had come from, he said he had no idea; the day before, he explained, a stranger had walked in and had sold him $13,000 worth of assorted merchandise.

Searching further, the Inspectors came upon ninety migratory-bird stamps. Now, this was extremely interesting. Migratory-bird stamps are not generally sought by philatelists. They cost three dollars apiece, and are sold, one at a time, to hunters, who have to affix them to their licenses before going out after any bird, like a Canadian goose, that can make interstate flights. And as the Inspectors knew, exactly ninety of these special stamps had been removed in the course of a burglary of the Suffern, New York, post office only five days earlier. The thieves evidently hadn't bothered to do any culling. What was more, there was some scribbling on the margins of these stamp sheets in Habib's office, and the assistant postmaster at Suffern was able to identify the handwriting positively as his own. Habib's goose was cooked.

The Nassau Street raid had been carried out as quietly as possible. The Inspectors wanted to learn what sort of customers Habib attracted when he had a fresh consignment of stolen goods. Late in the morning, a man who was quickly identified as a convicted bank robber strolled in and, on seeing the size and nature of the reception committee awaiting him, almost fainted. During the lunch hour, an even more striking personage materialized. It was a postal clerk, a teller from a lower Manhattan station, with an envelope in his jacket pocket containing $3,086, and another thousand dollars in his pants. He was a man with a twenty-five-year clean record as a hard-working postal employee, and he had $50,000 in fixed credit—the amount in cash and stamps, that was, that he was entrusted with in the course of performing his everyday chores. He said he had never been at Habib's place before, but when an Inspector went over to his postal station, three glassine envelopes were found in the clerk's work jacket with notations on them damagingly close to those on glassine envelopes that Habib had in his office. It also turned out that a thousand dollars of the clerk's fixed credit funds was missing. He was at once arrested.

From that point on, as far as the Inspectors were concerned, it was largely a question of tidying up the loose ends of their case. Habib pleaded guilty to one count of mail fraud and got a year and a day. Powers got eighteen months, and Holmes and Allison five years apiece. After Holmes was sentenced, he solicited further interviews with the Service, and on two occasions Inspectors went to call on him. The first time he explained how he concealed the glare of his torch when he went to work on a safe. He would drag a table up alongside the strongbox, he said, and drape it with empty mail sacks. Then he would crawl underneath and operate inside his improvised curtains, with a string tied to one leg, which Allison was supposed to tug on as a signal to stop. Holmes also said it was terribly important for thieves working inside a place to maintain radio contact with their outside lookouts. In the second interview, Holmes said he thought the locking mechanisms on post office safes were inferior, and he drew diagrams of ones that he thought would be much harder to circumvent. While he was at it, he confided that the new safes the Service had been installing since 1967 had caused him some trouble at first, but that after he'd examined the ones he'd removed at Richmond they hadn't been too difficult to cope with. He had some suggestions for improving *them* in general, and he passed these along. His recommendations were subsequently studied and analyzed, but not put into effect; the Service's final conclusion was that its own experts at fool-proofing could do better than Jimmy Jack Holmes.

# 4. The Five Hundred Billion Dollar Bubble

There is something clean-cut and comprehensible about crimes like hijacking and safe-cracking, which when they do not involve outright violence are easily distinguishable as antisocial. Many crimes are far less overt, and not only are not characterized by rude behavior but, on the contrary, may depend for their success on extravagant good manners and even courtliness. They are often committed in the hallowed names of the dead, who make excellent accomplices because they cannot be called as witnesses. Since there can be no one on earth who had no ancestors, and since practically everyone on earth is sorry he did not inherit more of what it has produced, the possibilities of invoking the names of the past for the chicanery of the present are limitless.

Some people have rich uncles, others wish they had, and still others—this perhaps the largest of the three categories—can readily be persuaded that they probably did have and, for a comparative pittance, can be rewarded with their rightful legacies. Is there anyone anywhere named Kelly who has not heard of the Mary Kelly Estate? It is uncertain just who she was, if she ever existed, but over the years thousands of individuals named Kelly or Kelley, whose names happened to appear in telephone directories, have been advised by mail that for a mere ten dollars or so they can receive documents entitling them to lodge a claim against the residual estate of one Mary Kelly, and there may well be letters to that effect in some unsuspecting Kelly's mailbox at this very moment.

There have been dozens of other notorious missing-heir swindles; anyone who is told he stands likely to inherit between ten and two hundred million dollars if he had an ancestor named Bogardus, Jennens, or Wertz should instantly beware. The granddaddy of all the bogus estates surely is that of Sir Francis Drake, since whose death on the Spanish Main in 1596 hundreds of thousands of Americans have been led to believe that his estate—worth by now in their rosy imaginations as much as $22 billion—was practically in their pockets. The names of 70,000 putative Drake heirs were uncovered in a single office in Chicago one day in 1935. In Canton, North Dakota, which had a population of 2,500 in the 1930s, 250 of the residents had paid money to be registered as Drake heirs. The chief beneficiary of their hopes was a man named Oscar M. Hartzell, who was finally sent to prison. He ended up in a hospital for mental defectives, but in his healthier days he lived handsomely for nearly twenty years—part of that time in England, after he was deported from the United States as an undesirable alien—off the money pressed on him by panting aspirants to the legendary Drake fortune.

If Mark Hopkins, the California railroad and real-estate magnate, had written a will before he died in 1878, nobody knows how many greedy and gullible people might have been spared a great deal of time, trouble, money, and grief; and a young confidence man from Virginia named David Ray Wright might, ninety-three years later, have been spared a conviction for mail fraud and a stay in a federal prison. Hopkins, a resident of Nob Hill, in San Francisco, where the stately Mark Hopkins Hotel now memorializes his name, was in his middle sixties at his death. On November 1, 1883, a California state court issued a final decree of distribution of his estate. One-quarter of it was awarded to his brother Moses, and three-quarters to Mary Frances Sherwood Hopkins, who was Mark's widow, or who at any rate was accepted by the court as his widow. The value of the estate, in 1883, was somewhere around $20 million—a considerable sum at that time, or any time.

Mark Hopkins died not only intestate but also childless, though to complicate the tangled web of his posthumous affairs there was a boy, Timothy Hopkins, who somewhere along the line was adopted by Mary Frances. As a further complication, most of the records bearing on Hopkins' past and on his property vanished during the earthquake and fire that ravaged San Francisco in 1906. Since then, spurred on in part by the absence of authentic documentation to refute their assertions, a large number of people have devoted large portions of their lives to seeking a piece of the legendary Hopkins estate, which in their fevered imaginations has swollen, depending on the degree of their wishfulness, to somewhere between $500 million and $500 billion. Not a few individuals have practically made a career out of trying to establish their own and others' eligibility to dip into this bottomless pot of gold. Among the arguments they have used to press their claims are the contentions that—the five years between Hopkins' death and the court decision notwithstanding—there were Hopkins siblings other than Moses who should have been taken care of in 1883, but who never even knew their rich brother was dead because Moses and Mary Frances were derelict in spreading the word; and that Mark may not have been married to Mary Frances at all but, rather, to an East Coast woman named Mary Ann Moss, who was either his lawful or his common-law wife and in any event a convenient stepping stone between his alleged fortune and the countless optimistic individuals who reckon her among their kin.

Periodically, over the years, the 1883 decree has been challenged in the courts by people who thought they were Hopkins' rightful heirs, and every time every court has dismissed every challenge. One petition was thrown out in 1926 on the ground of laches—that is, an inexcusable delay in making a claim. A generation later, a federal judge ruled once and forever that although there might have been some mischief committed in 1883, the 1906 fire had done away with all possibility of establishing it, and that since so much time had elapsed and so few facts could be verified, the issue was no longer moot. Judicial declarations of that sort have failed to dampen the ardor of, for instance, an elderly woman named Helen Kincaid, who was the nurse and does seem beyond doubt to be the heir of one Lydia Hopkins, the presumed daughter of Timothy Hopkins, whatever his relation to Mark may have been. Mrs. Kincaid professes to believe that Lydia Hopkins was both Mary Frances Sherwood's granddaughter and her niece. Another senior citizen who figures importantly in the Mark Hopkins demonology is Mrs. Estelle Latta, who professes to be a double grandniece of the Nob Hill man. One court case she filed was thrown out in 1949 on grounds of *gross* laches. For many years, Mrs. Latta engaged in the lucrative business of selling shares in the Mark Hopkins estate; for a mere one hundred dollars, she promised each of her customers one-hundredth of one-fifth of one-sixth of one-seventh of the estate, which came out to one twenty-one-thousandth. Inasmuch as she appraised the estate at sixty billion dollars, attributing to it landholdings in all but two of California's fifty-eight counties (she included the ground on which stands the Los Angeles City Hall), each of these tiny fractions was worth three million dollars. Many of Mrs. Latta's suppositions were outlined in a book she wrote called *Controversial Mark Hopkins . . . The Greatest Swindle of American History.* She considered herself among the swindled. The Securities and Exchange Commission thought otherwise. In 1965, it got a federal court in California to enjoin her permanently from further peddling of her peculiar stock. When Mrs. Latta persisted, she was arrested for violating the injunction and was put on trial in the spring of 1971. She suffered a stroke during the proceedings, and the case is still pending.

What has buoyed the hopes of all the claimants to the almost assuredly inaccessible estate of Mark Hopkins is, for one thing, a lingering uncertainty as to just who he was. What he did in California is generally stipulated by all concerned: He arrived there as a store proprietor not long after the gold strike of 1849; he teamed up with Leland Stanford, Collis Huntington, and Charles Crocker to develop the West Coast railroads, and he became very rich. Among his potential heirs, though, there is little agreement as to his origins. Of several Mark Hopkinses who have figured in American history, at least two of about the same age ended up in California at about the same time. A kind of Civil War has ensued over them. Helen Kincaid, for instance, has usually contended that the consequential Mark Hopkins, the one it pays to be related to, was a Northern Mark Hopkins from New York and Massachusetts. Estelle Latta and her followers have been more partial to the theory that he was a Southern Mark Hopkins, who was born in Georgia and later dwelt in North Carolina and Virginia. Mrs. Latta has even come up with an ingenious notion that ties together both these men: According to her, the Northern Hopkins married Mary Frances Sherwood in New York and brought her to California, where he died in 1876; his widow then became the housekeeper for the Southern Hopkins and on his death passed herself off as *his* widow.

To further ensnarl the all but incomprehensible series of purported interrelationships, there was also a nineteenth-century *black* Mark Hopkins, a scientist from whom quite a few white Southerners entered in the Mark Hopkins Estate Sweepstakes, to the amazement of the Postal Inspectors who most recently looked into the whole mixed-up matter, have blandly claimed to be descended—just in case he might somehow be a factor in the strange proceedings. The New England educator Mark Hopkins has not been much dragged in, conceivably because of his conspicuous nonidentification with worldly possessions: It was he who expressed the belief that the most admirable sort of academic institution consisted of a log with a teacher sitting on one end and a pupil on the other.

All things considered, it has been easier to claim some sort of connection with the principal Southern Hopkins than with the principal Northern one, which explains why so many of the participants in the perennial wild-goose chase have come from the

South. What keeps their hopes sputtering is their stout conviction that before the Georgia-born Mark took off for California, he wooed and won a Blue Ridge Mountain woman named Mary Ann Moss, who before she ran away with him was the first wife of a man named Henry Samuel Wright. As a consequence of their naughty alliance, there is hardly a Moss or a Wright east of the Mississippi and south of the Potomac who has not been stirred up at some time or other by the possibility that he or she might be a descendant, if merely a collateral one, of Moneybags Hopkins. There was once even a Mark Hopkins Society in North Carolina, and in that state's city of Durham, Estelle Latta for a time presided over a weekly newspaper column entitled "Mark Hopkins," in which she served up tidbits guaranteed to tantalize. In May, 1967, several hundred aspirants with Moss on their family tree gathered at Martinsville, Virginia, for a meeting chaired by W. Rex Moss, who was more or less the patriarch of and spokesman for the contemporary Mosses. His great-great-grandmother on one side was supposedly a sister of the Southern Hopkins, and his great-great-aunt on another side was supposedly Mary Ann Moss.

Among the Danville, Virginia, representatives of the Moss clan who attended the session at Martinsville were the members of one Wright family who also professed to believe that they were doubly connected to the chimerical fortune: Raymond Wright, a mortgage broker; his wife, Willye Sue; and their older son, David Ray, who was then twenty-five but grasping beyond his years. The mother looked like a typical genteel Southern belle until she opened her mouth, at which point she often turned sharp-tongued. The son, who also had an explosive temper and could be extremely curt with people who doubted his veracity, was married and had his own home, but he was much under his parents' sway; he worked, when he worked legitimately, as a salesman for his father, and although he was married, he worked closely with his mother on her various projects. None of the Wrights had criminal records back then, but both the mother and the son had guns, for which they had not bothered to obtain permits.

It is difficult, when dealing with confidence men and women, to sift fact from fancy, inasmuch as their stock in trade is the fabrication of plausible myths; but it seems generally accepted that when the Wrights first got involved in the Mark Hopkins game they were mainly motivated by fairly innocent greed—the desire to get rich quick by staking a claim to the will-o'-the-wisp estate. Indeed, in 1967 they paid Rex Moss five hundred dollars to be sure they'd be cut in when and if he steered the fabled treasure ship to port. It was not long afterward that they apparently concluded he was too poky and there was far more to be made by collecting money from others than by waiting around, as so many other hopefuls had for the better part of a century, to collect it from the estate. Raymond Wright was only minimally engaged in their subsequent shenanigans and was not ultimately indicted; in fact, on November 24, 1967, for reasons that are not clear, he went through the formality of ceding all his own claims on the estate to his wife, for a paltry ten dollars. Even so, that was ten dollars more than any living person's claim on the estate has yet been proved to be worth.

From that moment on, until, on December 22, 1971, they pleaded guilty to nineteen counts of mail fraud and one count of fraud by telegraph, Willye Sue and David Ray Wright managed to extract, from at least three hundred simple-minded victims in at least thirteen states, a sum that has been conservatively estimated by the Postal Inspectors who brought them to bay at $300,000—a modest enough yield by the standards of some confidence-game practitioners, but a robust one considering that the Wrights clipped some of their pigeons for no more than $250 apiece. Not a little of the money was removed from the pockets and bank accounts of their own trusting kin, and so dazzling was the picture the Wrights painted for them—each victim being promised a minimum of $1 million of "unclaimed assets" of the Hopkins estate, whatever they were supposed to be—that to this day many of the suckers refuse to concede that they were bilked at all but, rather, blame the Postal Inspection Service for having rudely and uninvitedly stepped in and pricked their golden bubble. Few of the victims, being largely millworkers, dirt farmers, housewives, and pensioners, could afford their losses. Some mortgaged homes to finance the Wrights, thanks to whom, instead of ending up with some of Mark Hopkins' savings, the victims squandered most of their own.

It takes hard work to be a successful confidence man, and the Wrights, whatever else they may have been, were not shirkers. Evenings and weekends were their favorite fund-raising times. The tools of their trade were not costly or burdensome. They merely had to plant the seed of greed and nurture it. To begin with, they had some fancy calling cards printed up, David Ray's proclaiming himself a "Genealogist" and his mother's identifying her as that and as an historian to boot. As a nice touch, both cards bore the legend "By Appointment Only." Both also were adorned by the seal of the Virginia Genealogical Society. The seal was authentic, but its use questionable; anyone can join the Society on payment of five-dollar annual dues, and most members would no more think of displaying its insigne on their business cards than would moderate contributors to the Boy Scouts display *its* insigne on theirs. To further impress prospects, the Wrights would sometimes claim to be "registered genealogists" in Virginia. Genealogy is important in that state—where the First Families of Virginia cherish their primacy—but in regional genealogical circles the Wrights had no standing whatever. They were hardly objective researchers; the only people they listed on family trees they got up were those who had paid for the privilege. In any event, stretching the truth came easily to the Wrights. David Ray, for example, a short, porcine fellow with a glib tongue and a shifty eye, claimed sometimes to be a graduate of North Carolina State (he had a 1966 class ring), sometimes to be a Doctor of Divinity (he had an honorary degree that he had bought from a Hollywood, California, mail-order diploma mill), and sometimes to have completed two years of business college and one of law (he had briefly attended some noncredit courses at a Danville extension school of the University of Virginia).

While soliciting prospects, the Wrights often carried with them a suitcase full of documents, a few of which they would let their customers glimpse. Principal among these, naturally, was an inventory of the assets of the estate to which they pretended to have a pipeline—assets, they would let on, that were unlawfully held by various banks and government agencies. One piece of paper they sometimes waved around was a photostat of a page of Mrs. Latta's book; the total of the stocks, bonds, and real estate on this particular list came to only $174,756,740.00, but that was not bad for starters. One had to add to this, the Wrights would now and then explain, most of the oil properties in California and all of the property on which Disneyland had been constructed, not to mention railroad stocks and bonds that had been worth over $30 billion in 1870 and would fetch only Heaven knew how much one hundred years thereafter; and seventy gilt-edged acres in downtown San Francisco.

These assets, the mother and son would go on to tell their dazed prospects, were merely what remained after certain substantial distributions that had already been made to deserving heirs—$25 million in cash to one unnamed man in Texas, for instance, and an unspecified sum to another chap who now had two Rolls-Royces and had fitted out his home with solid-gold doorknobs. From dirt farming, virtually overnight, to solid-gold doorknobs! Who could resist such a vision! Those lucky legatees were anonymous, but to lend credibility to their arguments, the Wrights were prepared to name some others. The roster was breathtaking: Harry S. Truman, Earl Warren, Ronald Reagan, and Lady Bird Johnson. The swindlers' proof of their payments was, by normal evidential criteria, gossamer. Their substantiation for President Truman's windfall was a copy of a letter *to* him from a crackpot accusing him of having received $3 million of the Hopkins money; in Mrs. Johnson's case, the Wrights brandished a copy of a letter from one crackpot to another in which she was named as a $15 million beneficiary. So swiftly were these papers produced and tucked away again that the victims who glanced at them usually had a chance only to take note of the well-known name and the mouthwatering figure. The Wrights were also fond of citing one judge who was supposed to be a $9 million Hopkins heir. In this instance, the evidence consisted of a photostat of a bond in that amount that a judge had posted in connection with serving as the executor of a large estate, but it was an estate that had nothing to do with Mark Hopkins. No matter; people who want to believe what they are told will seize at any straw of confirmation.

Digging into their suitcase, the Wrights would sometimes pluck forth some worn old railroad bonds that practically sang of authenticity and antiquity. These were genuine bonds—although not Mark Hopkins' and although all but worthless—that the mother and son had borrowed from one of their victims, on the pretext of cashing them for him. The Wrights' explanation of how they had acquired these securities was more romantic: They had got them by breaking a code in San Francisco, they asserted, and thus gaining access to a Wells Fargo safe-deposit box. And in the same box they had found Mark Hopkins' family Bible! And—guess what!—in its brittle pages they had seen inscribed the name of an ancestor of—guess who!—exactly the person they were talking to at that very moment!

Still another heady gambit was the disclosure, usually *sotto voce,* of the names of various renowned lawyers, among them Melvin Belli and F. Lee Bailey, who the Wrights would hint were handling the tedious legal details of their enterprise. The swindlers said that they had approached both attorneys and had paid them retainers, but neither man recalls performing any services for them. The mother and son nonetheless made it sound as though Belli or Bailey, or both, were working covertly on their behalf; once, Mrs. Wright phoned a woman prospect and said if she would look at such-and-such a page of her daily paper—where there was a picture of Belli escorting a client out of prison—she'd see the kind of legal representation she could expect if she anted up. As lagniappe, the Wrights would sometimes inform potential victims that among the fringe benefits of being a recognized Hopkins heir were free stays at the San Francisco hotel named after him;

whether or not this included drinks on the house at the Top of the Mark, at the establishment's summit, was not specified.

By the time the mother and son, working separately or as a well-coordinated team, had finished an hour or so of their rigmarole, an astonishing number of people were not only willing but eager to give them $250, which, at the outset, was the routine charge for "registering" as a Hopkins heir—though of course there is no need for any lawful heir to an estate to register in order to collect what he properly has coming to him. (Later, they sometimes hiked the initiation fee to $500.) Perhaps hoping thereby to avoid future trouble, Mrs. Wright instructed her victims to sign an awkwardly phrased statement reading, "It is understood by me that by contributing this $250.00 it is a gamble and that I will not blame her or anyone else if this money is not recoverable, or if the above mentioned estate is unsuccessful the decision to contribute the money is altogether mine." Willye Sue's husband would often notarize this gibberish, but he never affixed his notary's seal. Mrs. Wright, for her part, furnished a quid pro quo, declaring in a receipt of sorts that she would "honestly and truthfully" perform as the "duly appointed representative" of the party of the other part.

Once a prospect was hooked, it was usually a simple matter to hit him again. One gimmick was to persuade parents to register—at an additional $250 per capita—each of their children; the oil wells in the Hopkins estate, the Wrights would explain, were earmarked for the benefit of legatees' offspring, who were entitled not only to a lump-sum payment but to a veritable gusher of annual royalties. Then there were travel expenses. It was essential for the Wrights to touch bases at San Francisco, Sacramento, Houston, Boston, and other spots to pin down the slippery inheritance, and no duly appointed representative could be expected to undertake such missions for free. In the summer of 1971, for example, David Ray cajoled a minister and his brother-in-law out of $2,500, to underwrite an expedition to Massachusetts which was for the purpose of redeeming a $4.7 million Mark Hopkins insurance policy and retrieving deeds to a couple of large properties, one of which had some stables on it that all by themselves were appraised at $7 million. (The stalls presumably had solid-gold latches.) From Boston there was a telephoned plea for an extra $1,000, this to satisfy a handwriting expert who suddenly had to be hired. When still another call requested $2,500 more for "title research and filing fees," the brothers-in-law had the good sense to call it quits.

A sideline activity in which the Wrights vigorously took part was the signing of "contracts" with other pursuers of the Hopkins trove, each signatory pledging himself to split with the others whatever Hopkins proceeds might come his way. Whenever somebody in the field seemed to be on to a good thing, or said he was, the others would swiftly close ranks. Thus Estelle Latta, who usually collected other people's powers of attorney, gave her power in the fall of 1969 to a woman named Doris Taylor, a Mark Hopkins expert who was then in vogue. The following February, Willye Sue and David Ray signed a contract with Doris Taylor. Not long after that Doris Taylor sued Helen Kincaid, Estelle Latta's long-time rival, on some esoteric ground or another. A few months later, the Wrights signed up with Helen Kincaid, who was later to throw the contract situation into hopeless confusion by testifying in a courtroom that there were at least a half dozen such understandings extant with her name on them that were fraudulent.

In all their dealings with their victims, the Wrights stressed urgency and secrecy. It helped to preclude the leisurely perusal of proffered documents if the mother and son could convince prospects that there was an imminent deadline for filing claims on the estate and that in order to qualify for a bonanza, their names, duly registered, had to be submitted to the appropriate lawyers within a day or two—if not, indeed, within a few crucial hours. As for keeping everything hush-hush, when one victim—a man who had registered himself and three children and was about to notify relatives all over the country to hop on the gilded bandwagon—suggested that perhaps it would expedite a settlement if the F.B.I. were asked to help ferret out the elusive Hopkins funds, the

Wrights retorted solemnly that the government had to be kept in the dark; otherwise, to cover up *its* misappropriations of the inheritance, it might order the F.B.I. to do away with the lot of them. A few weeks afterward, revisiting this man late one evening, the Wrights took to ducking into his bathroom and flicking a light switch on and off. When asked what they were up to, they said they were reassuring some F.B.I. men posted outside that they were all right. But, the man said puzzledly, hadn't they given him to understand that the F.B.I. was *against* them? "Oh, it was, but now we have a couple of agents on our side," was the hasty answer.

The Wrights would swear some members of a family to secrecy, warning them not to tell their brothers and sisters of their impending good fortune, and would then go out and solicit the brothers and sisters. The Wrights' own close relatives were not exempt from their peccadilloes. One young woman named Grace Thompson—the names of all victims mentioned herein have been changed; they have suffered enough—met the mother and son at a family funeral and, not having $250 to register her name with them, offered to provide some secretarial work in lieu of cash. Her duties came to include making out checks to the Wrights from elderly victims who were too addled or too palsied to do more than scrawl their signatures. Sometimes the Wrights were careless; Miss Thompson got suspicious when she ran into a victim named Arthur Forrest, who'd been told by Willye Sue that she'd gone to San Francisco to confer with a famous lawyer at a time when Willye Sue had told *her* she was conferring in Boston. Miss Thompson was flabbergasted on learning the truth about her employer, and she told a Postal Inspector, "It's just beyond my comprehension that anyone could deliberately take money from their relatives for their own personal gain."

It is astonishing how many of the victims were related—if not to the Wrights, to each other. Nobody knows for certain how many victims there were. The Postal Inspection Service figure of three hundred seems low; Mrs. Wright once boasted of having bagged forty in a single day. Of seventy-nine victims particularized in the mail-fraud indictments—the Wrights did not discriminate; forty-four were men and thirty-five women—twenty-six were Forrests or their cousins or in-laws, and they constituted less than one-fourth of that single family's known dupes. The saddest thing was that so many of the victims volunteered, more or less, to be fleeced. One of the Forrests who lived in Virginia went to a North Carolina convocation of Mark Hopkins buffs in the spring of 1968, heard about the Wrights, and on his return to his home state looked them up. Mrs. Wright was enchanted to make his acquaintance and said almost at once that he could well be the missing link she'd long been seeking in a genealogical chain. (For a suitable price, she could spot a missing link at a thousand yards on a moonless night.) He could hardly wait to spread the good tidings among his local kinfolk, of whom there were quite a few; and one of them told an uncle in Illinois about the providential development. *He* rushed to enroll his six children—how he must later have regretted his prolificness!—and then phoned a brother in Indiana, who enrolled himself and his three children and phoned three more brothers. One family of Forrests got so enthusiastic that they let the mother and son use their home to recruit people unrelated to them. The more often some of the Forrests listened to the Wrights' spiel, though, the more baffling it sounded; and when the Forrests sought to clarify some of the discrepancies between one sales pitch and another, the Wrights' responses were disconcertingly evasive. Moreover, while none of the heirs' money seemed to be forthcoming, the Wrights' standard of living had markedly improved; David Ray was seen driving around Danville in a new baby-blue-and-white Cadillac. When a Forrest in Virginia told an Indiana Forrest of the Wrights' failure to transmit a promised receipt for some travel expenses, the Midwesterner and one of his sons flew east—still another travel expense they incurred—to confront the Danville pair. Mrs. Wright soothed them temporarily by presenting them with one of her "honestly and truthfully" forms. But as time dragged on and nothing happened, the Forrests grew increasingly apprehensive. They did some canvassing among themselves and their acquaintances and were startled to learn that although none of them had a firm assurance of ever receiving a penny, their ascertainable outlay to the Wrights had reached the sum of $51,475—$32,625 of this alone from 112 members of the Forrest family. That sobering revelation impelled a couple of them, in the fall of 1970, to ask the Postal Inspection Service what it knew about the mother and son and their machinations. Not long after this act of perfidy against the Wrights was revealed, one of the tattletale Forrests received in the mail an envelope containing two playing cards—the combination of an ace and a jack known in mordant gambling circles as a Dead Man's Hand.

Two Postal Inspectors then in the Washington, D.C., field office of the Service, Charles C. Cheezum and Norman E. Robbins, were assigned to the case. While they were not obliged to try to unravel every last twist of the knotty mystery of Mark Hopkins and his money, real or fancied, they had to establish enough misrepresentations in the Wrights' version of it to determine that they had used the mails to perpetrate a fraud. This was not as simple as it sounded offhand, for the Wrights themselves were understandably uncommunicative, and as the Inspectors called on one victim after another, they were hard put to get people to admit they'd been duped or to speak out against their defrauders. There remained too many lingering hopes that the Wrights might somehow someday make good on their pledges of paradise. Cheezum, for instance, got nowhere with one elderly man who ever since he had registered as a Hopkins heir had been buying coal by the bag instead of by the ton. Expecting at any moment to hear the good news from the Danville pair and to abandon his run-down shanty home for a mansion with eighteen-carat doorknobs, he didn't want to be encumbered with a surfeit of fuel. He had been buying coal by the bag for close to a year.

Persistence sometimes triumphs, however. Inspectors Cheezum and Robbins had first to convince the victims they called on that they really weren't ever going to lay their hands on any Hopkins money, let alone a single plain Hopkins doorknob; and then they had to convince them that their cooperation would, if nothing else, possibly save some yet unborn suckers from falling into the same glittering trap. Eventually the Inspectors rounded up enough potential witnesses—some of whom, of course, were feeling sufficiently vengeful to volunteer to testify—to make a solid case against the Wrights. On January 13, 1971, the Inspectors submitted their findings, and names, to the United States Attorney at Roanoke, Leigh B. Hanes, Jr., who presented the matter to a federal grand jury. It produced an indictment on February 8. The mother and son were arrested on February 22, and released on bond.

It takes more than a mere inconvenience like an arrest, though, to deter a true-blue confidence man from pursuing his vocation. The pattern of behavior is familiar: The jig is up, or nearly up; time is fast running out; whatever can be milked from a scheme has to be squeezed out in a hurry. And in these pressing circumstances, the stakes must be raised. So when, following their arrest, the Wrights approached one North Carolina beauty shop proprietor, it was for no mere few hundred dollars; they asked for $15,000, in return for which she was to receive, within a fortnight for sure, 10 per cent of their interest in the Hopkins estate, the total of which they then calculated, with uncommon prudence, to be $550 million. This prospect did not bite. The Wrights did much better with the male proprietor of a television business, who over a comparatively short stretch of time gave them—practically forced upon them—more than thirty checks amounting to $26,000; how could he refuse, on discovering that the name of one of his wife's progenitors had been discerned in Mark Hopkins' own Bible? The very same day that, at Danville, a pretrial hearing was held to take the testimony of thirty-two victims, David Ray was on the phone trying to lasso still another.

On September 16, 1971, the venue for the Wrights' trial was changed, at their request, from Danville to Roanoke; the United States District Judge who approved the shift also issued a temporary injunction forbidding either Willye Sue or David Ray to engage in any further solicitation. Eight days after *that,* David Ray checked into a motel at Knoxville, Tennessee, tore out of the local telephone directory the page listing twenty-eight Hopkinses, and called as many of them as he could. He invited them all to stop by his room that evening and hear something that could be of sensational pecuniary benefit to them. Fifteen of them showed up. Wright gave a brief outline of his version of the history of Mark Hopkins, and then revealed that of the giant estate $87 million had been earmarked for Hopkinses alone, including descendants of one of Mark's brothers, the Johns Hopkins after whom the university is named. (This was a new twist; there is no reason to believe that Johns Hopkins was related to Mark.) The fat melon was to be carved in Boston the following January, David Ray went on, and he was at that instant en route there to iron out a few of the remaining kinks. All he needed to accomplish this was a thousand-dollar advance from each of forty persons, every one of whom, in addition to doing him a favor, would within less than four months' time realize a cool million. It was an unrewarding evening, because a sixteenth Hopkins, who thought the telephoned invitation had a fishy ring, had notified the police of the motel assembly, and a plainclothesman was also in attendance. As a result, all David Ray realized for his efforts was to be arrested again, this time on the charge of trying to take money under false pretenses.

Sensing that the net was tightening, David Ray, after posting bail, skipped Boston and headed instead for Houston, where he sought unavailingly to engage the noted criminal lawyer Percy Foreman. Back in Federal court, on December 22, the Wrights, who were liable to a thousand-dollar fine and five years' imprisonment on each of the twenty counts of their federal indictment (the Knoxville charge was dropped after their conviction), cut the proceedings short by pleading guilty to all counts. David Ray was fined five thousand dollars and sentenced to one year in prison; his mother got the same fine and was put on probation for three years. By that time, the Internal Revenue Service had got into the act and had procured an indictment of its own against the son, the mother, and the father of the family as well; from this indictment, Raymond Wright also drew a five-thousand-dollar fine and three years' probation. The income tax charge must have been particularly galling to Mrs. Wright, inasmuch as a year or so earlier she had bragged to one of her prospective patsies that she herself had already reaped such a harvest from the Hopkins estate that she had money stashed away in safe-deposit boxes in five banks, and that the Internal Revenue Service—making this state of affairs all the more delightful—wasn't even aware that she existed. That one small secret at least is now out in the open.

# 5. The Cheese in the Mousetrap

By the time most swindles come to light, they have already resulted in grievous losses to people who hope to make a quick killing and in substantial profits to the swindlers themselves, who can be certain that among every group of individuals there is a hard core of the greedy, the gullible, the careless, and the irrational. Sometimes, though, the perpetrators of the schemes end up with scarcely any gains to show for their usually considerable pains. Such was the case a few years ago in California, whose soil has long proved hospitable to the nurture of deceit. A Santa Monica policeman, civic-mindedly tidying up a mess of papers strewn along the edge of a freeway, found among them some printed letters signed by Jack Dempsey and Groucho Marx, inviting the recipients to attend a testimonial banquet for Sandy Koufax at the Beverly Hills Hotel. Tickets were reasonably priced at fifteen dollars. A hasty check by a Postal Inspector to whom the undelivered mail was forwarded revealed that neither the prize fighter nor the comedian had authorized the use of his signature, and that nobody had notified the baseball player that the banquet was to be held in his honor.

A lot of detective work is pure drudgery. There are only a limited number of places, even in Southern California, that do job printing, and on methodically checking them out, the Inspector soon determined that a petty confidence man and shoplifter of long standing had had three thousand of the invitations made up; but these were so ineptly worded, and so few of them had actually been mailed, that he had had only one response—a $150 donation from a social club reserving a table for ten. The most unusual aspect of this undistinguished scheme was the eventual appearance, during a trial that culminated it, of Groucho Marx, who tried to convert a courtroom into a stage set. He asked the judge, for instance, if he could tell a few jokes. Save them for television, the judge informed him tartly. Finally, the judge dismissed him from the premises, but Groucho had the last word: Stalking out of the courtroom in his familiar duck walk, he paused at the door, waved an unlit cigar, and said, "Why did the man who picked me up this morning have handcuffs?" The biggest joke of all may have been on the criminal who launched the episode, because not only did he end up with 180 days in jail, but his printing bills just about canceled out his proceeds.

Direct-mail solicitation is a common and often lucrative sort of fraud. Over the years, alluring advertisements in newspapers and magazines have proved to be no less rewarding to the people who dream them up. In Miami Beach, not long ago, a man inserted an ad in a weekly magazine much fancied by photography buffs. He offered Polaroid 210 Color Pack cameras for $19.95 at a time when they were normally selling for vastly more. Someone who doubted that anybody in his right mind would make such a proposal had the good sense to ask the Miami office of the Postal Inspection Service what it thought of the ad's validity. Inspector Robert E. Crider got onto the case, and just in time: When he caught up with the originator of this particular scheme, there was no sign of any cameras, but there was $48,631.41 in his bank account and another $23,831.52 in his residence. And within the next few days a flood of mail came in—11,062 letters containing $174,323.10 worth of orders for nonexistent cameras. After all ascertainable claims had been paid off—some of the victims were so eager to get their bargain cameras that they had mailed in cash and neglected to enclose return addresses—there remained $17,018.51, which the Post Office Department conscientiously turned over to the Treasury Department, thus again contributing, in however minuscule a way, to a diminution of the national deficit.

What go-getting businessman would not welcome an invitation to take part, at practically no cost to himself, in the "World's Largest International Gift Fair," especially when it was to be held at Las Vegas? Between 1969 and 1970, some thirty thousand firms received a friendly communication from an outfit that called itself International Gift Shows, Inc., and purported to have offices in London as well as in Las Vegas and Los Angeles. International Gift Shows, it seemed, was putting on a mammoth exposition, which would feature a half million items from five hundred top-flight American manufacturers and still more from fifty-six nations abroad. "We will Jet you to Las Vegas and return you to your nearest airport, accommodate you at the new International Hotel for 5 days and 4 nights, along with 4 meals, the dinner show, lounge shows . . . a very enjoyable business trip, all for $199," said the eye-opening letters. What a bargain! Hundreds of the recipients of this good news scrambled to avail themselves of the opportunity, in a couple of instances sending their checks—altogether, they invested $250,000 in the Las Vegas lark—by special-delivery mail, since they had little faith in the postal service.

They had too much faith in International Gift Shows, which consisted of a couple of shrewd operators named Robert Craven and Edward Nelson. Nelson went to prison not long afterward for his part in the venture; Craven disappeared before he could be arrested and hasn't been spotted since. The two men had simply pocketed the deposit money people sent them, and would stall complainants by pleading that their expositions had had to be postponed for reasons beyond their control. Craven's methods of operation were consistent with the known facts of his life: On investigation, the Inspection Service learned that he had a criminal record going back more than twenty years, including convictions for issuing bad checks and failing to pay employees' wages. A distinctive feature of his record was that while he had been lucratively promoting "trade shows" for at least seven years, he had never actually got around to putting on a single one of them.

Still another teasing come-on involved the well-known weekly *TV Guide,* which in its various editions had a circulation in 1969 of 14.5 million, and which charged accordingly for advertising space. The originators of *this* scheme not only didn't end up with any profit but actually ended up out of pocket to the tune of some $25,000—thus achieving the unique distinction of trying to perpetrate a fraud in which, by the time it ran its short and shady course, the fleecers actually got fleeced. There were two of them, a pair of twenty-seven-year-old, personable, glib West German businessmen named Roland H. Graber and Hans Georg Aust, temporarily living in Hollywood, California. At the moment of their downfall, in the spring of 1969, Graber was by his own account an unemployed cookie salesman. Aust called himself a self-employed pollster. Earlier, operating out of a West Side apartment house in New York City, Aust had run a questionable enterprise in which he sold advertising space in a directory ostensibly distributed to Telex subscribers. Migrating westward, he had shifted for a while to a very special offshoot of the import-export trade. He would represent himself as a middleman for a European car dealer and would make small down payments on automobiles to be shipped and sold abroad. He would then unload the cars for whatever he could get and renege on the balance of the purchase price, explaining when anyone pressed him that the money was tied up in the red tape of foreign exchange and would be forthcoming at any moment.

By the start of 1969, Aust, whose own overt acquisitiveness was nicely complemented by an understanding of the latent acquisitiveness of many Americans, had a stake of some $30,000, and, with Graber's willing collaboration, devised a plan to make this money grow by leaps and bounds. Purporting to be making a tourist survey for a consortium of high-placed European travel agencies, Aust dropped in on a West Coast advertising representative of *TV Guide* and took a half-page ad in its April 5, 1969, editions. The ad cost $17,534. Graber tagged along while the arrangements were being made, ostensibly as the California agent of a travel agency called Flonex GMBH, which actually existed, but was in substance merely a dummy company that had been set up by Aust and had no discernible clients. The ad was placed on behalf of an outfit with the inviting name of the DeLuxe Vacationer Company, and it offered 2,000 prizes to readers who would bother to answer four easy questions: Did they prefer to take their vacations in summer or off season?; How many vacation days did they have each year?; Was their favorite vacation transportation by air, sea, or land?; and Had they ever been to Europe, did they hope to go to Europe, or had they no interest in Europe? Of the 2,000 prizes, to be awarded in a drawing held among the respondents, 1,998 were unspecified, but the first prize was to be a two-week all-expenses-paid trip for two to Acapulco and the second a similar fetching excursion to Hawaii. The ad was appropriately illustrated with sketches of Mexican guitarists and a Hawaiian surfer.

While waiting to hear from the readers of the magazine, Aust and Graber were not idle. They commissioned a couple of job printers in Hollywood to run up some handsome winners' certificates for them—not one for Mexico and one for Hawaii, but 28,000 for Mexico and 42,000 for Hawaii. Each certificate purported to be valid for a round trip to the designated destination and a stay at a luxury beach hotel, and there were all sorts of fringe benefits itemized: free entrance to a country club, free tennis, swimming, horseback riding, and, in the case of Hawaii, "One Full Day Fishing Trip in Luxury Sea Cruiser, lunch on board." Casting out bait was clearly much on Aust's and Graber's minds. On both varieties of certificates, there was a caveat that had the ring of authenticity: "Tips and beverages not included." As far as the two young Germans were concerned, though, the stipulation that counted went: "Note: According to regulations, a $25 registration deposit to secure your winner prize is required WITHIN 10 DAYS. This deposit will be FULLY REFUNDED to you on your day of departure."

The response to the *TV Guide* advertisement may have been slightly disappointing to its sponsors. Perhaps they had overestimated their audience; perhaps television aficionados are disinclined to read and write. Here they were with 70,000 winners' certificates ready to be mailed—along with a form letter signed by Graber congratulating the lucky winner and informing him that his certificate was good for one year—and only 57,000 people answered the ad. Still, that was not bad; 57,000 times $25 came to $1,425,000. So out went 57,000 letters to the alleged winners of the Hawaiian and Mexican excursions; the remaining 1,998 prizes were never mentioned again. The addresses to which the winners were to send their $25 registration deposits were those of telephone-answering services that the European entrepreneurs had arranged to use as mail drops.

The winners' certificates were mailed out from Los Angeles on May 18, 1969, and it may be a tribute to the sagacity of the Western Hemisphere that not all the Americans and Canadians who received them were taken in by them. (There might have been more responses, but readers of the Canadian edition of *TV Guide* had been instructed to send their entry blanks in the contest to a mail drop in Vancouver, British Columbia, and delivery of their letters was hindered by an airlines strike in Canada. Even so, there were enough inquiries from puzzled Canadian "winners" to prompt the Anti-Rackets Board of the Canadian postal service to start an investigation of its own, which it was happy to be able to terminate on learning that its counterpart across the border was already on the trail.) Why pay $25, some "winners" wondered, or, when it came to that, why pay anything, for a free prize? And why, if there were only two winners, would the letter of notification be printed? One woman on the sucker list had been to Hawaii, and she felt certain the promoters of the contest could never have been there themselves, or at any rate not to the island of Kauai, where, she declared in a letter that failed to include a registration deposit, "after two days on that rock you start losing your marbles. I'd hate to think what you would lose after ten days." Another woman and her husband, on receiving their certificate, consulted a lawyer, who told them to go right ahead and send in the money, because *TV Guide* was bound (as it was not) to stand behind the proposition.

But while some nervous Nellies were dragging their feet, there were 11,000 others who rushed to send in their $25—for a total of $275,000. Some were so excited about the prospect of their free holiday that they quit their jobs in order to give it their full attention. One man who didn't quit, being flat broke, expended a good deal of energy making arrangements; he borrowed the $25 from a brother-in-law, he urged his wife to charge a suitable wardrobe at their local department store, he got his boss to give him two weeks' off, and he persuaded his mother-in-law to set aside the time to take care of his children.

Aust and Graber had a couple of valid documents of their own, in the form of West German passports, and they probably planned to take their money and run—for all anyone knows, to enjoy deluxe vacations in Mexico or Hawaii. But they failed to reckon with the innate suspiciousness of some people to whom $25 is a sum not lightly spent. The California recipients of their beclouded largess received the good word on the morning of May 19. That same afternoon, Postal Inspector Charles J. Lerable was sitting in his Hollywood office when he got a phone call from a woman who said she'd won a trip to Mexico in a contest, and what did he think about that? "Congratulations!" cried Lerable, who had no reason then to believe the contest was suspect and who was rather envious, never having won any sort of prize himself. "A few minutes later, a second woman phoned in," Lerable recalls, "to ask what I thought about the authenticity of a trip to Hawaii she'd just won, and I congratulated her, too, though a bit less heartily, because it seemed a strange coincidence that both of the only two grand-prize winners should have elected to get in touch with our office in such quick succession. Then a third call came in. Three winners

—with only two prizes? Suddenly a light dawned, and I said to myself, 'Son of a bitch, we got a fraud!' "

Most Americans think of governmental bodies, even investigative agencies, as moving at a snaillike pace. The belief is wrong; properly stimulated, they can leap like cheetahs. Lerable had been around for a long time, and he knew how fast confidence men can move themselves, and how essential it is to head them off before they head for hiding. He enlisted a fellow Inspector, Maurice P. Jones, and they got to work and worked through the night, routing various surprised individuals from their beds—to begin with, the proprietors of the company to which the letters had been mailed. Then came officers of the bank where Aust and Graber had an account against which they drew checks to pay the mail-answering service, and next, after checking bank records, came the printing company where the winners' certificates and congratulatory letters had been run off. By the afternoon of May 20, only twenty-four hours after Lerable had got the first of his three edifying phone calls, Jones and he felt they had enough evidence that the two Germans were up to no good to pay them an inquisitive visit at a nicely furnished apartment the Inspectors had also located through the bank.

Aust and Graber were lounging around with two attractive young women when the Inspectors showed up, and, seemingly not knowing that Postal Inspectors have the power of arrest, and believing rather that this was some routine check of the efficiency of the postal system, they greeted the visitors warmly. "Ah, we're getting marvelous mail service!" exclaimed Aust, and Graber hospitably offered them a drink. Both men appeared to be taken aback when Lerable and Jones not only declined refreshments but advised the Germans that they had some questions to ask and anything they said could be used against them. Even that did not totally faze Aust and Graber. They said they were quite willing to talk, and signed a form waiving their rights not to have whatever they said put in evidence later on. Well, then, asked the Inspectors, how much did they calculate a two-week holiday to Mexico or Hawaii might cost? Aust said he thought maybe $400. It seemed a somewhat conservative estimate for two people on a two-week deluxe vacation, but the Inspectors accepted the figure, did some on-the-spot multiplication, and informed the men that they had used the mails to promise 57,000 persons free holidays worth $22,800,000. And where, they asked, had Aust and Graber anticipated getting such a sum? Well, the men said, they were being financed by a bunch of European travel agencies on whose behalf they had conducted their survey of tourist habits and preferences. And what were these agencies? The only name that was forthcoming was that of Flonex GMBH, which the Inspectors had already learned from their vigorous research was Aust's own flimsy concern. At that point, the Inspectors saw no need to prolong the conversation unduly. Jones pulled out a couple of pairs of handcuffs, which had a noticeably sobering effect on the discussion. The Inspectors did not detain the two young women, who they decided were merely under the impression that they were on a double date with a self-employed pollster and an out-of-work cookie salesman. "We're not entirely heartless," Lerable said afterward.

With the two men in custody, the Inspectors, with the concurrence of the United States Attorney, next obtained a search warrant and served it on the establishments to which the Deluxe Vacationer mail was addressed. The proprietors of the two offices quickly washed their hands of the affair and refused to accept any more deliveries, so the Inspectors—who are forbidden to open other people's letters but can at least impede their getting them—had a stop order processed through the office of the General Counsel of the Postal Service (in accordance with the civil statutes governing false representation), ordering the local Postmaster to impound Aust's and Graber's mail. By May 26, there was a lot of it to stop; eight thousand letters had already piled up in the Hollywood post office, and three thousand more were then in transit. By then, furthermore, Lerable and Jones had had phone calls from all over the United States. The national headquarters of the Better

Business Bureau had had five hundred inquiries from confused "winners," local branches of the Bureau had had thousands more, and there were countless additional calls from other Postal Inspectors, from Police Departments, District Attorneys, Chambers of Commerce, newspapers, and radio and television stations to whom holders of the first- or second-prize certificates had turned in search of enlightenment. (The switchboard at the main office of *TV Guide* was tied up for two weeks with anguished calls.) Lerable and Jones were able to assure all hands that the Deluxe Vacationer Company was no longer doing business, and that whenever possible the victims' letters, their remittances still safely enclosed, would be returned to the senders. All but 327 of the letters—those, again, bearing no return address—ultimately were sent back, accompanied by a gentle note from the Inspection Service informing the parties concerned that they had been hornswoggled. Lerable and Jones eventually received in turn quite a number of notes from victims who thanked them for their providential intercession, though one man complained that the Inspectors had stolen and cashed his check for twenty-five dollars. He was duly informed, rather coolly, that if he could furnish a photostat of his canceled check *that* would be investigated; he was not heard from again. "There is always some guy who wants to make a fast twenty-five bucks," Lerable says stoically.

Aust and Graber were indicted, on June 4, on fifty-nine counts of mail fraud (fifty-nine instances, that was, of deceived people having mailed them money) and one of fraud by wire (while Lerable and Jones were in the Germans' apartment, a phone call came in from a "winner" in Far Rockaway, Long Island, who had got their number through their mail drop and who wanted to know how soon he could embark). On June 30, the two defrauders pleaded guilty without a trial, and on August 11 they came up for sentencing. The judge was fairly lenient; by then, unable to post bail, the defendants had already spent nearly three months in prison, and moreover, nobody had lost any real money in their caper except themselves. Graber was given an eighteen-month suspended sentence, and was immediately deported. Aust, as the mastermind in the plot, got a two-year jail sentence, to be followed by deportation. He managed to escape from the federal correctional institution at Terminal Island for twenty-four hours in September, which was long enough to visit a girl friend but also long enough to have ninety days added to his prison term.

When Aust and Graber came up for sentencing, both men, in a bid for clemency, said that they were sorry for what they'd done. Their remorse was surely no more heartfelt than that of the thousands of individuals whose vacation hopes were so delightfully raised and so dismayingly dashed, and who would presumably henceforth have good reason to respect the wisdom of a legendary Chinese proverb: "You can always get free cheese in a mousetrap."

# 6. An Obstacle or Two

In the late 1920s, just before the stock-market crash, the nation's peddlers of shady securities were having a field day. It is safe to say that few, if any, firms entered into the spirit of things more enthusiastically than the Industrial Bankers Company, which, notwithstanding its high-flown name, was one of a number of unsavory brokerage houses that flourished before the Securities and Exchange Commission was set up to keep a supervisory eye on Wall Street. And among the staff of Industrial Bankers, probably none went about their work with greater zest than three customer's men named Otis W. Rowe, Leo F. Hampton, and Patrick Henry ("Packy") Lennon. Of these, Lennon was the most spectacularly successful; in 1930, when he was only twenty-nine, the New York *Evening Journal* paid him the tribute of captioning a picture of him "DON'T LET HIM SELL YOU ANY STOCK."

By then, however, Lennon was no longer associated with the Industrial Bankers Company. Even before the 1929 boom had fizzled, the concern had quietly shut up shop, soon after word got around that its officials (along with those of certain other companies) were about to be served with subpoenas for having hawked, at up to thirty dollars a share, large quantities of almost worthless stock in an outfit called the Inter-City Radio & Telegraph Corporation. In plugging Inter-City, Lennon and his syrupy-voiced colleagues had received a big assist from a rumor, assiduously circulated by those who stood to profit from it, that a couple of Hollywood producers were angling for a controlling interest in the company. The salesmen found perhaps their most avid customer for Inter-City in Augustine J. Cunningham, an industrialist of Rochester, New York, who, starting in 1926, bought 8,492 shares of Inter-City, at an average cost of $12.62 a share. The last batch of stock certificates Cunningham received—they were issued three weeks after the subpoenas were drawn up—were dated October 29, 1929, the day the New York Stock Exchange took its worst drubbing ever. By the time Inter-City folded, the following year, he had lost $107,147.27 in it, or about a tenth of the total amount invested in its stock.

Born in Rochester, in 1878, Cunningham was one of that city's most respectable and respected citizens. He belonged to its most exclusive urban club, the Genesee Valley, and its most exclusive country club, the Rochester. A bachelor in his early fifties, he lived alone, except for servants, in a mansion on East Avenue, in Rochester's most imposing residential section, only a block or so from the house then occupied by George Eastman, the founder of Eastman Kodak. Cunningham was genial, gentle, fastidious, and well liked. Daily, summer and winter, he sported a fresh flower in his lapel. He owned two identical dark-green Cadillacs, to be sure of always having an immaculate one on tap, and an old Cunningham car, a gaudy memento of the time when the firm of James Cunningham Son & Co., of which he had become president in 1909, was one of the pioneers in the automobile business. Founded by his grandfather in 1838 and originally engaged in the manufacture of horse carriages, the company began making horseless ones in 1904, and later switched to turning out high-priced automobile bodies for the custom trade. From the Civil War on, it had also produced various types of military equipment, including tanks and airplanes. After the Second World War, the firm, which once provided limousine bodies for the Pope and the King of Spain, began turning out, among other items, electronic switches. All in all, it had a long, honorable, and prosperous history—a history in which Augustine J. Cunningham, who remained its president until he died, in 1957, at the age of seventy-nine, played a long and honorable role.

Between 1951 and 1955, Cunningham was the victim of what may well be the biggest fleecing in the history of the confidence game. He was, in the words of one government official who later looked into the case, "a real pigeon." In the course of those four years, Cunningham more or less unblinkingly handed over $439,-121, in seventy-eight payments, to a smooth-talking cabal of criminals. In return for this investment, Cunningham expected to receive an amount that cannot be calculated precisely but that he seems to have believed might come to $28 million. As it turned out, he never got a penny. He was dealing with operators who are known among their kind as hundred-per-centers; that is, men who look upon everything they can extract from a sucker as pure profit.

Of the gang that worked Cunningham over, three of the principals were former customer's men of Industrial Bankers who had sold him Inter-City stock in the twenties, and it was his misfortune that in 1951 they remembered a lot about him while he remembered nothing about them. In the intervening years, all of the trio had served prison sentences, and so had had plenty of leisure to sharpen their memories of past patsies; they had kept sufficiently abreast of Cunningham's activities to feel reasonably certain that he was as easy a mark as ever, whereas he had probably not given a thought to any of them. Among the heartening indications that Cunningham's gullibility was still unsullied was an authentic report of his having presented one of the few extant Cunningham automobiles, valued by connoisseurs at between twelve and fifteen thousand dollars, to a pair of swindlers who visited him in Rochester and gave him in exchange a sheaf of strikingly unnegotiable securities. Here, for once, retribution had been swiftly meted out; the two swindlers were in such a hurry to put Rochester behind them that the ancient car turned over and one of them was killed.

In February, 1951, a dapper, dignified man of sixty called on Cunningham at his office. Introducing himself as Donald Peddit, he asked if he was correct in surmising that Mr. Cunningham was the gentleman of that name who had suffered so grievously in the bygone Inter-City fiasco. Why, yes, said Cunningham, he was indeed. "Capital!" cried Peddit, who had actually been in no doubt about the matter, since he was Otis W. Rowe, formerly one of the customer's men who had so energetically pushed Inter-City stock. (He was also formerly an inmate of the federal penitentiaries at Atlanta, Georgia, and Lewisburg, Pennsylvania, where he served time for mail fraud.) Not only did Peddit-Rowe know a good deal about Cunningham's financial past, but he and his fellow conspirators had done further biographical research on their pigeon and had analyzed their findings in a series of barroom seminars in Manhattan. They were aware, among other things, that Cunningham was an eminent Catholic—indeed, in 1932, the Vatican had conferred on him the Equestrian Order of the Holy Sepulchre of Jerusalem. Accordingly, before elaborating on the Inter-City matter, Peddit-Rowe tossed into the conversation the casual, though inaccurate, remark that he had a brother down South who was a bishop of the Church. Cunningham warmed to his visitor at once.

Then Peddit-Rowe got down to business. He wondered if Cunningham recalled Dr. Randolph Parker. No, Cunningham did not. This was no reflection on his memory, for the Dr. Parker his caller was about to describe had never existed. It seemed, Peddit-Rowe went on, that Dr. Parker, an inventor who was at one time connected with Inter-City, had died, leaving an extraordinary will. Reaching into his pocket, Peddit-Rowe pulled out what he said was a copy of the will, let Cunningham glance at it, retrieved it, and, when he left, an hour later, took it away with him. Cunningham never saw it again. The gist of the document was that Dr. Parker had bequeathed his estate, consisting entirely of patents in the field of communications and electronics, to the three investors who had been hardest hit by the collapse of Inter-City. Cunningham was one of them, Peddit-Rowe went on, and the two others were named J. J. Driscoll and Harry Hoffman. He didn't profess to know much about Driscoll but claimed to be a business associate of Hoffman, whom he identified as a real estate operator in Wheeling, West Virginia. He and Hoffman had made a preliminary investigation of the Parker legacy, he continued, and had discovered that some motion picture companies in Hollywood had been infringing on these patents, that the guilty parties were now prepared to make amends to Dr. Parker's three heirs, and that the settlement would come to something like sixty million dollars.

The conventional businessman would probably have either laughed off this story or consulted his lawyer, who could easily have ascertained that no such will had been probated and no such patents granted to a Dr. Randolph Parker. Cunningham consulted no lawyer and laughed not at all. Instead, after thanking Peddit-Rowe politely, he sat back to await developments, informing no one of this singular turn of events. He did not have to wait long. A few weeks later, Peddit-Rowe was back, bringing with him a neat, cheerful, ruddy man of fifty, whom he introduced as Harry Hoffman. It was a pleasant meeting. Hoffman and Cunningham exchanged commiserations about their losses in Inter-City, and exchanged congratulations on the windfall that was to recompense them so handsomely for the beating they had taken. Then Hoffman, suddenly growing solemn, informed Cunningham that there might be an obstacle or two. For one thing, he had been advised that he ought to obtain releases from certain other heavy investors in Inter-City, to avert any trouble when news of the huge settlement got out, and this precautionary step would, of course, require discretion, time, and money. For another, while officials of the delinquent movie companies were ready to make atonement, their attorneys were a slick, sly bunch, who might scheme up interminable delays; it would perhaps prove necessary to slip these shysters something under the table. Hoffman added that he had already put up substantial amounts of his own money to defray such expenses and that he hoped Cunningham would see his way clear to helping out, too, if the need should arise. In closing, he remarked that he had just moved from Wheeling to New York, and had an office in Room 1184 of a building at 11 West Forty-second Street, to which Cunningham could mail such trifling sums—and surely they would be trifling compared to a one-third interest in sixty million dollars—as might be required. Cunningham must have nodded sympathetically, for, as his later actions showed, Hoffman struck him as the personification of credibility. There were a few things he didn't know about Hoffman, though. One was that Room 1184 was not Hoffman's office but that he had been given permission to use it as a mail drop by a disbarred lawyer. Another was that Hoffman was Patrick Henry Lennon, whom the *Journal* had warned its readers against twenty-one years before and who, more recently, had been sitting in on the barroom seminars.

By the time Hoffman-Lennon made the journey to Rochester, he had proved himself to be one of the boldest and craftiest confidence men of his generation. According to a letterhead he had once had printed up when he was passing himself off as a public-relations expert, he was the author of a book entitled "Never SELL 'Em—Make 'Em BUY." While this was an adequate summary of his approach to business matters, he had never got around to writing the book. He had, however, composed several excerpts from nonexistent reviews, and these he also put on the letterhead:

> "A psychological treat," Chicago *Tribune*.
> "Hope he gives us more," Miami *Herald*.
> "Swell reading," Albany *Times-Union*.
> "A best seller, by a best seller," New York *News*.
> "Light, interesting reading," Cleveland *Plain Dealer*.
> "Would make a dandy novel and movie," Hollywood *Reporter*.

Since the nature of a confidence man's occupation automatically casts doubt on everything he says, not much credence can be given to any of the autobiographical data Lennon chose to reveal at one time or another. He once swore on oath that he was born in New York City, and it may have been true that, as he sometimes claimed, he was a plumber's helper during his boyhood and derived a taste for high living while working on the pipes in the Andrew Carnegie mansion, on East Ninety-first Street. Or it may have been pure myth. He seems to have done some amateur boxing in his day, and he indisputably built up a wide acquaintance in prize fighting circles. It was known that he once had a wife, who bore him two daughters, and that he abandoned all three of them about twenty years before he called on Cunningham, by which time he had taken to living with a middle-aged woman named Sally something. There was no question, either, that by then he had poor vision, and was an alcoholic, frequenting a string of second-rate saloons in the midtown area, a few of which he used as mailing addresses. Records not compiled by him also showed that he had been in jail, on and off, since 1926, serving terms for grand larceny, investment fraud, and other mischief. His most recent set-to with the law—and at this point the murkiness surrounding his pre-Cunningham career lifted somewhat—had occurred in 1945, when he pleaded guilty to charges of mail fraud and conspiracy following an investigation of the Federal Fyr-Ex Company, which was supposedly engaged in manufacturing and selling fire extinguishers but which turned out to be more interested in printing and selling shares of its stock. The case was of interest primarily because it revealed Lennon in the act of achieving new heights of artistry in his field of endeavor. While confidence men traditionally have a weakness for undoing widows and orphans, Lennon distinguished himself by selling some utterly valueless Fyr-Ex stock for nearly twenty thousand dollars to a woman who not only was a widow with four children but at the time was lying in a hospital bed in a plaster cast, since her back was broken. After she recovered, Lennon and some of his henchmen took her out to lunch, and during the meal he gave her a hundred-dollar bill—for which he had her sign a receipt—as a token of the splendid increments she might expect from her investment in Fyr-Ex. Before the meal was over, she excused herself to go to the ladies' room, leaving her purse behind, and when she returned she noticed that the bill was missing from it. She ventured to ask her host where on earth the hundred dollars could have gone, and he responded by demanding, "Are you questioning the honesty of these friends of mine?"

After pleading guilty in the Fyr-Ex case, Lennon was sentenced to a four-year term in Lewisburg, where he was appointed assistant to the Catholic chaplain. He was paroled in June, 1949, but he had become so attached to Lewisburg that in 1950, and again in 1951, he returned to the campus, in the role of an open-handed old grad, to attend the inmates' annual pre-Christmas party, bringing with him a number of entertainers and prize fighters. On both occasions, there was a banquet, and in 1951 Lennon, sitting at the head table with the prison brass, was prevailed upon to make a few remarks to the grateful inmates, who set up a chant of "We want Packy! We want Packy!" His table companions joined in the applause. They might have been bemused had they known that all that year, though on parole for most of it, he had been working as a full-time swindler, the leader of a group whose take had come to slightly over a hundred thousand dollars.

One of the contributors to that sum was Augustine J. Cunningham. Toward the end of April, 1951, he got a phone call from Hoffman-Lennon requesting a modest $1,600, and docilely sent a check in that amount to the Room 1184 address; in May, in response to similar requests, he sent three more checks, totaling $3,315. The squeeze was on. Room 1184 was actually occupied by Harold Schnuer, or, as he sometimes called himself, Harold Shaw. He was the disbarred lawyer who had agreed to let Hoffman-Lennon receive mail there, and since he had been a dummy officer of Fyr-Ex, he may have been aware of the nature of the correspondence. On thinking the matter over, however, he apparently decided not to run the risk of implicating Room 1184 in anything underhanded. At all events, early in June, Hoffman-Lennon started sending deputies to Rochester to bring back Cunningham's contributions. The problems involved in the Parker legacy, Hoffman-Lennon advised Cunningham, were turning out to be more complex than had been anticipated, and he was dispatching a bonded messenger—name of Shaw, Harold Shaw—to call for the money. Hoffman-Lennon added that this time, regrettably, Cunningham's one-third share of the expenses was considerably larger than any sum he had previously been asked to supply—$8,750, in fact. Cunningham gamely agreed to go along, and asked that the messenger report at noon at his house on East Avenue, where he retired each day for a solitary lunch, followed by a nap. When Shaw-Schnuer arrived there at the appointed hour on June 6, Cunningham handed him an envelope containing the money, mostly in hundred-dollar bills. Evidently, the problems were becoming more complex almost by the hour, for on June 11 Shaw-Schnuer again presented himself at the mansion on East Avenue and was given $14,706, and on June 15 he was back to pick up $16,666—bringing Cunningham's outlay for the nine days to $40,-122.

Shaw-Schnuer, who was receiving about a thousand dollars for each trip to Rochester—a fairly princely rate of pay for a messenger, even an ostensibly bonded one—would probably just as soon have kept shuttling back and forth all summer. By the time of the June 15 dole, however, Hoffman-Lennon had detected, from his telephone conversations with Cunningham, that the old man was getting balky. He thereupon invited Cunningham to come to New York for a meeting with the third co-heir, Driscoll, who, he said, had just arrived from his home in Tulsa, Oklahoma, and had checked into the Fifth Avenue Hotel. A man who registered as J. J. Driscoll, of Tulsa, had indeed just moved into the hotel; he was Boston Jimmy Knowles, an old-time confidence man. On Sunday, June 23, Cunningham came down to New York, called at the hotel, and was directed to the Driscoll suite, where he had a reassuring meeting with Driscoll-Knowles, Peddit-Rowe, Hoffman-Lennon, and a man who was introduced to him as George V. Arlen. Driscoll-Knowles was even more indignant about the costly delay than Cunningham was. Why, he said, he had already shelled out $125,-000 of his own money to those grasping lawyers in Hollywood! But he had no doubt everything would turn out all right. Cunningham, who had so far put up a mere $45,037, was much solaced by the fact that a man who had put up nearly three times as much was still so sanguine, and three days later, by way of demonstrating his own rekindled faith, he sent Hoffman-Lennon, via Shaw-Schnuer, $12,500 more.

Apparently chastened by Cunningham's momentary symptoms of apostasy, the boys eased up during the next few months, clipping him for a mere $23,500, largely on the pretext that it was needed to pry a quick $2 million out of the movie people in partial payment of their debt. When this payment failed to materialize, Cunningham again began to show signs of bridling, and Hoffman-Lennon was prompted to improvise a new twist in the plot. Driscoll was dead! He had been killed in an automobile accident, and his widow was proving sticky; it might cost $50,000 to dissuade her from gumming things up. (Boston Jimmy Knowles did die, two years later, of a heart attack. His widow said she had thought he was an advertising man.) Cunningham thereupon came through with $9,000, and Driscoll's widow, he gathered, was mollified.

Early in 1952, Cunningham was told that he could expect a full settlement almost immediately. In March, while he was still waiting for it, Hoffman-Lennon again fell back on the partial-payment gimmick; this time the payment was to be a measly $1 million, but Hoffman-Lennon glossed over the comedown by promising $450,000 of it to Cunningham. The prospect produced another $9,000 from Cunningham, but, after waiting a few weeks for his $450,000, he once more became irritable. That spring was a trying one for Hoffman-Lennon; having exhausted the lure of the instant partial payment, he scraped what seemed to be the bottom of the barrel in June by telling Cunningham, on his word of honor, that if he would make one last contribution to the war chest, in the amount of $12,500, there would be no further appeal for funds. On the twenty-sixth of that month, Cunningham sent Hoffman-Lennon a check for the amount requested.

While waiting for time to blur Cunningham's memory of the last few pledges and promises, Hoffman-Lennon retired into the background and pushed a potent substitute into action—another veteran of the boiler-room squadron at Industrial Bankers and of the federal jails. This was Leo F. Hampton, who, setting himself apart from the others by using his real name, journeyed up to Rochester, dropped in on Cunningham, and confided that he had happened to hear about the Parker will and that he personally considered the chances so rosy that he had paid $40,000 for a fractional interest in Hoffman's stake. Cunningham was so heartened to find an outsider eager to get in on the legacy that he gave his visitor $37,784 to help speed the day when the movie companies would at last disburse.

Now and then, as the months rolled expensively by, Cunningham jotted down on the backs of envelopes the sums he had shelled out. The money coaxed out of him by Hampton brought the total to $136,821, and he was definitely losing his zeal along with his cash, but he was still willing to listen to a persuasive argument from time to time—enough so that by the end of 1953 the envelope-back ledgers showed that he had spent more than $300,000 in pursuit of the elusive Parker millions. He had doled out a big chunk of this—$80,000—in August of that year, moved by an exceptionally persuasive argument from Hoffman-Lennon, the nature of which, unfortunately, is not known. As it happened, Hoffman-Lennon neither asked for nor received the whole $80,000, but the fact remains that Cunningham paid it out. The negotiations for this touch began in mid-August, when Hoffman-Lennon called Cunningham to say that he would need $30,000 on the nineteenth. Cunningham called his bank, the Security Trust Company of Rochester, and instructed one of its representatives to have the sum ready for him in cash by that date. Not long afterward, Hoffman-Lennon called back and said he was sorry but there had been some new developments and he would now need $50,000 on the twenty-sixth. In his alarm—or, conceivably, elation—over the way things were going, poor Cunningham misunderstood, and notified his bank to set aside $50,000 over and above the $30,000.

On the twenty-sixth, George V. Arlen, whom Cunningham had met in the Fifth Avenue Hotel and whom Lennon had met originally in the Lewisburg penitentiary, turned up in Rochester to pick up the money. Nobody is certain what Arlen's real name is. He called himself George Chapman, Ralph Di Cozza, J. J. Stanton, and Reynard Curtis Gardner, but he seems to have been born, in 1900, as Sidney Gottlieb. He began his criminal career, at the age of thirty, as a member of a gang of toughs who stole a million dollars' worth of securities by hanging around Wall Street brokerage-house delivery windows, posing as bona-fide messengers; eventually, he queered the act by making the mistake of offering to sell some of his loot to a detective. Now, at fifty-three, he had at last become a bona-fide messenger, of sorts. Cunningham escorted him to the bank and gave him the $80,000, in hundred-dollar bills. Arlen-Gottlieb must have been startled at getting $30,000 more than he'd expected, but composure is essential to a successful confidence man, and he retained his. When he reported back to Hoffman-Lennon, he again did not bother to mention the extra $30,000. Instead, he kept it, and shortly afterward set himself up in the brokerage business, for the purpose of dealing in Canadian uranium stocks of doubtful merit.

Cunningham did not maintain a balance large enough to cover such hefty withdrawals, but his credit at the bank was practically unlimited. Its president, Bernard E. Finucane, was a fellow club member and a personal friend of his, and, in any case, the bank held, and had set aside as collateral against his loans, a fat portfolio of first-rate securities that Cunningham had acquired when not diverted by flings into Inter-City and the like. Banks are required by the Federal Reserve Board to report all cash transactions involving more than $10,000, and when Cunningham withdrew the $80,000, an officer of the Security Trust informed the Federal Reserve that Cunningham was a highly respected gentleman of independent means and of excellent character, and that the bank's president had discussed these transactions with him. Finucane had, but he had managed to learn not much more than that

Cunningham was involved in an exceedingly promising business venture.

Arlen-Gottlieb was not the only emissary who betrayed Hoffman-Lennon. A year later, he sent his "secretary" of the moment—a man who called himself Frank O'Brien—to Rochester to pick up $9,000. When O'Brien got there and learned how painless such extraction was, he was inspired to attempt it unilaterally. A couple of days later, without telling Hoffman-Lennon, O'Brien returned to Rochester and said another $14,000 was needed at once. After a certain amount of gloomy head-wagging, Cunningham yielded. When Hoffman-Lennon next called Cunningham and said the $9,000 entrusted to O'Brien had proved insufficient and could he please send some more money, the industrialist replied, "But I gave your secretary another fourteen thousand." Hoffman-Lennon almost dropped the phone, but recovered quickly and said yes, of course. He never saw O'Brien again—or the $14,000.

Shortly after New Year's of 1954, Hoffman-Lennon called Cunningham to inform him that he was closing the office in Room 1184, because he had a lot of traveling to do in their joint behalf, and that, if necessary, he could be reached by mail through another secretary, Miss Catherine Curran, whose address was the Hotel Flanders, 135 West Forty-seventh Street, New York City. Over the next twelve months or so, Hoffman-Lennon introduced several new devices for keeping Cunningham in line. For one thing, he told Cunningham that Peddit, the man who had first brought the glad tidings of Dr. Parker's will to Rochester, had died and that, in common decency, his widow had to be taken care of. It was true that Peddit-Rowe was dead, having hanged himself in the lobby of a Queens apartment house where a woman he went around with lived, but he had no widow, and neither the Queens woman nor his professional associates bothered to claim his body at the morgue. Around this time, also, Hoffman-Lennon recruited to his ranks a cold-blooded ally named Harold Paul Odom. Most confidence men look down on ordinary forms of lawlessness as vulgar, preferring skulduggery of the lofty sort in which brains are essential to success. Odom, however, was of a different cut. Born in 1895, he had a record dating back to 1919 that included burglary, cheating at cards, horse touting, and drunkenness. At race tracks, equipped with a portable radio transmitter, he sometimes took part in post-race betting schemes. Whenever the Pinkertons, who knew him well, caught sight of him, they would throw him out. Nonetheless, he was a suave, imposing man, and when he went up to Rochester, under the name of William Ryan, Cunningham took to him instantly. The newcomer portrayed himself as having $70,000 tied up in the fight to straighten out Dr. Parker's patents, and also as a man with some useful connections in Washington—a lucky break for Cunningham, he pointed out, because sooner or later the federal government was bound to show an interest in the case, over taxes and whatnot. By way of showing Cunningham his standing in government circles, he produced a "Dear Bill" letter written on the stationery of Joseph W. Martin, Jr., the then Speaker of the House of Representatives, and supposedly signed by the Congressman, who, the text hinted, was eager to see the Inter-City affair resolved in favor of those who had lost the most as a result of it. Cunningham felt that here, at last, was reason to anticipate speedy progress; it did not occur to him that the letter might be a forgery on a stolen letterhead, which is what it was. Ryan-Odom, who hoped to poach on the other criminals' pigeon-trapping preserve, told Cunningham to sit tight—he'd soon be hearing from him.

Toward the end of 1954, Hoffman-Lennon telephoned Cunningham, seemingly in a state of such gleeful excitement that he could hardly contain himself. Their ship was in! Well, all but in. It appeared that, to escape paying certain stiff taxes that might be levied against all concerned, the Hollywood interests had decided to reimburse Dr. Parker's heirs covertly, and at that very moment an armored car, with Ryan in charge, was lumbering east from California with a cargo of $50 million in cash, of which Cunningham's share had been computed at $28 million. All Cunningham had to do now was to wait until the truck pulled up at his front door and, after Ryan dropped off the $28 million, stash it away and keep mum about the whole business.

On December 23, Cunningham received an agitated phone call from Ryan-Odom. The most awful thing had happened! To save time, the truck had crossed into Canada at Detroit, and, on reentering the United States at Plattsburgh, New York, had been halted and searched. The money had been confiscated, and Ryan-Odom was in jail at Plattsburgh and needed nine hundred dollars to bail himself out, so that he could go and reason with the authorities. Although a glance at an atlas would have made even the acquiescent Cunningham wonder why anyone looking for a time-saving route from Detroit to Rochester should choose to go by way of Plattsburgh, he hastened to send off the nine hundred dollars by Western Union money order. The plight of Ryan-Odom was not as pitiable as Cunningham thought. Instead of being a prisoner in an upstate border town, he was a free man calling from New York, having arranged with Western Union to forward to him at the Governor Clinton Hotel, at Seventh Avenue and Thirty-first Street, any money telegraphed to Plattsburgh.

There are four basic rules for success in a confidence game. First, find a suitable victim: that is, one who has money to spare but who craves more, who is in the habit of keeping his affairs to himself, and who is elderly and therefore has a good chance of dying before he can testify against you. Second, milk the victim as long as you can. Third, if the going gets rough, let him think he is involved in something slightly improper, so he will be afraid of getting in trouble himself if he speaks up. And, fourth, when you figure that either his gullibility or your luck is played out, drop him cold. The armored-truck tactic, with its overtones of tax evasion and currency smuggling, fulfilled Rule No. 3, and, by even a conservative interpretation of Rule No. 4, the time had come to pull out, or so thought three of the principal conspirators—Ryan-Odom, Hampton, and Arlen-Gottlieb. But Hoffman-Lennon, although he did lay off the old man for one seven-month stretch in 1955, couldn't afford to quit permanently. With his friend Sally, he had been living high in New York, where they occupied a suite at the apartment hotel known as Ten Park Avenue, and in various resorts in Florida, California, and Cuba. Stored for him here and there in Manhattan saloons were about twenty hatboxes, each containing a slightly used gray homburg, for he couldn't tolerate a soiled hat and would buy a new one whenever he detected a spot on the one he was wearing. In New York, his daily routine began at eight in the morning, when he dropped in at Frawley's Bar & Grill, on West Forty-eighth Street, just as it was opening. After four or more hours of steady drinking, he would summon a Carey limousine or two and invite everybody in the place, friend or stranger, to accompany him out to the race track. There he would give each of his guests two hundred dollars to bet with, and on the way home he would stand them all a dinner.

On August 19, 1955, Hoffman-Lennon called Cunningham up and said that the confiscated money would be released to them by the end of the month if they just had $30,000 to pay off the one remaining official who was making things difficult. It had been quite an ordeal, he went on; he and the others had already spent so much on bribes that Cunningham's share of the fortune had dwindled from $28 million to $10 million—a harsh note that he may have injected in the belief that the old man would be more cooperative if he was made to face a semblance of reality. Whatever the motive may have been, the maneuver didn't work, for although Hoffman-Lennon said that he was willing to put up half of the $30,000, Cunningham declined to put up the rest. Hoffman-Lennon assured Cunningham that he would see things in a different light if he fully understood the details of the case, and said he would send a close friend named Robert Clarke to Rochester to explain them. On August 25, a man who introduced himself by that name called on Cunningham and remarked at once that his dearly beloved late wife had been a devout Catholic. Cunningham was touched, but he refused to part with any money. The next day, Hoffman-Lennon tried flattery. Telephoning Cunningham, he said his friend Clarke had returned from Rochester with such high regard for the industrialist that he was going to put up $5,000 of the required $15,000 himself. After letting this sink in, Hoffman-Lennon added that he could round up $9,400 from another outside source if Cunningham would come through with the balance of six hundred dollars. Whether it was the flattery or the fact that in the eyes of a man who had already contributed nearly half a million dollars to the cause this was a paltry sum, Cunningham sent along a check for the six hundred. At the time of this call, Hoffman-Lennon knew only that Clarke's mission had been fruitless, but a day or so later he received a brief letter from him, which said nothing about admiring Cunningham but warned that "Mr. X" could be skinned no longer. As Clarke summed it up, "One thing is certain. The man is absolutely dead."

To Hoffman-Lennon, however, the six hundred dollars proved that the man was still alive, and on the very day that he received Clarke's diagnosis he again called Cunningham. Bad news, he told the old man; the outside source he had been counting on for the $9,400 had backed down, and Cunningham would simply have to come through. Very much alive, Cunningham not only consented but became so filled with a sense of urgency that, at Hoffman-Lennon's suggestion, he called up the Security Trust and asked his friend Finucane to have a correspondent bank in New York deliver $9,400 to Robert Clarke at the Hotel Ambassador before the day was out. Finucane would have no part of it, though. Cunningham had already borrowed $323,000 from the bank, and its directors had decided that, collateral or no collateral, he would get no more until he told them what he wanted it for. After refusing Cunningham's request, Finucane again implored his friend to throw some light on the situation. Cunningham thereupon realized uneasily that he did not have much light to throw, and, hoping to find some, he put in a call to Clarke at the Ambassador, and found that the hotel had never heard of the man. That was too much even for Cunningham, who now told Finucane all he knew, and on September 2, with Cunningham's reluctant blessing, the bank president phoned the F.B.I. office in Rochester and arranged for Cunningham to stop by the next day.

The F.B.I., of course, can act only in cases that present some federal angle within its jurisdiction, and as far as its Rochester agents could make out, this was not one of them. Cunningham did, however, mention having used the mails on several occasions to send money to his tormentors, so on September 8, the F.B.I. turned the matter over to the Postal Inspection Service. The Cunningham case was entrusted to Charles Miller, then stationed in Rochester. Miller found it hard to believe that anyone in his senses—as Cunningham definitely was—could have been so badly taken in, but Postal Inspectors have become gloomily reconciled to the fact that as long as confidence men exist, they will not lack for victims.

It did not take Miller long to find out how thoroughly the old man had been bamboozled. No Dr. Parker had been associated with Inter-City, and nobody in Hollywood had heard anything about infringements on patents held by a man of that name. No armored truck and no William Ryan had been taken into custody at Plattsburgh. Tulsa, Oklahoma, had never heard of a J. J. Driscoll, nor Wheeling, West Virginia, of a Harry Hoffman. A large part of the world Cunningham had fancied himself living in for the past few years suddenly vanished. While this negative information was being funneled into Rochester, Miller showed Cunningham a whole gallery of police photographs of criminals named Hoffman, Driscoll, Arlen, Ryan, and so on, and was finally rewarded when Cunningham recognized a picture of Hampton, the one principal who had considerately not burdened himself with an alias. Cunningham remembered addressing some checks to Hampton at the Hotel Capitol, on West Fifty-first Street, and Miller, inquiring there, learned that the man had been a guest of the hotel for a while but had recently moved. Miller thought it reasonable to assume that unless they had somehow been alerted, most of the men he was looking for were lurking in Manhattan, since during their negotiations with Cunningham that appeared to be their normal habitat. So, bringing Cunningham along, he settled down for a couple of weeks in the Hotel New Yorker. Miller figured he could probably pick up valuable background information in New York. The Inspector in charge of the state, Henry B. Montague, went beyond that. He lent Miller the active aid of two of his staff —Martin Kogel and George Forster. Sundry tips and leads indicated that, after leaving the Capitol, Hampton had holed up in some other West Side hotel, and undismayed by either the abundance of such establishments or the possibility that Hampton, too, had begun using another name, the three Inspectors undertook to make a methodical search of them all. To their considerable relief, this was not necessary, for they had examined the records, and shown Hampton's photograph to the desk clerks, of no more than forty or fifty hotels when they found him, registered as Richard E. Hampton, at the Empire, at Broadway and Sixty-third Street; to clinch matters, the handwriting on his registration card was found by laboratory analysis in Washington to match that on a receipt he had signed for Cunningham. Shortly after midnight on October 16, the Inspectors grabbed him.

At first, Hampton would say little, though he did concede that he had gone to Rochester to obtain money from Cunningham—but only as an envoy, he insisted, for a man named Joe Fortuna. Had he never heard of Harry Hoffman? No. Was he sure of that? Well, maybe the guy's name *had* been Hoffman. Who was Hoffman? No idea. At length, however, Hampton consented to let the Postal Inspectors take a look at the contents of a safe-deposit box he had at the Empire, and there they found $4,950 in cash and a book of blank checks issued by the Marine Midland Trust Company of Central New York, in Syracuse, to one R. E. Baker. More important, they also found on him an address book, and among the names was Odom's. It was easy to ascertain that Odom had a criminal record, and to obtain a picture of him, which Miller showed to Cunningham. "That's Ryan," the old man said. The Inspectors got nothing further out of Hampton, who was arraigned and locked up in Rochester's Monroe County jail in default of $20,000 bail.

Odom was a cinch to find. The Inspectors sent out an interstate request for information about him, and learned almost immediately that for the past five days he had been in custody in Cumberland, Maryland, having been arrested on a burglary charge dating back to 1949. Concurrently, the Syracuse police were trying to trace him because he had abandoned a car in a parking lot there —a Cadillac fitted out with radio equipment, for use in receiving news flashes from race tracks. The car also contained a check-writing machine, a pair of cowboy boots, and a briefcase crammed with blank power-of-attorney forms, unused envelopes bearing the frank of the Speaker of the House, an Ontario fishing license, and a batch of stationery sporting the letterheads of hotels, including the Caribe Hilton, in San Juan; El Rancho, in Port-au-Prince; the Jaragua, in Ciudad Trujillo; the Grand, in Yarmouth, Nova Scotia; and, anticlimactically, Hampton's recent Broadway retreat, the Empire. Odom was even less communicative than Hampton. Just about all he would say about anything was that the Monroe County jail—where he joined Hampton when he, too, was unable to post $20,000 bail right away—was a dump. Odom, with picturesque contempt for the honor-among-thieves tradition, soon figured out a way to leave that depressing environment. Hampton, it seemed, was eager to have his $4,950 transferred to his account in the warden's office—possibly so he could buy cigarettes or toilet articles, possibly so he could get himself a bail bond. Odom had a son in Connecticut, and said he would be glad to ask the young man to fetch the money if Hampton would give him the key to the safe-deposit box at the Empire. This Hampton did, his idea being that Odom could keep a couple of hundred dollars for his pains. The son got the cash, all right, but his father never let Hampton get his hands on it. Instead, Odom seems to have used it to bail *himself* out.

Meanwhile, Miller had been seeking to identify Hoffman through the woman he had once called his secretary—Catherine Curran, of the Hotel Flanders. Suspecting that if he approached her directly she would deny everything and tip off Hoffman, he asked his two New York colleagues, who were better acquainted in midtown hotel circles than he was, to approach the management of the Flanders secretly and have the three of them assigned a room adjoining the one occupied by Miss Curran, who proved to be a former showgirl. The Inspectors were joined by two New York City detectives—Robert Collins and Neil Maison. After the investigators had settled themselves there, Cunningham called Miss Curran from his room at the New Yorker and told her it was imperative that he get in touch with Harry Hoffman at once. Miss Curran gave him an evasive answer, hung up, and, as Miller had anticipated, hurried out of her room and headed for the lobby. The men in the next room followed, hoping that she would lead them to Hoffman, but instead she entered a phone booth in the lobby. Miller reached into the booth, tapped Miss Curran on the shoulder, and took her to the main Post Office building for questioning. The session was not a very illuminating one. Miss Curran said that she knew Hoffman only casually, from a chance meeting at Hogan's Irish House, a saloon on West Fifty-second Street between Broadway and Eighth Avenue, and that he had paid her a few hundred dollars for secretarial services.

When it appeared that Miss Curran would reveal nothing of any great importance, the investigators persuaded her to authorize them to search her room. Back at the Flanders, they found among her belongings some mail addressed to Patrick H. Lennon—a name that, as Postal Inspectors, they found far more illuminating than anything Miss Curran had divulged about the case. Cunningham readily picked out a rogues' gallery likeness of Lennon as that of the man he had known as Hoffman, and the chase was under way. It didn't move fast, though, for Miller and his colleagues soon found themselves handicapped by the circumstance that the very people—bartenders, bellhops, taxi drivers, and the like—on whom investigators rely most heavily in tracking down the Lennons of this world were tacitly declining to cooperate; plainly, those who knew the fugitive were fond of him. From their evasive manner, the Inspectors suspected that Lennon was still in New York, and they took to lounging around his known haunts, such as Hogan's and Frawley's. He must have been tipped off, however, for he didn't show up.

Then, on November 4, Lennon surprisingly turned himself in. He wasn't talking, though. All Miller could get out of him in answer to any question was "No comment." Lennon, too, was held on $20,000 bail, but, unlike his two predecessors, he was able to post the sum at once. His arrest left only two principals in the case unidentified—the men Cunningham knew as Peddit and Arlen—and by mid-December the Inspectors, with the aid of Schnuer, whom they located by studying the tenancy records of Room 1184 in the West Forty-second Street office building, had accounted for that pair, too. Peddit, Schnuer revealed, was the late Otis W. Rowe, whose death could be easily confirmed, and Arlen was Gottlieb, or whatever the name was. The latter presented more of a problem, for he had disappeared from his home, but Miller quickly learned that Gottlieb's wife was a patient in a hospital, and the inspectors nabbed Gottlieb as he was trying to slip in and visit her. Gottlieb was released on $20,000 bail. No charges were pressed against Schnuer, since he had been only a messenger and had made no misrepresentations.

Few victims of confidence men, as investigators everywhere are well aware, can be prevailed upon to stand up and testify against the men who fleeced them—in some instances because they shrink from becoming publicly known as suckers, in others because they don't want their families to learn the bleak truth. After Lennon and his associates had been rounded up, Miller learned that, more or less concurrently with their Rochester operation, they had been preying on at least seven other citizens—six men and a woman—from whom, between 1951 and 1956, they took $309,736.41. Added to the nearly half a million they got from Cunningham, this brought their total known income for the five-year period to $748,857.41. Of the eight, though, only Cunningham had the gumption to admit his foolishness openly, and the names of the seven second-string pigeons used here—most of them are dead—are not the ones they sign, or signed, their checks with.

The first of these diversionary targets to come to light was one who, if he accomplished little else, at least made plain the seamy callousness of his persecutors. On the day after Lennon was arraigned, the story of Cunningham's experience appeared in the newspapers, and a few hours later Miller, back in Rochester, received a phone call from a private detective. The man had, he said, been retained by attorneys representing the estate of Peter F. Billings, who had died in New York the previous May, at the age of eighty-seven. For some years prior to his death, Billings, a retired and retiring businessman, had lived, with his wife, in the penthouse of a fashionable East Side apartment hotel and in homes they owned in Massachusetts and Florida. According to the detective, Billings' executors were looking into certain disbursements that, unknown to Mrs. Billings, he had made between 1948 and 1952 to a will-o'-the-wisp coterie of men, two of whom were named Odom and Hampton; two others were named Parker (he turned out to be Arlen-Gottlieb) and Patrick (it didn't take a very astute investigator to guess that this was Patrick Lennon). After promising the detective to look into the matter, Miller went right over to have a talk with Hampton in the Monroe County jail. When he asked the prisoner if he had ever heard of Billings, Hampton admitted that he and his confreres had had a patron by that name. Not long after Miller left the jail, he wrote a letter to his fellow Inspectors, Kogel and Forster, saying, "It seems apparent indeed that we have broken into the operations of a loosely knit association of old-time confidence men who have been fabulously successful in their criminal ventures during recent years."

Technically, Billings fell short of qualifying as an ideal subject for swindlers. To begin with, he seems to have been more philanthropic than avaricious. Then, too, he was not a man who readily parted with large sums of money. But in spite of these black marks, he did fit the orthodox pattern in some ways—his age, for example, and his wealth and his reticence. In any case, during the six weeks before Christmas of 1951, Billings wrote sixty checks, and no fewer than nine of these helped to make the swindlers' Yuletide a festive one. A year or so earlier, Billings, in a shaky old hand, had written an acquaintance of theirs a letter, enclosing a check for $2,200 and explaining, "This is a lot of money, for me, but I send it on faith in you as an honest man and in Patrick, though I barely know him. . . . Mr. Patrick is evidently one who knows what he is doing and I have faith in his doings." The addressee was a man named Addison B. Gatling, who had undergone a serious operation on his vocal cords and could talk only by means of a voice box hooked into his throat. Billings was a soft touch for the afflicted, and Gatling had been sponging off him since 1948. For three years, Gatling, working alone, had wormed several thousand dollars in small amounts out of his benefactor. On June 11, 1951, however, while downing a few at Frawley's Bar & Grill, Gatling ran into Lennon, an old drinking companion, and told him about Billings' generosity. From then on, things were never the same. That afternoon, in fact, Gatling called on Billings, accompanied by Lennon, who, though he was just starting in on Cunningham—a messenger of his was collecting in Rochester at that very moment —had decided that the octogenarian sounded too good to pass up and too old to defer. Gatling introduced his companion to Billings as Thomas J. Patrick, a close friend of his, and then Lennon took over. Professing to be, like his host, a businessman solicitous of Gatling's welfare, he profusely thanked Billings for having done so much to sustain it. But, he said, there was no need of continuing to give money away in this fashion; he had in mind a plan whereby Billings, in return for a small investment, could make Gatling self-supporting. Patrick-Lennon's proposal was that Billings buy some land he knew about in Skaneateles, New York, and build a refreshment stand on it for Gatling to supervise. The site was ideal for the purpose, he said, and he would gladly attend to the details of purchase and construction if Billings would cover the costs, which would not be exorbitant; as a matter of fact, he thought a mere five hundred dollars would be enough to make a good start on the project. Thoroughly taken in, Billings wrote out a check to him for the five hundred.

As always when Lennon was masterminding a financial venture, one thing led to another. Opportunely, the newspapers reported that uranium ore had been discovered near Skaneateles, and Patrick-Lennon persuaded Billings to buy more land there—enough, say, so that if it turned out to contain no ore, they could at least build a veterans' rest home on it, again with Gatling as supervisor. To Billings, the possibility of acquiring a rich uranium deposit for almost nothing was titillating, while the prospect of helping not only Gatling but veterans, too, was irresistible. Soon, however, he was being called upon to write checks for many less alluring purposes—title searches, options, tax surveys, fees, retainers. Gatling took fright when he realized that the small-scale handouts he had been accustomed to had mushroomed into large-scale thefts, and he dropped out of the picture. Lennon didn't mind seeing him go, for by then he had been joined in the pillage by several old cronies, notably Hampton and Gottlieb, alias Arlen in the Cunningham operation and alias Parker in this one.

In December, 1951, six months after Billings had agreed to build Gatling a refreshment stand, he paid out $20,000 to Lennon and his colleagues (who were simultaneously extracting $9,000 from Cunningham). Even so, on January 11, 1952, Lennon, Hampton, and Gottlieb, who were basking in the sun at Coral Gables, Florida, found themselves strapped, and Hampton had to run over to Billings' winter place, in Orlando, and hit him for $7,500 more. In all, Billings paid out $78,369 in his effort to make Gatling self-supporting, and he had nothing to show for it but a tenuous claim to a $4,200 piece of property in Skaneateles and a $25,000 promissory note from Thomas J. Patrick, payable on demand.

In the summer of 1953, it was generally agreed among the boys that Billings was simply too feeble to bilk any further, and for a time they all dropped him. But on July 5, 1955, Gottlieb, unaware that Billings had died six weeks earlier, took it into his head to have one more try, and wrote to Billings not as his old friend Parker but as a stranger named Arlen, an independent oil operator. He explained that he wanted to let Billings in on a uranium find in British Columbia, and added, "I shall try to talk with you personally in the near future to give you a more comprehensive picture of this fabulous operation." A few days after posting this letter, Gottlieb learned that Billings was dead. Anything but abashed, he immediately wrote to Mrs. Billings. In his first paragraph, he said he had just heard of her husband's death. Then, without wasting time on condolences, he repeated verbatim the text of the earlier come-on letter. Mrs. Billings had the good sense not to reply.

Leonard P. Quinn, a sixty-seven-year-old consulting engineer with offices in Long Island and New York, lost nearly $100,000 more to the gang than Billings did—$171,968, to be exact—but then his motives were less humanitarian. Inspector Miller got the first clue to his misfortunes while going through satchels full of documents, many of them self-incriminating, that the cocksure Lennon had left, along with his twenty hats, in midtown bars. In one suitcase were some calling cards bearing Lennon's name and Quinn's, and Miller presently went to see the engineer. Quinn revealed—in confidence, of course—that toward the end of 1950 a New York state senator had introduced him to Lennon, who represented himself as a chap with exceptional political and social connections, through which he could land the engineer some big contracts, and would, for a mere 15 per cent commission. Quinn snapped at the bait, and invited Lennon to make free use of his New York office, which, he explained, he himself rarely visited. In April, 1951, the month when Lennon began to tighten his clutch on Cunningham, he wangled three checks, totaling $2,100, from Quinn as advances against the fat commissions he was sure to be earning any day now, and the parade was on. While Quinn was still waiting for Lennon to turn up his first engineering contract, the latter approached him with a tip on a deal of another kind—a chance to make a profit of $200,000 by purchasing for next to nothing the rails of an abandoned streetcar line in Portland,

Maine, and selling them as scrap. A few months later, Lennon, affecting acute chagrin, reported to Quinn that the deal had fallen through, because a woman who owned part of the land the rails were laid on had refused to come to terms. Quinn was sorry to hear this, for through Lennon he had already invested $5,583 in the project, or thought he had.

In 1952, Lennon, without producing a single contract, got Quinn to give him $4,850 more in advances against commissions. ("Oh, what a long-drawn-out pull this game is!" he wrote in a letter to the engineer.) Early in 1953, assuming an air of grave contrition, Lennon told Quinn that he was sorry he had thus far let him down so badly, and said that to reimburse him he would be happy to give him a mineral-rights lease he owned on some land near Center, in Shelby County, Texas, which he inaccurately described as a big oil-producing region. But, Lennon went on, he was afraid it wouldn't be much of a gift, because while several big oil companies were clamoring to buy up leases in the vicinity of Center, this particular lease didn't cover quite enough acreage to interest them. Then, as if a happy solution had just occurred to him, he brightened and said that, come to think of it, his brother-in-law, George Arlen, owned some leases of the kind the oil companies *were* interested in—possibly, to help a relative make amends, George would be willing to part with them for only a fraction of their value. Quinn wound up by paying $27,250 for the leases and an additional $35,440 to make them acceptable to the oil companies, a course that entailed straightening out certain liens, attachments, mortgages, and whatnot, conducting a geologist's survey, and hurdling still another obstacle Lennon dreamed up—Indian rights.

In August, 1954, Lennon thought it was time for Quinn to meet a Texan, and he produced one in Odom, who got himself up in a big-brimmed hat and snappy leather boots, and appeared on the scene as Paul E. Devaney, a Shelby County oil-lease broker. Quinn, who was beginning to have his doubts, boldly asked if he might see Devaney-Odom's credentials, but when the visitor replied apologetically that he had left his wallet at his hotel, he let the matter ride. Devaney-Odom thereupon declared emphatically that he could get the whole messy lease business tidied up for a 5 per cent commission—$4,000 of which he would need in advance—on whatever price Quinn might finally be paid for the properties. Quinn wrote out a check for $4,000 on the spot. A few weeks later, Devaney-Odom told Quinn that he had a buyer lined up for the leases—a man by the name of Harrington, a real big wheel, representing a giant oil syndicate. Harrington, Quinn was advised, lived in Rochester, at 1026 East Avenue—a whimsical touch on Odom's part, for the address had the oilman living almost on Augustine Cunningham's lawn. Quinn never got a chance to meet Harrington, though Harrington frequently telephoned him, and it would have been awkward if he had. For Harrington, like Devaney, was Odom. After Harrington had joined the cast of characters, Quinn gave him and Devaney—that is, Quinn gave Odom—$54,885 for this and that, including more Indian rights.

It may be recalled that when the Postal Inspectors opened Hampton's safe-deposit box at the Empire Hotel, they found a checkbook belonging to R. E. Baker, together with $4,950 in cash. The minor puzzle of the checkbook was cleared up when Quinn identified Hampton from a photograph as a man named Baker, whom he had met through Devaney-Harrington-Odom. On being informed by Baker-Hampton, a bit player in this particular drama, that he himself had invested in the oil-lease deal, Quinn gave him $42,160 to clear up the usual assortment of snarls. Naturally, Quinn never received the leases he had paid for—nor did he receive much of anything else, except a fraudulent death certificate. This came his way in the summer of 1955, after Odom had grown tired of playing a double role in a single swindle. As Harrington, he telephoned Quinn to tell him sorrowfully that their dear friend Devaney had suffered a heart attack and passed away aboard a train at Buffalo. Quinn must have been overcome by grief, for he apparently did not pause to reflect on how odd it was that Harrington, a big wheel in the oil industry, should ask him for

$2,180 to ship Devaney's body back to Texas. Instead, he instantly reached for his checkbook, and the death certificate arrived shortly afterward. Whether it occurred to Quinn that it was also rather odd for one friend to mail such a document to another upon the death of a third is not known; possibly Quinn thought it would help him establish a business expense for income tax purposes. If he did, he soon had more and greater expenses to keep on file, for Harrington bullied him into buying off Devaney's widow and brother—in the amounts of $21,000 and $5,000, respectively. Lennon, Odom, and Hampton might have gone on conning Quinn for widows' mites and Indian rights practically forever if Miller had not broken up the cabal.

As for the smaller fry among the ring's victims, two were doctors—a circumstance that came as no surprise to Inspector Miller, since medical men, for some reason, are especially vulnerable to the wiles of confidence men. One of the two was Dr. Roger Phillips, a distinguished eye surgeon, who in the fall of 1954 was unlucky enough to have Lennon for a patient. By then, Lennon's eyesight had become so bad that he had to rely on friends to tell him which horse was leading in the stretch. Dr. Phillips removed one of his eyes but restored the other to normal vision, and a few months later the patient showed his gratitude by letting the doctor in on an oil deal in New Mexico. "This could and I am assured it will be colossal," Lennon wired him. Among the papers Lennon left lying around in luggage was a forged letter he had written to himself on stationery taken from the surgeon's office. Presumably composed as a come-on for some other doctor, the letter started off "Dear Pat" and, after calling attention to an enclosed check for $1,600, continued, "At breakfast this morning, Mrs. Phillips said, 'Pat bought our first Cadillac with his Kentucky operation; and our farm with his Texas operation; let us hope that New Mexico will be as good as Kentucky and Texas was.' " As if it were not bad enough to have his wife's grammar debased, Dr. Phillips was taken for $4,399.66.

The second doctor on Lennon's list was Nathan C. Traven, a

general practitioner in New Jersey. Lennon entered his office one day in January, 1953, and presented a business card identifying him as a vice-president of the Hathaway Steel Corporation, a concern that he and Gottlieb had invented. Lennon sold Dr. Traven on some imaginary oil leases in Texas and New Mexico, and even after his arrest for defrauding Cunningham made the papers, he continued to extract money from the physician, collecting about a dozen payments over a period of six months—while he was out on bail—by stoutly maintaining that he was implicated in the case only because Odom had appropriated his identity. Miller noted in a memo to one of his associates that Lennon's success in keeping Dr. Traven in line against such odds was illustrative of his "almost diabolical ability to gain one's confidence." Dr. Traven ended up $25,989.75 poorer.

While Miller accepted as a matter of course the presence of two doctors in Lennon's net, he was startled to find, as he went on sorting out the papers, that also enmeshed was a lawyer—a species generally avoided by confidence men. Youthful specimens of the breed are considered especially undesirable, yet this man, James B. Griffin, Jr., was only in his early thirties when, in April, 1955, from his home in Ohio, he wrote to Lennon, inviting "Pat" to his forthcoming wedding. In the letter, which was never answered, Griffin then turned to a less festive matter; some creditors were pressing him, he said, so could he please have, no later than May 1, $5,000 of the rich returns Lennon had guaranteed him on his investment in 320 acres of oil-and-gas land in Sierra County, New Mexico? Griffin told a Postal Inspector who interviewed him after the Cunningham case broke that he was sure he'd get the money sooner or later, because Lennon had happened to mention that he himself had invested in 320 acres adjoining Griffin's; what's more, Lennon had given him a promissory note for $4,085, payable on demand. The interview did nothing to make Griffin realize that he'd been hornswoggled. Right up to the time of his death, in an automobile accident, in the spring of 1956, he kept on sending Lennon money. Lennon took him, in all, for $25,000.

Even after Lennon was convicted of swindling Cunningham, Joseph B. Marsula, a resident of San Francisco who was a schoolmate of Lennon's and had always liked him enormously, remained unshakably convinced that his friend would sometime repay what he owed him. The debt amounted to $2,240—a sum that Marsula, in the spring of 1955, sent Lennon for reinvestment, having raised the money by selling thirty shares of Crown Zellerbach common. Lennon had asked Marsula for $2,250, so, in a sense, this victim was ten dollars ahead of the game.

And, finally, there was the case of Jennie Frederick's aunt. Jennie, a waitress at the Belmont Plaza Hotel, put Lennon in touch with her aunt, who proved the validity of his slogan "Never SELL 'em—make 'em BUY." Lennon worked her up to such a high degree of investor's fever that even after he practically beseeched her to lay off some oil leases in New Mexico, stating bluntly, "This is a highly speculative field, and I do not think it is something for a woman in your position to place her money in," she insisted on going right ahead. Lennon took her for only $1,500, which may have been all she had.

In March, 1956, Lennon, Hampton, Odom, and Arlen (under that name) were indicted by a federal grand jury for mail fraud and conspiracy in connection with the Cunningham case—the only one in which the authorities felt that they had enough evidence, and enough cooperative witnesses, to convict the swindlers. Their prosecution was assigned to Donald F. Potter, a young Rochester lawyer then serving as an Assistant United States Attorney. A trial was set for May, but was postponed for a month when it developed that Lennon was critically ill in Bellevue; he had been admitted late in April, suffering from a severe umbilical hernia, and had subsequently been found to be afflicted also with cirrhosis of the liver (he told the examining doctors that he regularly drank two quarts of whiskey a day), jaundice, swollen ankles, and probable cancer of the pancreas. Miller and Potter came to New York to see for themselves what shape he was in, found him bright yellow and tight-lipped, and were told by the doctors attending him that the chances of his ever leaving the place alive were exceedingly slim. (Another man who called on Lennon was Dr. Traven. It was a nonprofessional visit for him, but not for Lennon. Sick as he was, he managed to wheedle five hundred dollars from the well-wisher sitting at his bedside, with the understanding that it would be invested in a pending bonanza in Alaska.)

Lennon's trial, accordingly, was severed from that of the other defendants, against whom Potter was anxious to proceed while Cunningham, then seventy-eight, was still available as a witness. Hampton pleaded guilty, and was sentenced to two and a half years, which he served mostly in the federal penitentiary at Milan, Michigan. Odom and Arlen went to trial in July, 1956, before Judge Harold P. Burke, the senior United States District Judge for the Western District of New York. (Cunningham not only testified against Odom but was conned by Odom into posing with him for a photograph, in which the two men were shown beaming, as if they had just jointly swung a big deal.) Both defendants were convicted and sent to the federal penitentiary at Lewisburg—Odom for three years, Arlen for five. Arlen went down fighting. He insisted on conducting his own defense, although the judge urged him either to retain a lawyer or to accept a court-appointed one. Evidently, Arlen hoped that if he had no lawyer he could use that deprivation as grounds for an appeal. But the judge anticipated this gambit, and warned Arlen so often of his rights to have counsel that when he was found guilty and did make precisely such an appeal, the Appellate Division threw it out. Three days after Odom and Arlen were sentenced, Lennon, his health astonishingly improved, decamped from Bellevue. Potter at once asked Judge Burke to revoke his bail, arguing that otherwise he was likely to drink himself to death before a verdict could be rendered on him. The request was granted, and Lennon was picked up at Hogan's Bar by Inspectors Forster and Kogel and taken to Rochester, where, on September 6, he, too, pleaded guilty. He was sentenced to five years in the penitentiary at Milan.

None of the money the confidence men got out of their eight

victims was ever recovered—there was no proof that Hampton's (or Odom's) $4,950 came from swindling—but Cunningham, before he died, may have derived some scant satisfaction from the knowledge that his lawyers were able to charge off part of his losses as an income tax deduction, just as they might have if his property had been struck by lightning. After Lennon was sentenced, he told Miller, at the close of a sweeping confession, "I hope when this is over to try to make something of the few remaining years of my life"—which, coming from him, might have seemed ambiguous, but which the Inspector construed as meaning that he planned to go straight. A year or so later, a lawyer for Billings' estate, perhaps encouraged at hearing of this, journeyed to Milan in the hope of tracking down some of the thousands that were intended to set Gatling up in business. The lawyer asked Lennon a hundred and fifty questions, and Lennon refused to answer any of them. Without any help from Lennon, however, Billings' executors found that Packy and his allies actually had bought a piece of land at Skaneateles, and, after interminable legal wrangling, the old codger's estate was declared owner of the property.

In December, 1956, seven months before his death, Cunningham telephoned Miller to report that he had just received a long-distance call from Hampton. "Isn't he supposed to be in prison?" Cunningham asked, and Miller replied that Hampton undoubtedly was there. "Well," Cunningham went on, "a man whose voice sounded exactly like his called me from a pay phone. I heard the operator ask him for a dollar forty-five. He's in an awful jam and needs ten thousand dollars. It cost him that much to defend himself." Miller pointed out gently that Hampton had pleaded guilty and hadn't spent even a dollar forty-five on his defense. "Well, anyway, he needs ten thousand to put his children through a good Catholic school," Cunningham persisted. Aware that Hampton was then seventy years old and had abandoned his family some thirty years before, Miller told Cunningham to leave everything up to him. By then, there was no way of tracing the call, so the

Inspector got in touch with the warden at Milan, who assured him that not a single pay phone was on the premises but Hampton definitely was. Miller could only surmise that a swindler was still at large who had the accurate hunch that there was one more drop of blood to be squeezed out of the credulous old man.

# 7. The Incorrigibles

*"I knew that money gained in a dirty business such as this never did anybody any good, but it has been awfully hard for me to break away from the con racket since I started it in 1920. I have always seemed to be able to talk people into turning over money to me on almost any kind of representation I might make. This has been my downfall. I hope when this is over to try to make something of the few remaining years of my life, and I know that I can do so."*

—From a sworn statement by Patrick H. Lennon to Charles A. Miller, made on September 20, 1956, just before Lennon went to prison for mail fraud.

Whether or not imprisonment leads to the rehabilitation of criminals is moot, but there is one variation of the species that year in and out is as implacably recidivist as it is disarming—the dyed-in-the-wool confidence man. Except for his perseverance, there is nothing more characteristic about the skilled con man than his confidence in himself. A few years ago, one who, like Packy Lennon, dealt largely and larcenously in fake oil leases was about to appear before a grand jury that subsequently indicted him. He had been apprehended by Karl Fein, a veteran Postal Inspector who, it sometimes surprised the people he tangled with, had a law degree. Fein spent more than forty years in the postal service, and nothing about confidence men surprised him. He rather respected them as professionals who were continually playing a game against the Inspection Service. It is an all-or-nothing game; either the con men win or they lose, and when they lose a round they often shrug and go off to jail without any hard feelings. One fellow for whose incarceration Fein was mainly responsible received permission to get married by a prison chaplain, and he invited the Postal Inspector to be his best man. Fein declined; he didn't think members of opposing teams ought to get that chummy off the playing field.

Now, in the grand jury proceedings, one of the con man's victims appeared to testify against him—a chap who not long before had squandered sixteen thousand dollars on some spurious oil deal. Espying the victim, the con man told Fein he'd bet him five dollars he could clip that pigeon once again if he had a chance. Fein asked the United States Attorney who was prosecuting the case if it would be all right to give the predator a private word with his plucked prey, and the prosecutor said he didn't mind; it would be interesting to see what happened. Five minutes later, the *victim* asked for a private word with the two law-enforcement officials: Would they have any objection, he wondered, if before taking the stand he bought a few more oil leases, because he had just heard of a really smashing investment possibility. Fein, congratulating himself on not having been sucked into a larger bet, paid the con man his five dollars.

Knowing well the incorrigibility of most confidence men, Inspector Miller was startled into wakefulness at 8 A.M. on the morning of April 4, 1962, when, as he was riding drowsily on a Washington, D.C., bus, heading to work in the Fraud Division, he glanced out a window and saw Packy Lennon, jaunty in homburg and chesterfield, striding along the sidewalk. Lennon had been released from prison two years earlier, and Miller hadn't been sure what he'd been up to in the interim, but whatever he was up to in Washington, the Inspector surmised, it was probably not in the public interest. Miller hopped off the bus at the next stop, walked back, accosted Lennon, and invited him to his office for a catch-up chat. Lennon said he couldn't spare the time; he had to see some friends. Well, then, what about lunch? Lennon begged off. "But don't worry," the con man told the Inspector. "If anybody tries to skin me, I'll get in touch with you instantly." Then he walked off, laughing. Miller had nothing to hold him on, except general principles, but the next morning the Inspector sent a warning memorandum about his newly met old acquaintance to the Service's field office in the capital: "It is most unlikely that he is engaged in honest work in Washington, and it is believed that Inspectors handling fraud cases in this area which involve questionable investment schemes should be apprised of Lennon's presence."

On June 6, two months later, Miller learned that his hunch had been correct. Inspector William J. Hegarty wanted him to talk to a troubled woman of sixty-one who was in his office. She was Dr. Helen Dwight Reid, the Coordinator of Seminars in the College of General Studies at George Washington University, and she had come to report her concern about $36,325.85 she had recently invested, at the bidding of a fellow academician named Harry Hicks Hornblower, in New Mexico oil and gas leases. Miller at once sent for some mug shots of Packy Lennon, and while awaiting them said he assumed that Dr. Reid could identify Hornblower all right. Well, not exactly, the woman said abashedly; the fact was she had never laid eyes on him. They had conducted their business by mail and telephone, and although at her request Professor Hornblower had made several appointments for face-to-face meetings, something had always come up at the last moment to require their cancellation. Now, looking at Lennon's photograph, Dr. Reid said she certainly knew *him;* he was Charles Chalk, a courier who had come around several times to pick up some money for Hornblower. She remembered Chalk well because she hadn't liked his looks, and she had told the Professor as much. (Oh, Chalk was an all right sort, the Professor had assured her; he was a kind of old family retainer of the Hornblowers whom the Professor kept in pocket money by giving him casual errands.) This rare aspersion on Lennon's physical appearance may have hurt the disembodied Hornblower's feelings, for Harry Hicks Hornblower,

Inspector Miller was already certain without pictorical confirmation, was none other than Patrick Henry Lennon himself.

Dr. Reid was strikingly different from the ignorant, unsophisticated kind of woman on whom con men often prey. The only child of a successful electrical engineer, she had graduated from Vassar in 1922, got her M.A. and Ph.D. in political science at Radcliffe, and taught at, among other institutions, Bryn Mawr. She had been a Carnegie Fellow in International Law, and, in 1945, a consultant to the United States delegation to the founding meeting of the United Nations in San Francisco. In 1956, with an initial grant of $250,000, she had established the Helen Dwight Reid Educational Foundation. She had worked for a number of federal agencies—the Office of Education and the Foreign Operations Administration, among them—and had not long before returned from a stint in Indonesia, where she had been a special adviser on higher education. On June 27, 1961, when her discomfiture began, she was on leave from George Washington University, working for the State Department—in, of all places, its Division of Intelligence and Research.

A spinster, and a fervent disciple of the Christian Science church, Dr. Reid got a phone call that evening from a man with a terribly nice voice who said he was in New York and hoped he wasn't ringing at an inconvenient moment, but he had something significant to convey to her. He was, he said, Harry Hicks Hornblower, Professor of Geology, Emeritus, of the University of Kentucky, and he was confident she would be sympathetic to an important, but so far deliberately unpublicized, philanthropic venture in which he was privileged to be playing a minor consultative role. Did she have a minute to hear him further? Unfortunately for her, Dr. Reid did. Well, Lennon went on purringly, a small number of distinguished American Christian Scientists had banded together in a unique investment scheme, one increment of which was to be a suitably splendid memorial, at Albuquerque, New Mexico, to Mary Baker Eddy; in view of Dr. Reid's well-known concern for the Mother Church, it had been thought she might like to join this elite group.

The project was called "Operation Faith." There was an opportunity, if the group moved rapidly enough, to get hold of some New Mexico oil and gas leases that were ridiculously underpriced; and Hornblower's geological expertise enabled him to assert unequivocally that this was a once-in-a-lifetime chance. Ten per cent of the proceeds were to be allocated to the shrine for Mrs. Eddy, and this tithe alone would probably amount to a million dollars. For the nonce, the other participants in this testimonial enterprise wished to remain anonymous, but he could let her know in strict confidence that among them—indeed, it was he who had given the Professor Dr. Reid's name—was former Senator Owen Brewster, of Maine. And if she felt inclined to join in, would she be good enough to mail a check for $250, as a demonstration of good faith, to Hornblower at the Commodore Hotel in New York?

Dr. Reid was impressed, and flattered. She had known Brewster for years. The Senator and his wife had attended her Christian Science church when they were in Washington, and she had entertained them at her home. It apparently did not occur to her to ask Brewster, who was then back in Maine, about Operation Faith. Instead, she sent the $250 the next morning. Over the following eleven months, she favored Lennon with two dozen additional payments, half by check and half in cash. (On each of her checks she neatly inscribed "Operation Faith," presumably to help her accountant at tax-filing time; once, when she asked Professor Hornblower why he insisted on some installments in cash, he muttered something about tax advantages, and she did not pursue the point.) In return for her $36,325.85, she did actually receive leases covering 280 acres in Chaves County, New Mexico. The leases cost her an average of $164.28 an acre. Lennon had got them, for $3.12 an acre, from a shady lease broker in Washington who had paid $1.32 an acre in New Mexico. Inspector Miller later ascertained from the United States Geological Survey that the leases were for land eighteen miles from the nearest well-drilling, and that by the most generous estimate the leases were worth twenty-five cents an acre. The kind of land she had invested in was contemptuously described, in knowledgeable oil-and-gas circles, as "goat pasture."

In his prime, Lennon was likened to an irresistible force meeting a movable object. Once he latched onto a victim, there was no stopping him. In Dr. Reid's case, he started off in suitably low gear, shifted almost imperceptibly into high, and cruised smoothly for nearly a year until he ran out of gas. "This is the Professor," his importunate calls would begin, and always there were new details and complications to be reckoned with and paid for—lawyers' fees, recording fees, filing charges, whatever came into his mind. He got $716 from the political scientist on July 10, and another $625 on July 12. (Temporarily short of cash, Dr. Reid borrowed the latter sum from the State Department Credit Union.) Later that summer, he demonstrated *his* good faith by actually sending *her* some money. This was represented as a preliminary return on her investment, and though it amounted to a mere $133.33—that made it seem as if she was getting a fraction of something much bigger—it had the effect of persuading her to send him much larger sums just about whenever he asked.

Dr. Reid left the State Department in October, 1961, for a holiday in Europe. Soon after her return, in December, she heard from Professor Hornblower. Lennon read the papers, especially the obituary pages, and now he wanted to commiserate with her on the Christmas Day passing of their dear mutual friend Senator Brewster. But even in adversity there could be advantage, Hornblower reported; the Brewster share of Operation Faith was now available, for a comparative pittance, to his erstwhile co-investors. Within less than a month, Dr. Reid had divested herself of an additional $8,507.50. She paid this in six installments, one of these to an alcoholic drifter (Martell brandy was the staple of his diet) whom Lennon had picked up in a New York saloon. This emissary had investigated Dr. Reid in *Who's Who in America*, had learned she was born in Glasgow, and had been inspired to call himself Robert Burns Thayer. The name must have been effective; one day in February, she gave the poet's earthy namesake $14,000 in cash. Meanwhile, she continued to honor Professor Hornblower's requests for checks, a couple of which, at his instructions, she mailed to a "Judge Joseph Murphy" at an address which, although of course she didn't know it, was that of a tavern frequented by Lennon in New York.

It saddened Dr. Reid that, no matter how often she asked the Professor, she never seemed to be able to obtain any fixed address for *him*. He did once communicate with her on a letterhead with "Operation Faith" printed on it, as well as the initials "H.H.H." There were also three geographical locations—Albuquerque, Los Angeles, and Ogden, Utah—but no street addresses. When reproached by Dr. Reid for his seeming inaccessibility, the Professor would explain that his business—and hers, too, naturally—required him always to be on the move. (There were reassurances forthcoming from other sources, too, about his circumstances and his character. Once Charles Chalk—Lennon, of course—told Dr. Reid that Professor Hornblower—Lennon, of course—had lamentably suffered a stroke, but had gone to a Christian Science service and had immediately been cured.) On one occasion, Dr. Reid was told by a voice on the phone to stand by the next day for a call from Melbourne; at the appointed hour, the Professor called. He was in Australia, he said, attending a brother's funeral.

Sometimes, Dr. Reid balked at giving the Professor any more money, but her resistance was weak, and before he was through he might even make her feel guilty about her recalcitrance; why, he would say chidingly, how could she hesitate to send along a mere couple of thousand dollars when he had already put up thirty or forty thousand of his own to maintain her parity with her fellow investors? Just exactly how big a stake Dr. Reid had in the joint venture was never entirely clear to her. Early in the game, she stood to net $96,000, according to the Professor's jovial estimate. Then in September, 1961, a smooth-talking gentleman, never identified, came around to see her. He claimed to be representing an oil company, and wondered if she would consider selling her

New Mexico holdings for $300,000? Dr. Reid had at that point a net investment of only $2,567.67, and the proposition sounded attractive, but she thought she'd better check it first with the Professor (who of course had sent the chap around), and he said no, she should hang on, they could make a much better deal than that.

On June 5, 1962, Dr. Reid had a busy day. That morning, Charles Chalk stopped by to introduce an oil specialist from Delaware whom Professor Hornblower specially wanted her to meet. This was a man named Edwin O. Keller, who didn't know much about oil but had known Packy Lennon since his bucket-shop days, and had not long before been reunited with him at the men's bar of the Waldorf-Astoria in New York. Keller, it seemed, had been asked by the Professor to pick up $10,000 from Dr. Reid, which was needed in a hurry to help grab up the Operation Faith interests of Francis V. Du Pont, of whose demise in Wilmington two weeks before Lennon had also been apprised by the obituary pages. The Professor had hoped to come around to collect that trifling sum himself, but he was simply too busy closing their deal. (Lennon was busy; he was trying to recruit a septuagenarian Christian Scientist in Washington, a retired engineer, into Operation Faith; and the old man had already come through with an initial love offering of $1,600.) Dr. Reid gave Keller a check for the $10,000. That was a Tuesday, and it was her habit to give small dinner parties on Tuesday evenings. She had to excuse herself to her guests briefly a few hours later when the Professor called. He wanted to thank her for the latest check and to advise her that, now that their partner Du Pont had been sadly promoted to another world, her profit in Operation Faith would probably be $953,000.

Dr. Reid had already begun to have some misgivings about her adventure. Since March, whenever she sent the Professor cash, she jotted down the serial number of every bill; and just a week before, after handing a check to the ill-favored Chalk, she had tried—too late, as it turned out—to stop payment on it. But nine hundred and fifty-three thousand dollars! "What should my foundation do with close to a million dollars?" she asked her guests when she returned, a trifle flushed, from the telephone. She did not expand on that teasing pronouncement, but one of her guests, an old friend who was also a trustee of her foundation, stayed on after the others had left, and finally, for the first time, she blurted out the whole story. The friend said there were two things to be done first thing the next morning. She should call her bank and stop payment on the latest check, and he would call the F.B.I. The F.B.I. forthwith referred him to the Postal Inspection Service, and within a matter of hours Dr. Reid was peering at Packy Lennon's photograph.

When Dr. Reid asked the Postal Inspectors what she should do next, they suggested that she sit back and wait to see how Lennon-Chalk-Hornblower et aliases reacted to her change of mind and heart. He reacted two days later with an oh-ye-of-little-faith phone call so drenched in sincerity that Dr. Reid was almost swung back to his side. But then she remembered Inspector Miller's firm advice, and instead of yielding to Lennon's importunities she merely pretended to yield; she said she'd give Keller the ten thousand in cash if he'd stop by on the morning of June 13. When Keller arrived at Dr. Reid's university office that day, Miller was already staked out in her coat closet, and Inspectors Hegarty and H. J. Simon were hiding down the hall. Dr. Reid handed Keller a sealed envelope containing a check for $10,000, and he gave her a receipt for it without bothering to open the envelope. If he had, he'd have noticed that the check wasn't signed. Miller had asked Dr. Reid to try to engage Keller in conversation, and when she did, he confided to her that he was on his way over to the Attorney General's office on a mission for the Du Ponts; he couldn't tarry too long, because he had to pick up the presidents of the Chase Manhattan Bank and Hornblower & Weeks, who were going along with him. The eavesdropping Miller was not surprised by the name dropping; this was hundred-proof pure con-man intoxicant. Keller did pause long enough to confide also that in the past his old friend Harry Hicks Hornblower, whom he had known for fourteen years, had had some fantastic successes in gas and oil leases; why, he could remember one time when a $150,000 investment had been transformed into $8 million. On that cheery note, he prepared to depart, and at that point the Inspector, whose solitary confinement in the closet had been getting increasingly uncomfortable, sprang forth and pounced on the unsuspecting messenger.

On being advised that the game was over and that Lennon's participation in it was no secret, Keller resignedly said that he was supposed to turn over the envelope to Packy at 1 P.M. at the men's bar of the Statler-Hilton. Miller said he'd be happy to substitute; in fact, he added as he was handcuffing the messenger, he *insisted* on substituting. So at lunchtime it was Miller who materialized at the bar, where at a table Lennon was sipping a half-and-half mixture of Scotch and milk; the Inspector thought sadly that his old adversary's liver must be acting up. On spotting Miller walking toward him, Lennon said, "I guess I'm in trouble again," and he began doing something with his hands under the table. After the hands had been ordered up into sight, and had been cuffed, Miller collected some scraps of torn-up paper from the floor. Pieced together, they formed a check for $8,106.69, made out to P. H. Lennon from E. O. Keller. Lennon explained that this was to have been used to help further fleece the elderly engineer, with whom he had a date that very afternoon; on perceiving that two-thirds of the $12,000 needed to buy some Mary Baker Eddy Operation Faith oil leases had already been put up, the old gentleman might reasonably be expected to furnish the paltry remaining one-third. There was indeed a checking account in Keller's name at the bank in question, but it had a balance of only fifty-five cents.

Inspectors Miller and Hegarty, after advising Lennon of his rights, with which by that stage of his career he was well acquainted, asked him if he would mind answering a few questions, and he said not at all.

"Did you ask Dr. Reid for money when you made your first call to her in June, '61?" Miller asked.

"Why, of course," said Lennon.

"You were not a university professor?"

"Of course not."

"Who is Judge Joseph Murphy?"

"Me."

That was to be Packy Lennon's last fling—save an abortive attempt, during a pretrial hospitalization for sclerosis of the liver, to con a German-speaking doctor in Illinois by pretending to be an oil-lease salesman named Schweppenhauser. Lennon was given a ten-month-to-five-year prison sentence for his Hornblower hoax, and he died—so far as is known, unregenerate to the end—in a federal hospital not long afterward.

To make an appealing personal impression, even if only by telephone, is a first principle among confidence men. Occasionally, however, one of them surfaces as the exception to prove their rule. Such was a Brooklyn operator, who pretended to be a rabbi, a fellow of such calculatedly disagreeable mien and disgusting comportment that people once exposed to him would go to costly lengths to avoid a repetition of the experience. It was his practice to arrive unheralded in a small town with hardly any Jewish population except for one or two local and, the "rabbi" hoped, well-to-do businessmen. The transient would stop at the post office or police station, professing to be a holy man with high-level connections in Israel who was momentarily out of funds and needed a night's lodging. When his scheme worked, he would end up as the overnight guest of the leading local Jewish family. Returning to Brooklyn, the wayfarer would strike up a correspondence with his host, soliciting funds for this or that nonexistent synagogue or yeshiva. If the host didn't contribute—and of course, since the rabbi played one-night stands, there were dozens of hosts—then the guest would suggest that he pay another call, to plead his worthy cause in person. The host would usually be good for at least a token gift to avoid laying eyes on him again; anything would be better than *that.*

One inveterate confidence man whose polished exterior stood

him in good stead for many years was Edwin Cole, of whom a federal judge declared while ordering a five-year sentence for him when he was sixty-eight, "I am well aware of your age. I am equally well aware that when you get out of prison you will be back at the same game again. This is the fourth of a series of serious felonies by which you have mulcted people out of hundreds of thousands of dollars, in many cases from people who could ill afford to lose the money. Weighing your age against what you have done, I am imposing this sentence. Your history indicates that there is not much hope of your ever being rehabilitated."

If confidence men got pensions for protracted work, Cole would have been comfortably retired by then; he had already devoted more than thirty years to his exacting trade. (Earlier, he had dabbled in selling real estate and ginger ale, but he had found these legitimate pursuits unworthy of his formidable talents.) Cole had grossed well over a million dollars, and almost always by the same technique—"a basic scheme," according to Inspector Tarpey, who would later command the army that conquered Clifford Irving, "as old as fraud itself." Cole's slight variation on the theme was that whereas some con men have a trace of compassion, and will milk their victims merely to their next-to-last cent, he would wring them until they were bone dry. He had no qualms about transforming people into paupers; his only brother, a musician, spent the last eleven years of his life on welfare, at the same time that the nonwelfare Cole, whom Inspector Tarpey once apostrophized as "a major professional criminal," was spending much of *his* time at a suite in the Plaza in New York.

Cole, who had a wife but whose work required him to leave her on her own periodically, was a familiar figure in many hotels. While toiling in New York, he was partial to the Plaza, where, in the late 1950s, he was a welcome guest: Even by the lofty standards of that establishment he was a big tipper. He was frequently to be seen darting in and out of the E. F. Hutton brokerage office then in the hotel, and he was a valued customer of a lobby gift shop. His spendthrift habits not unnaturally caught the eye of one of the shop's clerks, a young Frenchwoman who had once won a beauty contest in France. She had come to the United States as a fashion model and had married a small-scale American businessman, who will be known here as Grimsley, and who, while generous as he could be, was bound to suffer in comparison with the elegant and open-handed Mr. Cole.

Cole did not so much con "Miss France" as let her con herself. Greed, like water, usually finds its own level. She had observed him practically commuting between her shop and the Hutton office; and she had assumed, as he wished people to assume, that he was not merely wealthy but knowledgeable about investments. So one day she asked him timidly whether he thought her husband and she should invest a few thousand dollars they had saved in a new issue of Ford common. Cole said they shouldn't: There were far more worthwhile ways for prudent people to augment their savings; he was flattered that they had solicited his humble advice; he would be glad to help; come to think of it, why didn't the Grimsleys dine with him at the Plaza one evening, if they could spare the time? Mrs. Grimsley knew the Plaza well, but she had never eaten there; on hastily accepting the invitation, she could not help reflecting that the meal would probably cost Mr. Cole more than she earned in a week.

At dinner, once the small talk was out of the way, the eager Grimsleys brought up the subject of investments; and after a show of reluctance their host said that if they were all that anxious to get onto a good thing, perhaps he should mention that he had a half interest in a potential gold mine called the Patchogue Transit Mix Corporation, over on Long Island. Talk about quick profits! The way Patchogue was going, he might soon *buy* the Plaza. Unfortunately, most of the company's cash was tied up, as was his own; anybody who could see his way clear to lending Patchogue $1,600 for short-term working capital would get a handsome return. The Grimsleys almost fell over themselves giving him the $1,600, and within forty-eight hours he had returned it, along with a $200 profit. Well! That was more than enough to take *him* to dinner. But the gallant gentleman would have none of that. Instead, he treated them again, and this time disclosed that Patchogue Transit had a chance to land a huge contract with the Atomic Energy Commission, but needed $4,500 for immediate cash outlays; this would be returned, with a suitable profit, naturally, in increments of $500 weekly as phases of the job were completed.

The Grimsleys put up the $4,500, and got back six payments of $500 each. Then, at a third dinner, Cole explained that there might be a slight delay before further remittances were forthcoming; Patchogue had run into unexpected problems with labor and materials. But there was no need for them to worry; he himself had incalculably more than they riding on this particular venture, and he frankly believed that a little patience now might result in a lot of profits later. Meanwhile, had they heard about some of the marvelous uranium stocks that were currently available, at practically fire-sale prices, in Calgary and Edmonton? They hadn't, but thought they might be able to borrow $10,000 from Grimsley's parents—virtually their entire life savings—to take advantage of this situation. "I am sure you realize I am sincere," Cole wrote them on Plaza notepaper the next day, advocating haste. "I only wanted to help you because you both are fine people, respectable and refined." How was *that* for hospitality—all but a thank-you letter from the host to his guests! They swiftly gave him the $10,000. They were a mite surprised to hear, on inquiring how their uranium stocks were doing, that at the last minute Cole had switched their money to a real estate project outside Wilmington, Delaware, where he had been offered a piece of a vast new shopping center. In a chauffeured limousine that Cole often hired while at the Plaza, he drove Mr. Grimsley down there and showed him around the construction site, an impressively proportioned one. Enjoining Grimsley to share with nobody, not even his wife, the secret intelligence, Cole told him that the Du Ponts were also in on this one. Thus reassured, Grimsley not only forgave Cole for abandoning Canada but, on the ride back, volunteered to put another $8,500—all that his wife and he had left—into Delaware.

"The money will be used to borrow for us both $50,000.00," Cole wrote Grimsley somewhat incoherently on its receipt, "so we can keep in full our obligation to your mother and Pa immediately so you and Adrienne will be working on velvet."

Since that was the last of the Grimsleys' resources, that was the last they heard of Cole. He checked out of the Plaza, they were stunned to learn, without leaving a forwarding address. (He did leave an unpaid bill of $539.85, some of it deriving from their banquets *à troix*.) Inasmuch as Cole had used the mails in the course of swindling them, a friend urged them to lodge a complaint with the Postal Inspection Service, which up to then, surprisingly, had never heard of him. Grimsley recalled from his auto trip south that Cole seemed quite at home around Wilmington, so Inspector Tarpey, who was then in charge of that area, was instructed to track him down. Tarpey reasoned that for Cole to have been living it up as he was at the Plaza would have necessitated his hitting someone else shortly before he smote the Grimsleys, and the Inspector began making inquiries around Delaware hotels. He soon ascertained that just before Cole went to New York, he had been staying at the Lord De La Ware Hotel, outside Wilmington. The secretary-treasurer of the hotel knew him well, and also was sadly acquainted with Patchogue Transit Mix; he had invested $8,500 in that company. Cole had led him on much as he had mesmerized the Grimsleys—taking $3,800 from him and swiftly returning $4,000; taking $8,000 and returning $9,000; taking $11,500 and returning $14,000; and then taking, seriatim, a total of $78,000 and returning nothing, unless one counted a slide rule with "Patchogue Transit Mix" stamped on it. The hotel man was also involved in the big new shopping center, which explained to Inspector Tarpey how Cole knew so much about that. Tarpey learned, moreover, that while Cole was working over the hotel man, he had also been enriched to the tune of $62,500 by a half dozen other residents of Wilmington.

Inasmuch as that city had been so good to Cole, Tarpey figured he'd find him there sooner or later, and he finally did. The con man was staying—with, for a change, his wife—at a not quite first-class hotel there, and was in sorry financial straits. What he had done with all his money was unclear—perhaps he had invested it in Canadian uranium stocks—but he was patently broke; at the time of his arrest, he owed that hotel $1,000, and he had no discernible assets. He could probably have extricated himself from that awkward situation by finding a new victim, but he was clapped into prison before he had a chance, and he ended up there. It was a sad commentary on Cole's acceptance of pauperism as an inevitable concomitant of the American way of life that his wife, like a number of other individuals who had been consequential in his career, ended up as a pauper herself: She became a ward of the New Castle County Welfare Department.

A dedicated confidence man cannot afford to brood about the plight of his close relatives. Another old pro, Kenneth P. Chamberlain, could attribute a not inconsiderable part of his considerable success to his deception of his own brother. Chamberlain sometimes trafficked in fraudulent licensing agreements on inventions and patents, but his specialty was altering stock certificates. He would get hold of certificates made out in the amount of one to five shares of a stock, and would multiply the number of shares on them by as much as a hundredfold. Then he would sell the bogus certificates, representing himself as an officer of the corporation involved and promising at least a 9 per cent return on every investment. His brother, who had founded a plastics company, gave Kenneth $8,800 worth of stock in it. Chamberlain asked for this in the form of fifty-five certificates—he was putting them away at intervals for his children, he said—and after altering the numbers on them he peddled them for $151,600. It was integral to his scheme that he would agree to repurchase any shares at any time on thirty days' notice; that gave him a month to resell his goods. He also sent out dividends himself, with accompanying notices on counterfeited letterheads, drawing checks on bank accounts he opened, one for each company he handled.

Chamberlain came a cropper when he was hawking shares in a manufacturing company of which he professed to be an executive. He, too, found Delaware an agreeable environment—there must be something about the state, which has so long served as nominal headquarters for absentee corporations, that attracts swindlers—and while staying at hotels there would sometimes engage the public stenographers on the premises. When a young woman there inquired into the stocks he was dictating dividend letters about, he said that they were normally purchasable only by company employees, but that inasmuch as she had been doing company work, he would declare her eligible. He let her have fifty shares for $550. He must have forgotten about her, because he neglected to send her a quarterly dividend she believed she had coming, and she wrote about its absence directly to the company. Its president answered; her name, he said, did not appear on any shareholder list, and would she be kind enough to send a photostat of her stock certificate, so he could investigate the matter? The fifty-share certificate turned out to be one that had originally been issued to Chamberlain—who had formerly been a free-lance sales agent for the outfit—in the amount of five shares. (He had received 11,000 shares of the stock, in lieu of other compensation, worth at the time of transmittal $2,300; and by doctoring the certificates had reaped $57,080 from this source.) The angry public stenographer besought the help of the Postal Inspection Service, and when one of its laboratory technicians exposed her certificate to ultraviolet rays, the alterations on it were incriminatingly vivid.

Chamberlain's career ended soon after that. It might not have been so successful while he was pursuing it had many of his victims—who altogether entrusted some $400,000 to his dubious stewardship—known that although he had reasonably solid academic and religious credentials, having once taken a course in business administration and having served as a church deacon, he had in his prime also become, extracurricularly, an accomplished amateur magician. But then, what topnotch confidence man isn't?

# 8. The Importer

Late in November, 1958, two upstate New York men, who shall be known here as Robert Williams and Joseph Sutton, received a beguiling letter from a Montreal firm called the Tasty Treat Frozen Foods Products Company. The two men were brothers-in-law, whose families shared a double house, and who both had modest jobs with a wholesale florist. A couple of years before, to augment their incomes, they had begun baking butter crackers in an outbuilding next to their house; working evenings and weekends, they could turn out weekly a hundred dozen boxes of crackers, which they sold, mostly to stores in their area, at a wholesale price of $2.64 per dozen boxes. Williams and Sutton were eager to make baking their full-time occupation someday, so they had taken a few ads in trade magazines in the hope of broadening their business. The letter from Montreal, which had presumably been prompted by one of these ads, asked if they would be interested in selling their product in Canada—"a very profitable outlet." If so, the letter continued, Tasty Treat would welcome a reply. The part-time bakers answered with alacrity, and within a week they received a telephone call, collect, from Montreal. The caller, whom they later described as "a very persuasive and seemingly sincere person on the telephone," identified himself as Robert Davis, of Tasty Treat. He was a purchasing representative, he said, for two hundred Safeway supermarkets in Canada, and he wished a sample order of two hundred boxes of butter crackers rushed to him by air freight, prepaid. Williams at once complied, taking the crackers to the nearest airport and paying for their northward passage.

The next day, another collect call came in from Davis. There had been a mixup, he said, and the crackers had arrived collect. Williams and Sutton should therefore wire him $87.43, to reimburse him for the shipping costs, in care of his representatives, Associated Business Brokers. Davis added reassuringly that this trifling matter would be straightened out when the bakers submitted their invoice; what was important at the moment, he said, was that the crackers were wonderful—better than he could have imagined. Would they please send him, as rapidly as possible, a thousand dozen boxes, via the New York Central Railroad? The import duty on crackers, he went on, came to 50 per cent of the wholesale price, and in order to expedite the passage of the second shipment through Canadian customs, would Williams and Sutton please also wire $1,320 to a firm called United Food Business Brokers, which helped Safeway handle *big* deals? Davis explained smoothly that Tasty Treat and Safeway didn't like to be bothered with a slew of bills; they preferred to make one all-inclusive settlement with each creditor, and the cracker men had merely to tack the $1,320 on to their invoice.

The brothers-in-law had no immediate access to this much cash, but on the strength of their rosy prospects Sutton borrowed $2,000 from a bank and dispatched the $1,320 to United Food Business Brokers by telegraphic money order. Williams wangled a week's leave from his regular job, temporarily hired four extra bakers, and began turning out butter crackers in myriads. The thousand dozen boxes were soon packed off to Montreal, and Sutton wrote Davis, "The privilege of serving you has of course necessitated our having to take on additional help, expand our plant, and purchase more materials. . . . We look forward to long service, with a sound mutual profit basis." So did Davis, it appeared; in still another call, he ordered another thousand dozen boxes of crackers. Before these and an additional $1,320 could be transmitted, though, Sutton happened to talk with a knowledgeable exporter about Canadian customs charges, and was perplexed to hear that the rate on crackers was not 50 per cent but 17½ per cent. When the indefatigable Davis next called, to ask if all was going well, Sutton inquired about this discrepancy. Davis said that Sutton had been misinformed, and that a clarifying telegram would follow. None did, and after a few days of ominously unenlightened waiting the partners got on the phone to Montreal and tried to reach first Safeway, then Tasty Treat, then Davis, then the two impressively named brokerage firms. The Montreal operator had no listing for any of them. Thoroughly alarmed, Williams and Sutton asked to be connected with the Montreal police, whose representative listened to their story, sighed, and said that the partners had almost surely been hoodwinked by a man named Hyman David Novick.

Williams and Sutton jumped into a car that same afternoon and, by driving all night, reached Montreal the next morning. At police headquarters there they were handed, from a fat dossier, a photograph of Novick—alias Davis, David, Hammond, Edwards, Gibson, LeDuc, and at least a hundred other names. They looked up the telegraph clerk who had disbursed their $1,320 and showed him the picture, and he said that that was the payee, all right. The partners' efforts to track down Novick were unavailing, but they did get hold of his lawyer, who declared that if they had changed their minds and didn't want to proceed further with their business dealings, his client would be perfectly willing to pay them back, in installments. The brothers-in-law gloomily consented to this, anxious to salvage whatever they could from the debacle—including, if possible, their crackers. The thousand dozen boxes, it developed, were in a railroad depot at Montreal, from which the New York Central wouldn't release them until somebody paid some storage charges. Eventually, Williams and Sutton got the crackers back to New York State, although quite a few of them had been bruised beyond recognition during their futile round trip. After several months, and many nagging letters and phone calls to Canada, the partners had received $250 from Novick through his lawyer. They calculated their total loss, including phone calls, shipping charges, storage charges, and incidentals, at $2,040. It took them a couple of years to pay off the bank loan.

The rascal who put such a crimp in the dreams of these two hard-working small entrepreneurs was a confidence man who, for the sheer consistency of his approach—and perhaps for the total size of his take, too—deserves to be remembered as one of the most resolute crooks of our time. In something over twenty years, Novick fleeced thousands of lambs, most of them Americans, most of them manufacturers or processors, and most of them people who had never marketed goods in Canada and were apt to be naïve about the ramifications of international trade. When the occasion presented itself, however, he was not above fleecing his compatriots as well, or, for that matter, Europeans, Asians, and Latin Americans. His gross income from his operations has been estimated at as much as a hundred thousand dollars a year, and since his expenses were comparatively trifling, his net must have been substantial. (He did not appear to be an especially free spender, though, and just what he did with all his winnings has never been clearly ascertained.) His history impressively illustrates how a poor, uneducated boy can, with perseverance, gumption, and gall, make millions. It also illustrates how a crook who maintains a vague semblance of business legitimacy and concentrates on fleecing out-of-towners—or, preferably, foreigners—rather than local people, can avoid prosecution almost indefinitely.

Many a veteran criminal is readily identifiable not merely by his fingerprints but by his *modus operandi.* Novick's high-flying method varied little over the years, and he operated with such relative impunity that one of the investigators who brought him to earth, after years of more or less helplessly following his devious activities, remarked, "It could be that this guy did what he did for so long that he got the impression there was nothing wrong with it." What he did—which was no more wrong than plain stealing—was to strew bait around the way a fisherman strews chum, and to haul in all the fish, big or little, that went for it, except those that resisted too hard. His bait, nearly always, was a fat import order and the promise of more to come; his catch was, at the least, a sizable sum in fake shipping and customs fees, collected in advance, and, at the most, the fees plus the proceeds of the sale of unpaid-for goods that shippers less persistent than the two cracker bakers could not or did not recover. When a potential victim would begin asking about written confirmations of orders, conventional credit references, cash on the barrelhead, or other pesky details, Novick would wash his hands of the troublemaker and turn elsewhere. As is true of most successful confidence men, Novick was immensely assisted in his work by the almost pathetic anxiety of many of his patsies to get rich quick (they would respond, for instance, to come-on letters that were cheaply multigraphed and not even signed), and by their disinclination to seek revenge, which would presumably be costly, take a lot of time, and as like as not entail a public confession that they had behaved foolishly.

Novick, like Picasso and other durable artists, went through various periods, during each of which—presumably after a close perusal of certain trade magazines—he would concentrate on a particular commodity. There were his potato-chip period, his sauerkraut period, his vending machine period, and his boat period, to name a few. But fundamentally his tastes were catholic, and, given the opportunity, he could, like a cornucopia in reverse, ingest anything: lampshades, yeast, shoe polish, pumpkins, plastic garment covers, baby shoes, valise locks, fur-lined leather gloves, toothpicks, buttons, umbrellas, unshelled almonds, olive oil, neckties, corned-beef hash, frozen banana purée, raisins, oysters, salted peanuts, harmoniums, beer, doll strollers, shoelaces, paper bags, toy trains, and wallpaper cleaner. At the time he conned the cracker men, he was predominantly in his baked-goods period. A couple of weeks before the unfortunate brothers-in-law were first set to dreaming of an export bonanza, a Rhode Island food broker who specialized in breadstuffs had written to H. David, of Tasty Treat, "We remain quite frankly 'in the dark' concerning the various tie-ups with such as Tasty Treat and Associated [Business Brokers] and the like, but your assurance that this is common procedure [in Canada] is satisfactory for us at the moment. . . . We do hope this will be the beginning of a successful business relationship." The names of such optimists were easy enough to cull from *Chain Store Age, Milk Dealer, Fuel Oil News, Boys' Outfitter,* or whatever trade paper Novick happened to pick up, and if his direct-mail campaigns brought results from even a tiny fraction of his prospects, he must have felt few regrets at not having time for more inspiring reading matter.

In Canada, it is a simple procedure to register a company name. Practically all one needs to do is go to the office of a prothonotary —the equivalent of a county clerk here—and sign a piece of paper, and once this is done, one can open a bank account in the company's name. Safeway Stores, Inc., was a widespread and well-known chain in the United States and also had some stores in western Canada, but it had never extended its operations to the Province of Quebec, where Novick for the most part operated. He had an unsuspecting woman, the landlady of a rooming house he sometimes used as a business address, register Safeway Chain Stores as a subsidiary of his previously registered United Food Business Brokers. On paper, the domain of United Food Business Brokers was indeed imperial; besides Safeway Chain Stores, it had offshoots called A-P Supermarket, Krogers Supermarket, and Thrift Chain Stores. Novick usually shied away from exactly duplicating a bona-fide company's name. He produced a variation on J. C. Penney by spelling it "J. C. Penny"—an orthographic distinction that was, of course, hard to perceive in a telephone conversation. In addition to registering a long succession of brokerage firms (among them Fidelity Customs Brokers), Novick was inspired to set up outfits called Canadian Tariff Registered, Federal Customs Clearance, Dominion Customs Clearance, and Canada Customs Clearance. What inexperienced American businessman, with visions of a vast new market opening out before him, would hesitate to dispatch a certified check to something as official-sounding as "Canada Customs Clearance," especially when he had been instructed to do so on behalf of Safeway or J. C. Penny by a sugary-voiced representative of the Greater Universal Sales Company, the Consolidated Buying Group, the Canadian Sales Company, or the American-Canadian Buying Group Syndicate? All these, of course, were Novick, but even after his victims realized that they had been gulled, some of them found it difficult to grasp that in this shadowy, polynomial fraternity there was not *some* upright member. The president of a plastics company in Puerto Rico, who had stayed up all night to get a rush order ready for Novick, and had also wired him $2,367.70 for supposed customs fees, soon learned that he'd been had, and thereupon dashed off a letter to Associated Business Brokers that read, in part, "How is it possible for a crook like Davis to utilize a legitimate company like yours in this nefarious undertaking which involves a company as large as the Safeway food chain? Faithfully yours . . ."

There was considerable flexibility in Novick's *modus operandi* when it came to disposing of the goods he received. If he thought he could make a quick sale, he was likely to engage an honest customs broker to pay the duty on a shipment and move it along to him. Since Novick frequently worked out of a one-room office or mere rented desk space, he tried to be waiting outside his business address with a truck or station wagon when the merchandise materialized, but now and then he got his signals crossed. A woman who ran a telephone-answering and mail-receiving service, and among whose clients was a Mr. Hyman, of Dominion Departmental Distributors, was astonished one day to have delivered to her cramped premises a one-ton backstop for a baseball diamond. Inasmuch as Novick never paid for any goods, if he could possibly help it, whatever he sold, even at rock-bottom prices, was sure to bring him a nice profit. On a single day in January, 1954, the "Articles for Sale" column in the classified-advertising section of the Montreal *Star* carried six separate listings directing interested parties to call the same number—Novick's. There was a white enamel meat chopper available for $12; some assorted toys for $9.95; a portable refrigerator, said to be worth $69.50, for $22 (the ad called it a sacrifice); some skis, a fishing pole, and an automobile ski rack, all for $9.50; an electric clothes dryer, worth $389, for $175; and a rotary aluminum collapsible clothes-drying reel, worth $11.50, for $5 (another sacrifice). All these items, presumably samples that Novick had requested pending larger orders, were proclaimed, no doubt truthfully, to be either new or never used.

Sometimes Novick just couldn't be bothered with picking up his consignments—although it is suspected that now and then he would go to a customs auction of unclaimed goods and purchase, at *really* rock-bottom prices, wares he had abandoned himself. In the late 1950s, he was partial to perishables, and those sent to him often perished. Once, he let a whole railway carload of oranges rot. During a two-month stretch in 1958 alone, he is known to have ordered, and in time received, two carloads of dried peas from the state of Washington, worth $18,440.43 (the shipper also sent him $4,200 in cash, for duty), a carload of blueberries from Maine, and a carload of canned tuna from California. A Mr. Hammond, claiming to represent something called Dominion Stores, had contracted—in an informal, conversational way, of course—to pay $29,082.35 for the blueberries, or around $8 for each of 3,645 cases. Hammond-Novick resold these to no-questions-asked customers for as little as $4.75 a case. The tuna was worth $20,817.16, F.O.B. California. Novick ordered it toward the end of the year, and on December 31 its delighted seller conveyed warm New Year's greetings to his new customer. A few weeks later, the by then mortified fishman hired the Pinkertons to try to find his fish. The detectives were lucky; they retrieved 1,793 cases out of a total of 2,265. The shipper lost not only the 472 remaining cases but $1,362.50 he had laid out in shipping charges, $4,649.15 he had advanced for duty, and $1,790.25 he had spent on attorneys' fees, detectives' fees, storage, handling, and whatnot—plus $150 he had

had to pay to Novick's attorney. The fish packer was thus out $12,289.58, and the sales manager who, after accepting the first collect call from Novick, had enthusiastically started the transaction rolling, perhaps dreaming of a year-end bonus, was out of a job.

More often than not, Novick would have several dozen live prospects on his string at once, and before wrapping up a deal he might make eight or ten long-distance calls—collect, of course—to each one, changing his name and his companies' names to suit the circumstances. He was sometimes so busy that after an answer to one of his form letters came in, it might take him several months to make the first phone call requesting a sample—with the usual intimation that if the sample was satisfactory a blockbuster of an order would follow. It was indicative of the extent of his business that on a single day several years ago one reputable customs broker cleared through Montreal on Novick's behalf six shipments of merchandise: chocolates from Ohio, clothespins from Vermont, popcorn from Philadelphia, cookies from Iowa, black pepper from New York, and a batch of something called a cocktail mélange (apparently consisting of crackers and canapé paste), also from New York. What Novick may have harvested through other channels that day is not known. The records of Canada's two telegraph companies, the Canadian National Telegraph Company and the Canadian Pacific Telegraph Company, reveal that during one twelve-month period they handed over to Novick a total of $21,-995.34 in cash, wired him by 122 United States firms. Customs records for approximately the same period show that merchandise worth $100,340.76 passed through Montreal en route to Novick. Any records that Novick himself may have maintained have not come to light, and nobody knows how he kept track of what he was doing. He must have had either a fantastic memory or an elaborate reminder file. And, at that, he made an occasional slip. Telephoning a Maryland food processor from whom, in nearly two dozen calls, he had tried to pry loose a carload of blueberries (this was after his satisfactory Maine blueberry deal), Novick identified himself as Mr. Davis. The man at the other end replied, "But I thought you said the other day your name was Hammond." Novick did not get those berries. On other occasions, he pressed too hard. A Pennsylvania manufacturer who was all set to send him a hundred dozen potholders and a hundred dozen dish towels was put off by Novick's insistence that, because a Montreal Safeway had to have the items in twenty-four hours, they must travel by air. Having paused long enough to ask himself why a big chain store would want to pay air freight on dish towels and potholders, the prospective shipper thought better of the whole thing. In at least one instance, Novick revealed suspicion-provoking ignorance—or, it could be argued, irrelevant knowledge—which saved an Ohio food broker from parting with a carload of canned peaches and another of canned fruit cocktail. On behalf of the supposed Safeway, Davis-Novick ordered No. 10 cans. That designation, as the broker well knew, applied to very large cans, intended for use in institutions, and not normally offered to the public on supermarket shelves. Why would Safeway want No. 10s? The broker did some checking, discovered that there was no Safeway in Montreal, and thereby averted a No. 1 headache.

Until Novick's legerdemain with companies, customs, and carloads was finally halted, it attracted hardly any public attention in Canada, but in police, postal, and customs circles, and among such private monitors of Montreal business probity as Dun & Bradstreet and the Better Business Bureau, his name had long been one to groan at the mention of—although for many years, and for various reasons, the principal one being the unwillingness of his victims to give formal testimony against him, not much more than groaning was done. The Better Business Bureau's branches in both Canada and the United States had been on to him, and warning their members about him, for a good twenty years. As early as 1942, the Better Business Bureau of Montreal circulated a list of some of his current creditors. (Among them was a New York manufacturer of check-writing machines, but Novick was probably interested in the latter merely as merchandise; he was never much of a man for writing checks.) Some years later, the Montreal Bureau had a wire from its counterpart in Calgary reporting that a retailer there was confused because a Montreal outfit called Dominion Departmental Distributors had telephoned an order for three hundred dollars' worth of a kind of stationery that the Calgary man knew for certain was readily available right in Montreal. Calgary asked Montreal to look into Dominion Distributors. Montreal wired back, "REPLY NOVICK NEED WE SAY MORE?"

Perhaps to no single group of Canadians was Novick more of a pest than to the country's Post Office Department. It is not as easy to prosecute anybody for mail fraud in Canada as in the United States. In theory, mail fraud is an offense punishable under the Dominion's Criminal Code, the enforcement of which is the responsibility of the various provincial governments. These authorities can and occasionally do take action in mail-fraud cases, but only if a victim lodges a complaint. In practice, the Post Office is usually on its own. It can and does investigate such complaints as *it* receives, but it cannot initiate prosecution. Its only strong recourse, when someone uses the mails for seemingly crooked purposes, is to suspend that person's postal privileges by means of what is called a prohibitory order, which among other things bans transmission of mail to a specific name and address. A letter directed to a prohibited name and address is supposed to be returned to the sender marked "Non-Transmissible"; if it lacks a return address, it goes to the dead-letter office. A prohibitory order is usually temporary, and before it goes into effect there are various channels through which someone thus singled out can appeal his embargo. Beginning in 1940, temporary prohibitory orders were invoked against a variety of Novick's names and addresses, and from 1954 on he enjoyed the distinction of being the only person in history against whom the Canadian government had proclaimed a general and permanent prohibitory order, making it illegal for him to receive any mail anywhere in Canada under any name at all. (Technically, he couldn't send out mail, either, but to enforce this restriction would have entailed unmanageably strict surveillance.) The Post Office became so staunchly determined to refuse him its services that an unrelated and perfectly law-abiding resident of Montreal named Hyman Novak sometimes had a terrible time getting *his* mail. As for Hyman Novick, the prohibition meant, among other things, that his home phone had to be listed under the name of his wife, Mrs. Rose Novick; if it had been listed under his, the telephone company couldn't have sent his bills through the mail. Canada's Department of National Revenue, the equivalent of the American Internal Revenue Service, once begged its federal cousin the Post Office Department to let it send Novick, by registered mail, a notice of nonpayment of taxes; the Post Office Department regretfully but firmly declined.

It is understandable, therefore, why Hyman Novick preferred to have money sent him by telegraph; by mail, he couldn't legitimately get so much as a Christmas card. Not that he seems to have cared. On Christmas Day of 1958, he was on the phone, representing the Canadian Sales Company for Safeway, conferring with a nut company in South Carolina about fancy seedling pecan halves worth $3,450. The pecan people were also apparently loath to let a mere holiday impede the flow of fancy seedling halves, for their shipment, and their bill to Safeway, went out that same day. The Post Office hadn't yet heard about this Novick front, so the bill came back with the envelope stamped "Not in Directory." The Carolinians then wrote to the Canadian Sales Company. Since the postal authorities were on to this disguise of Novick's, that letter came back marked "Non-Transmissible." The nut men did ultimately get a Christmas present; they managed to recover their entire shipment, and thus were nicked only for $862.50 they had wired Novick for customs duty and an additional $500 or so in other expenses.

It is a rather widely held belief in Canada that United States citizens tend to trust Canadians, en masse, more than they trust Europeans, Africans, Asians, or, when it comes to that, other United States citizens. Possibly the red-coated image of the Royal

Canadian Mounted Police (most of whom are not mounted, and wear khaki) accounts in part for this attitude; the indications are that it is hard for folks below the border to conceive of the existence of chicanery in any nation watched over by the Mounties. Such faith may have contributed something to Novick's success, but the major credit for it belongs to his mastery of the telephone, an instrument he played with consummate virtuosity. (In placing calls, he sometimes used slugs, but his long-distance colloquists were naturally unaware of this raffish habit.) Telephonically, he radiated such assurance and authority that it just didn't occur to people to doubt him. In appearance, Novick was a squat, unprepossessing man, the sort of person no stranger would dream of playing cards with on a ship, but on the phone, during working hours, he exuded velvety charm. The exact status and listing of the telephone at his residence—a comfortable one, in a good neighborhood—must actually have been of little consequence to him, for he seems to have toiled at home only rarely. By and large, he preferred pay phones, though he sometimes made calls from the premises of various landlords or janitors who, for somewhere between three and ten dollars a month, let him use their places as business addresses. A postal investigator tracking down the connection between Novick and his then newly formed Dominion Departmental Distributors arrived at the dingy establishment to which that company's mail was going just as a call came in from a North Carolina businessman who had been told by a Mr. Gordon, of Dominion Distributors, to call a Mr. Stevens, of the Montreal office of Dun & Bradstreet, at that number to check on Mr. Gordon's reliability. With Mr. Novick absent, Mr. Stevens was unable to vouch for Mr. Gordon.

There were few such slip-ups in Novick's telephonic shell game, and when one seemed imminent his masterful long-distance manner usually forestalled it. A Brooklyn meat packer who wanted to communicate directly with Safeway about some detail of a pending transaction was cowed by David-Novick's admonition "Don't you dare! Any business with them will be done through me!" A

North Dakota manufacturer of infants' garments did have the nerve to make such direct contact—with the authentic Safeway's headquarters, in California—but unfortunately he was a little late. He had already sent Novick's Associated Business Brokers, which was collaborating in this particular undertaking with Novick's Mackontire Sales Company, 180 dozen baby garments, worth $2,-298.60, along with a duty *pourboire* of $1,980.61. The infants-wear maker had also shelled out $584.17 for phone calls, telegrams, and freight. "Our entire capital was spent on this deal, and additional financing is not available," this luckless victim later told an investigator, "so our loss is indeed great."

Sheer inability to get Novick's complex instructions straight saved some companies. A California manufacturer of sports equipment, giddy at the prospect of selling a batch of water skis worth $7,101 to the Hudson Bay Company—Novick did not bother to explain that this was not the famous *Hudson's* Bay Company but his own homonymous invention—carefully made out an advance-customs-clearance check for $3,195.45 to Canada Customs Clearance, but instead of sending the money to the Montreal rooming house whose address Novick had given him, he sent it to the genuine Canadian customs, in Winnipeg, which promptly returned it.

Some concerns had scarcely put their money in the mail when they found out they'd been duped, and then frantically tried to get their checks back. Postal officials in Montreal became accustomed to receiving telegrams like one that came in one afternoon from a postmaster in Georgia: "URGENT YOU WITHHOLD DELIVERY BROWN CLASP ENVELOPE 10″ × 13″ SENT AIRMAIL SPECIAL DELIVERY TO CANADA CUSTOMS CLEARANCE 796 RICHMOND STREET MONTREAL FROM . . ." That particular envelope contained a rug company's certified check for $2,893.40. Queen Elizabeth was touring Canada at the time, and in all the hubbub attendant to the royal visit the envelope was delivered before the wire, and the check was cashed. On one exceedingly rare occasion, though, an American merchant not only escaped being swindled by Novick but may have swindled him, if only on a minor scale. The intended victim was a baking powder manufacturer in Indiana. His company was already on the hook for a sample shipment to Novick and for some petty cash to speed this through customs, but when Novick ordered a carload of baking powder, the shipper made some inquiries and learned what Novick's true Dun & Bradstreet rating was. Novick soon telephoned, and this time, for once, it was not a collect call; with a carload at stake, Novick apparently had decided not to be a cheapskate. He talked on and on, in his most ingratiating manner, for nearly an hour, while the man at the other end, chuckling to himself, looked at his watch and happily computed the extravagant toll charges the Canadian must be running up. Then the Indianian abruptly told Novick he knew he was a crook, and the latter abruptly hung up. Of course, he may not have been out of pocket at all, for it is impossible to determine whose phone he was using or whether he ever actually paid for the call.

Not much is known about Novick's origins. He was born in Montreal in 1915. He went through the ninth grade in school, and then joined his father in the dry-goods business. In 1936, he started his first independent business, a lingerie shop, and went bankrupt in a year, with liabilities of $950 against assets of $600. After that, he was briefly employed by a knitting mill, and then started a textile-importing business. In 1939, he went bankrupt again. This time, his assets were less than $200 and his liabilities were undetermined, the reason being that he had quite a few creditors in the United States who had sent him goods on consignment but did not come forward to press their claims. Up to this point, Novick had had a career that was hardly auspicious, let alone lucrative, but he was far from discouraged, for he had learned a vital business secret; he had come to realize just how benevolent—and greedy—American businessmen could be.

Early in 1940, Novick established the Vogue Textiles Corporation. The room it occupied happened to be around the corner from Simpson's department store, a distinguished Montreal house, and Vogue's letterhead bore a photograph of Simpson's façade. (Later, one of the many *noms d'affaires* Novick employed was Simpson's Departmental Stores.) Vogue, which described itself imaginatively as the "largest exclusive distributor of women's full-fashioned hose in the British Empire," listed as its officers several of the founder's relatives—setting a precedent for a number of later Novick creations. It is unclear precisely how much any of these titular officers knew about what was going on. Novick's wife once claimed never to have heard of a company that listed her as president; conceivably, she, like many other wives, habitually signed without reading any papers that her husband thrust before her. The Vogue era turned out to be an unlucky one for Novick. On several occasions, he advertised in the newspapers for secretarial help, specifying that the applicant's duties might include some modeling. One young woman, after an interview with Novick, had him arrested on an indecency charge, and on April 23, 1940, he was sentenced to fifteen days in jail and fined two hundred dollars. Only a few months later, he was in court again, and this time he was convicted on each of eleven charges of cheating customs by undervaluing goods imported from the United States, and was fined fifty dollars and costs. By this time, too, the Post Office was after him, inquiring how he could assert in correspondence that he had offices in Quebec, Toronto, Winnipeg, Calgary, Edmonton, and Vancouver when all the evidence indicated he was operating practically out of his hat. Before long, Novick received his first prohibitory order. Among other complaints that had come to the postal people was one that went, "While there is no danger of our company or any of its branches falling victim to this clumsy attempt at securing merchandise on credit, it seems to us that as good citizens we should make an effort to safeguard others, especially as the office of Dun & Bradstreet informs us that they have had reports on the activities of this fake firm from time to time during the last few years. It is quite evident that the mails are being used in an attempt to defraud, and certainly to obtain goods under false pretenses, and something should be done about it." But it was to be nearly twenty years before anything really effective *was* done.

Vogue went bankrupt in February, 1942, its known liabilities exceeding its assets by some $12,500, and Novick at once moved over to the Redfern Textiles Corporation, which he had forehandedly registered more than a year earlier. To judge by *its* letterhead, Redfern was quite an outfit. It was "represented from Coast to Coast," and it had not only a separate Import Division but a separate General Purchasing Department within the Import Division. Although the Second World War did not otherwise impinge on Novick, he went all out for victory on Redfern's stationery, which carried pictures of airplanes and warships, along with the phrases, in red-white-and-blue lettering, "Buy Victory Bonds," "Keep 'Em Flying," and "Remember Hong Kong." (There was also a small printed notice stating that, in view of the international situation, Redfern waived any liability for contingencies beyond its control, such as strikes, lockouts, fires, floods, explosions, and war.) As soon as the Post Office became aware of the new company, it got in touch with Novick, who replied, on a sheet of Redfern Patriotic, "There seems to be some tendency on the part of certain people or firms to lay complaints just for the sake of causing annoyance." The next move—not long after Novick had received two hundred gross of thimbles from an American sucker ("Yours for victory," Redfern's soliciting letter had concluded)—was a prohibitory order against Redfern. Novick folded up the firm, to the distress of the thimble man and seventy-four other creditors, to whom he owed a total of $8,545.01. Waiting in the wings, however, were the Empire Export Company, the Toy Creations Company, the Commercial Clearing Company, and H. De Novick Agencies ("Manufacturers' and Mills' Representative"). When the Post Office began looking into these concerns, Novick once more donned his martyr's cloak. "Must I be sentenced for life without a chance to try to carry on business again?" he pleaded. Unmoved, the Montreal authorities temporarily suspended the postal privileges of these four companies, and Novick's, too, but after Novick appealed, as was his right, the order was reversed, notwithstanding one postal investigator's flat assertion, "This man is incorrigible." Novick had argued that he was merely a businessman whose various enterprises had been launched in anticipation of an expansion of foreign trade at the end of the war, and that if he couldn't use the mails he might be reduced to the awful status of a wage earner. Over the next few years, prohibitory orders against him and his companies were issued and withdrawn in dizzying succession. Once, the Montreal Post Office felt obliged to send him a formal apology, because a letter to a firm of his had been branded "Non-Transmissible" during an interlude when there happened to be no prohibitory order in force.

Toward the end of the war and in the early postwar years, Novick's stationery blossomed out with representations of both hemispheres, and his global outlook was further attested by alluring letters he dispatched to exporters in England, France, Denmark, Germany, India, Japan, and a number of other distant markets. He must have found the response heartwarming. From the Netherlands he received beach hats and bathing suits; from Italy, cotton sewing thread (to the value of $7,350); from Switzerland, sewing machines and sweaters; from South Africa, standing lamps and cocktail bars. The commercial attachés of embassies in Ottawa, to say nothing of their dependent consulates in Montreal, devoted a staggering amount of time to answering queries about Novick companies from irate merchants in their homelands. Meanwhile, Novick was not neglecting the United States as a field of endeavor, and the United States consulate in Montreal soon came to regard him as its *bête noire*. By 1952, the Montreal Better Business Bureau was plaintively advising the postal authorities, "Something should be done which will permanently curb this man's activities, which are being carried on through this country's mail to the detriment of Canada's international reputation." By then, though, Novick—probably less because he was worried about his nation's worldwide image than because the foreign mails were so poky—was cutting down on his overseas activities and entering his ice cream period, which began as a purely local manifestation. He started up a company called Pony Boy, to peddle ten-cent ice cream bars around Montreal from tricycle carts during the summer months. He advertised in the city's papers for route boys ("must be aggressive and honest"), mentioning a pay rate of thirty-five dollars a week. For many of the boys who bit, the experience was disillusioning. One lad later had reason to recall that while he was riding up in an office-building elevator to be interviewed by a Mr. Roberts, of Pony Boy, he was told by the operator, "Watch it. He is a big liar." The boy was hired, and he set to work under the impression that he had a weekly sales quota of three hundred ice cream bars. After working six eleven-hour days, he came around for his pay, and Roberts-Novick gave him a check for eighty-two cents, saying he had fallen outrageously short of his stipulated goal of three hundred *dollars'* worth of sales. Novick had neglected to get a peddling license from either the police or the municipal health department, and as a result his venders sometimes suffered the humiliation of being arrested and fined ten dollars, which they had to pay out of their own pockets.

Pony Boy did not merely sell ice cream; it advertised, in both American and Canadian magazines, for food machinery of all kinds, and food machinery of all kinds was soon streaming toward it, including fifteen ice cream makers from Missouri, forty-eight popcorn poppers from Florida, three coffee makers from South Dakota, and three more from British Columbia. For this last order, Novick agreed to pay six hundred dollars, but when the bill came in (the Post Office had not yet stumbled onto his latest name and address), he sent it back unpaid and—without so much as the expenditure of one of his letterheads—bearing the marginal notation "Shipment received in broken condition." Conversely, when one customer paid *him* seven hundred dollars for a vending machine and later came around and said he couldn't figure out how to make the contraption work, Novick retreated behind an icy caveat emptor. Novick insisted on cash in advance from both buyers and sellers, and when there was any delay in a payment he thought he had coming to him he could get quite testy. One year, he sold some cheap identification bracelets—in which his own investment was almost certainly either nil or negligible—to a store in Vancouver. He shipped them on November 8 and they arrived on the twelfth. Novick's first invoice went out on October 28, and by November 15 the purchaser had received three demands for payment. Hell hath no fury like a bilker balked.

Several months after the inception of Pony Boy, with the postal authorities as usual denying Novick's privileges, he moved the firm to a boardinghouse that made a particularly satisfactory headquarters. One of the mailboxes in the entryway had a defective lock. It belonged to a Miss Gordon, a fellow tenant who went off to work every morning before the postman arrived. Novick observed this state of affairs, and soon mail addressed to a Mr. T. Gordon was pouring into the building. The mailman would put it in the box marked "Gordon," and after he had proceeded on his rounds Novick would remove it. The scheme worked smoothly until Miss Gordon felt ill one day, stayed home, got to her box first, and found it bulging with airmail letters from the United States. More or less concurrently with being Pony Boy, Novick was Push Button Merchandising, and not long afterward he became Twentieth Century Merchandising, London House Distributors, Chuck Wagon Ice Cream, and, in an ultimate burst of inspiration, Good Humour Ice Cream. (Good Humors were not sold in Canada.) During this frosty stretch, moreover, Novick also found time to check in at the Mount Royal Hotel in Montreal as Mr. Holt, of Holt Business Brokers, a firm that welcomed inquiries from persons interested in obtaining, for a suitable fee, attractive franchises for marketing frozen foods. This business opportunity was publicized mainly through newspaper ads, placed (though never paid for) by Gibson Advertising—Novick. Gibson-Novick also inserted ads for Good Humour venders ("The sky's the limit," "A gold mine on wheels," "All sales are quick and strictly cash") in a number of publications whose readers might logically be looking for spare-time income in a seasonal and not excessively taxing line of endeavor. When one publication that had never heard of the Gibson agency requested advance payment for an ad, it swiftly received a check drawn on the Bank of Nova Scotia. The check bounced.

Toward the end of 1957, Novick entered a period in which he began to concentrate on impersonating existing giant companies, usually American, and he turned for assistance to his brother Nathan. Nathan, nine years Hyman's junior, was then thirty-three, and his only noteworthy accomplishment had been an arrest for theft, at the age of eighteen. A bachelor who now and then affected the alias Romeo David (it is hard to see why; he stood five feet seven inches and weighed 220), he seems to have lacked his brother's business acumen, but he could run errands, lug crates of canned goods, sign registration papers, and—until the postal authorities began clamping down on him, too—receive mail. There was a lot of that going back and forth. In 1958, one Montreal job printer was stuck with four batches of letterheads worth a total of $1,023.46—ten thousand sheets each for Grand Union, J. J. Newberry, J. C. Penny, and the National Tea Company. The order had been placed by a Mr. Hyman, of the MacIntyre Sales Company (not to be confused with the Mackontire Sales Company), who had given as his reference a Mr. Nathan. A few months after receiving all this stationery, the elder Novick instructed another printer to prepare some batches of letterheads inscribed, variously, United Chain Stores Buyers Association, Marshell Fields of Canada, Fruit Credit Exchange, Fur Credit Bureau of Canada, Credit Dairy Bureau of Canada, and Lumber Credit Bureau of Canada. Marshell Fields–Novick must have been anticipating a spate of requests for his credit rating.

In this period, as the cost of living kept going up, Hyman Novick raised his sights and began to think increasingly in terms of carload lots. But even with blueberries and tuna moving merrily along international rails, and with Nathan around to lend a fraternal hand, the pickings were not easy. The United States Post Office

Department had now entered the picture and was more and more vigorously thwarting Hyman with its equivalent of prohibitory orders—fraud orders. Our Postmasters at border points had standing instructions not to pass along to Canada any mail addressed to any of dozens of Novick aliases. The list was admittedly incomplete; as our Department of Commerce, which regularly tries to keep American businessmen apprised of fraudulent activities in various fields, once observed in a Novick bulletin it circulated, "We realize, of course, that you cannot keep abreast of Mr. Novick's new aliases, but thought you might want to know about these." And with the Montreal postmen also becoming more and more difficult, a brand-new name at a brand-new address was sometimes good for only one exchange of correspondence. Many Montreal mailmen now went about their work carrying Hyman Novick's picture—and in due course Nathan's, too. When a postman found himself burdened with thirty or forty communications from the States addressed to a spot that did not customarily reap such a haul, he would show somebody there a Novick photograph, and if it turned out to be a likeness of the chap who had recently arranged to get his mail at that address, the stuff was withheld then and there. For a while, Hyman was changing addresses faster than he could write letters. One cracker company in New Jersey was favored with a letter from Tasty Treat on which two Montreal return addresses had been typed and then crossed out, to be replaced by an address in Quebec City.

Montreal embraces three hundred square miles and contains nobody knows how many rentable rooms, but it was getting too small for Hyman Novick. After trying Quebec, he tried Ottawa, Toronto, and Cornwall, Ontario. Later, he rented boxes at post offices in Lacolle, Napierville, and Sainte-Geneviève de Pierrefonds, all in the Province of Quebec. But the postal investigators gave him no rest. In desperation, he climbed into his car on December 16, 1958, and drove the thirty miles from Montreal to Champlain, New York, just across the United States border. There, as Edward Barton, of the American-Canadian Buying Group Syndicate, he rented a post office box, for $2.20. This was to lead to his undoing.

Champlain, a town of 1,500, had a small post office, which was then staffed by a lady Postmaster and a girl clerk. Most American post office functionaries are acutely conscious of large stamp sales, because as their volume of business expands, the official classification of their post office can be upgraded, and with it their own salaries. Barton received a lot of mail at Champlain ("The box would often overflow," the Postmaster said afterward), but the trouble of handling it was more than offset by his habit of purchasing there all the stamps he used for his outgoing mail, which the Postmaster estimated at ten thousand pieces a month. She had no reason to suspect anything fishy, for neither Barton nor his imposingly named syndicate had yet appeared on any list of fraud orders. But Barton-Novick was not to be a patron of the Champlain post office very long. Early in March of 1959, while en route from Montreal to Champlain, he was detained at the border by American Immigration men. Having been notified by an alert Dun & Bradstreet agent that Novick was frequenting the area, they had looked into his record and come up with his ancient conviction on the indecency charge. This, they thought, might render him legally inadmissible to the country, and they insisted upon holding a hearing on the matter before letting him in again. Novick retreated to Canada, where he telephoned the Champlain post office and asked to have his mail forwarded to a Montreal address. A day or two later, the breath of the Canadian postal investigators again hot on his neck, he sent a telegram giving a substitute forwarding address. Before the wire giving the second address arrived, Champlain had forwarded 237 pieces of mail to the first address—an office whose door Novick had padlocked as he fled. Among the items that accumulated in the corridor outside it were 150 cases of canned goods, heaped in disarray.

Since Novick's Vogue Textiles days, the why-doesn't-somebody-do-something-to-stop-him refrain had been reprised so often that to people who had kept more or less abreast of his shenanigans it had a hollow ring. He wasn't all that easy to stop. Not only was the Canadian Post Office limited in what it could do, but there really weren't any piercingly loud gripes against him. There were relatively few Canadian victims, and most of his American victims had been victimized just once (though one uncommonly trusting Pennsylvania manufacturer of nightwear and children's garments had sent him five separate shipments, breaking off relations only when the unpaid tab of Dominion Departmental Distributors—represented in this instance by Fidelity Customs Brokers—reached what was, for that exporter, the enormous sum of $2,500). The majority of his American dupes seemed less inclined to go to Canada and corner him than to lick their wounds at home, and if they wouldn't come and complain voluntarily, the Canadian government couldn't subpoena them. On and off, there was talk of the Province of Quebec's setting up something called a rogatory commission that could send a committee to the States to take affidavits against Novick, but this plan got nowhere; reportedly, some of Quebec's provincial satraps expressed themselves as not being overly concerned if a few grasping Americans now and then took a drubbing.

Novick was not, of course, totally unsusceptible to pressure. In the spring of 1959, after the real Safeway chain, in the United States, had engaged the Winnipeg law firm of Aikins, MacAulay, Moffat, Dickson, Hinch & McGavin to ask the Montreal law firm of Common, Howard, Cate, Ogilvy, Bishop, Cope, Porteous & Hansard to help it *do* something, Novick had an attorney named Harry Blank send the American Safeway a notarized statement in which the woman who was legally responsible for Novick's Safeway promised not to use the name any longer. On the rare occasions when a victim showed fight, like the brothers-in-law who baked crackers, Novick would make partial restitution, but as a rule only after considerable harassment. A Georgia company that had sent fifty miniature Model T Fords, worth $250 apiece, to the Novick *frères* late in 1959, along with a certified check for $6,492 made out to Dominion Customs Clearance, took the pair to court in Montreal and got a judgment against Nathan (in whose name Dominion Customs Clearance happened to be registered) for $8,-262—the $6,492, plus $1,770 in shipping costs. The court impounded $4,158 that Nathan had inadvertently neglected to withdraw from a Dominion Customs Clearance bank account, and ordered him to make full restitution and also to pay costs and interest.

That action was a civil one, not a criminal one, and while the verdict was financially damaging to the Novicks, it did not, per se, affect any of their other operations. However, once Hyman had made the move to Champlain the situation was different. There Novick had been defrauding United States citizens from a United States post office, and our Postal Inspection Service, to which prosecutions for mail fraud are routine, swung into action. By the time it did, Novick, still awaiting the Immigration hearing that would determine whether he could resume business at Champlain, had swung into his potato-chip period, operating from some new Montreal mail drops. The National Potato Chip Institute reproduced and widely distributed a copy of his American-Canadian Buying Group Syndicate form letter, which, the Institute announced, "is being sent to many Chippers." Some Chippers had already been clipped.

Inspector Charles Miller was assigned to the case. He had two problems to solve: First he had to get sufficient evidence for an indictment against Novick, and then he had to get Novick. Looking over various lists of Novick's victims, Miller found five of them in Brooklyn, all dealers in foodstuffs—syrup, honey, fruit extracts, coconuts, and clams. True, none of the five had suffered grievous damage. Altogether, Novick had relieved them of a mere $646.75 in samples and $610.05 in cash. But their sales managers were all willing to testify about how they'd been gulled. (One of them, whose letter to the Canadian Sales Company had come back stamped "Non-Transmissible," had written to Associated Business Brokers asking them to get hold of Canadian Sales for him; that letter had come back identically marked. He was a frustrated and vengeful salesman.) Miller submitted his findings to the United States Attorney for the Eastern District of New York, in Brooklyn, and the prosecution was assigned to Assistant U.S. Attorney Marie McCann. In May, 1959, an indictment against Hyman Novick was handed down. He was charged with twelve counts of mail fraud and five of fraud by telegraph.

Obtaining physical custody of Novick was another matter. Miller had hoped that his man would reenter the United States for the pending Immigration hearing, but Novick, through his attorney, kept getting his appearance postponed, and it became evident he was not likely to cross the border of his own accord. Extradition seemed the only recourse, but here new complications arose. Never in Canadian history had the courts approved the extradition of a Canadian for mail fraud. In 1951, an old extradition treaty between Canada and the United States had been amended to classify mail fraud as an extraditable offense, but the only time Canadians had been indicted in the States on that charge, in 1954, a judge of the Superior Court of Canada named W. B. Scott had refused to extradite them. True, that case was, in its legal ramifications, quite different from Novick's, but nonetheless our Department of Justice, aware of this discouraging precedent, was leery of getting turned down again. In fact, so determined was the Department not to be rejected on some trivial technicality that not until eleven months after Novick's indictment did the United States ask Canada to issue a warrant for his arrest. When it did, the protocol was tortuous; for a simple affidavit taken in the United States to be acceptable at an extradition hearing in Canada, it must be executed in triplicate before a United States Commissioner, and the Commissioner must then append to it something called an Exemplification Certificate, the authenticity of which must be sworn to by a United States District Judge, whose credentials, in turn, must be vouched for by a Clerk of a United States District Court. (Clerks always seem to end up in the driver's seat.) While Inspector Miller and U.S. Attorney McCann scrambled around lining up documents and witnesses and judges and clerks, Novick—who apparently had not heard of the indictment, which was sealed—was not idle himself. He was importing 105 dozen raincoats from Indiana (plus $1,415.29 in cash), for instance, and $2,250 worth of cheese from Wisconsin (plus $1,055.22). He was also going full throttle into his boat period. After what must have been some notably diligent reading of boatbuilding trade magazines, he canvassed manufacturers in at least ten American states, several of whom came through with robust gifts—he got as much as $6,268.50 in cash from a single concern—and a few of whom also sent boats. He unleashed such a broadside attack on the American boat industry that at the time the United States Department of State was entering into negotiations with Canada for his apprehension it was also persuading the United States Department of Commerce to issue a special bulletin urging all hands in the maritime field to keep a sharp lookout.

In April, 1960, a warrant for Novick's appearance before an extradition hearing was issued by the same Judge Scott who six years earlier had looked unfavorably upon the extradition of Canadians for mail fraud; moreover, it was Judge Scott who was to rule on Novick's case. Novick presented himself, and the proceedings, once begun, dragged on for six argumentative weeks. (Novick was able to keep in touch with boatbuilders by making calls, during recesses, from a pay phone in the courthouse corridor.) The principal witnesses imported from the United States for the occasion were the Champlain Postmaster and her assistant, and their positive identification of Novick as the Edward Barton who had rented the box from them appeared to carry considerable weight with the Judge. In any event, while there was no ruling on Novick's extraditability in the matter of his twenty-odd years of machinations from Canada, Judge Scott did decree that Novick's less than three months of machinations from Champlain constituted grounds for handing him into American custody.

In September, 1960, Miller and a colleague, Postal Inspector Robert Crider, drove Novick to New York City, where the Canadian was arraigned and, somewhat to the Inspectors' consternation, at once released on bail. Novick was even allowed to go back to Canada until a trial date should be set, once he had promised not to leave the Province of Quebec and to return to New York when summoned. He promised nothing, however, about going into retirement. Seven months passed before his case came up for trial, and early in that period *El Universal*, a daily paper in Mexico City, accepted a collect call from a Canadian who wanted to place two advertisements, each costing fifteen hundred dollars. The first was for the Hudson Bay Company, in Montreal, which was eager to hear from Mexican exporters of textiles, footwear, toys, canned fruit, or anything else; the second was for the Hutson Bey Company, which had the same Montreal street address as Hudson Bay, and which wanted blankets, towels, sheets, pillowcases, handkerchiefs, underwear, parasols, veils, canned foods, handbags, and anything else. When *El Universal*, following telephone instructions, mailed its invoice to the Montreal address, the bill came back marked "Non-Transmissible." But meanwhile the ads had run, and they had had drawing power; before Hudson Bay and Hutson Bey had been spotted by the weary Canadian postmen, at least one Mexican businessman had sent along a check for $7,365—though some fast footwork on the part of the Mexican consulate in Montreal kept it from reaching its destination.

To some close observers of Novick's career who wondered how he would handle himself in a confrontation with a prosecuting attorney, his trial, held in Brooklyn, was a sad letdown. By now, the charges against him had been reduced to four counts of mail fraud. Also, Miss McCann had been reassigned to Washington, and the prosecution had been taken over by Assistant U.S. Attorney Joseph Marcheso. Inspector Miller had been in touch with some 150 American firms that had been bamboozled, and had dozens of witnesses ready to testify to their misplaced trust. But when the time came, none of these people had a chance to get in any retaliatory licks, for Novick simply pleaded guilty. Some of his victims felt as if they had been further cheated. On being sentenced to four years in a federal prison, Novick burst into tears, whereupon

Judge Jacob Mischler, who was trying the case, announced from the bench, "For twenty years you have conned hundreds of American companies, and I have no doubt you are capable of trying to con me." Even before Hyman Novick was sentenced, the Canadian government, perhaps jogged into action by its neighbor's example, had arrested Nathan, on charges of fraud and attempted fraud. Ultimately, he was convicted and given a suspended sentence. At the penitentiary in Danbury, Connecticut, the mail of Hyman Novick was not subjected to any prohibitory order; he enjoyed the same limited and strictly regulated postal privileges as any other federal prisoner.

A decade later, after Novick had finished serving his term, the *Weekend Magazine* of the Toronto *Globe and Mail* ran a feature story entitled "Canada's Greatest Con Man" that began:

> Not long ago, a Montreal firm sent a letter to a number of businessmen in Spain pointing out the lucrative trade prospects here:
>
> "Our buyers service over 3,000 stores in Canada and are interested in your product," it stated in part. "Please send us several dozen samples, air freight prepaid, to show our customers."

# 9. The Malpractitioners

Along the quicksandy course of American history, marching in stride with get-rich-quick schemes, which stimulate man's hope of solvency, have been get-well-quick schemes, which no less stimulate his hope of survival. Incalculable sums have been forwarded through the mails—with no calculable improvement in the physical or mental condition of the forwarders—by hopeful individuals who either are or think they are afflicted with cancer, arthritis, obesity, headaches, impotency, baldness, or general malaise. The remitters are often those members of society who can least afford such frivolous disbursements, the poor or the elderly or the elderly poor with in many instances little or no access to competent medical practitioners. Also, the sort of people who are apt to be beguiled by mail-order promises of a longer or sexier life are further apt to be those who rarely get large quantities of mail, and who find especially welcome communications from strangers who profess an interest in their vigor or vitality. Every year, the Postal Inspection Service causes to be indicted, or stops the use of the mails by, hundreds of promoters of nostrums, panaceas, and pills with curative powers unknown to chemistry. Sometimes the victims of quack medical schemes sign installment-plan contracts committing themselves to interminable regimens of treatment. If they welsh on a payment, as they often do on discovering they've been bilked, their bilkers are apt to send around collectors who threaten them with deprivation of Social Security benefits or welfare allowances or whatever unless they cough up. Inasmuch as it was the victims' ignorance that got them into their predicament to begin with, they are rarely smart enough to realize that there is no more authenticity to the collectors than there was to the contracts.

Not all fraudulent medical practitioners go to jail. Since 1872, the Postal Service has had the administrative authority, under a civil statute, to stamp "Return to Sender" on mail addressed to promoters who are demonstrably using false representations. The procedure is most commonly resorted to in the case of mail-order quacks. People who thus get their money back are not always grateful; they are sometimes infuriated at being refused permission to support a person like Mrs. Florentine C. Robards, a Sacramento housewife who used to advertise in a Tijuana, Mexico, newspaper with a large readership among Spanish-speaking Southern Californians. Mrs. Robards could cure *anything* ("Whatever is your difficulty, I will help you"), and her fee for a diagnosis, made solely on the basis of what a person wrote her about himself, was a modest one dollar. Her fees for treatment were slightly higher. To be apprised of her backache remedy (one teaspoonful of honey, followed by an identical dose of vinegar) cost thirty dollars. For forty dollars, she diagnosed one correspondent's symptoms as indicative of "chronic rheumatism and arrigmia in the heart," and she prescribed potassium chloride and iron phosphate tablets, a dosage that full-time medical practitioners had trouble evaluating, since they had never heard of that cardiac irregularity.

Medical frauds are ageless, and in the nineteenth century their inventors would sometimes frighten their victims into gratitude by nearly slaying them before they saved them: They would send out pills at intervals, and the first batch would produce such dreadful aches and pains that their swallowers would practically beg for the rest, after consuming which they would just about end up where they'd begun. Nowadays, quackery is a good deal more sophisticated, and its practitioners work on the mind as much as on the body. "Avoid fabulous doctor fees—lose weight by listening!" went the text of one fairly recent advertisement. The reducing agent was a $3.95 phonograph record, which was supposed to transmit hypnotic reducing suggestions to the auditor's subconscious. It sold very nicely, because fat people are always searching for ways of slimming down without diminishing their intake of food. This same unremitting quest resulted in the book *Calories Don't Count*'s becoming a best seller in the early 1960s. Its author, Dr. Herman Taller, and some associates followed up by selling half a million dollars' worth of safflower oil tablets, until they were convicted of mail fraud.

Hearing aids are exceedingly popular among these peddlers of flawed goods, because most of the people who need them are old and sometimes also addled. When four Iowa men went on trial for mail fraud not long ago, of twenty-two victims who testified against them, fifteen were over seventy, six were over eighty, and one was over ninety. Several not only had hearing problems but were nearly blind. The four Iowans would, like most defrauders, take money from anyone who responded to their newspaper ads or to the promotional literature passed out at their booth at the Iowa State Fair; but the people they most liked to mulct were those who lived alone, had some funds, and were in a position to allocate these without having to ask anybody else's advice. (The hearing-aid pushers were quite aware that any sane person's advice would have been: "Don't.") One eighty-two-year-old woman who nicely filled that bill of particulars applied for the free hearing test that the promoters pledged in their come-ons. The test, she reported later, consisted of two salesmen yelling at her in her living room. Then they badgered her into signing a contract. The only hearing aid she had ever got was an ear plug that didn't work; her oppressors had got all the money she had set aside to pay her taxes.

In most instances, the proprietors of the Central Iowa Hearing Aid Center, the Transistor Hearing Aid Company, the Electronic Hearing Aid Company, and various other names that the quartet used to make themselves sound dependable, actually did furnish their victims with devices of one sort or another. But these were usually second- or third-hand aids in new cases. They rarely worked well, if at all, and when the people who'd bought them complained about this the salesmen would offer to accept them as trade-ins on newer models—at, of course, an extra charge. At a time when brand-new, first-class hearing aids could be bought from reputable dealers for about $500, Central Iowa or Transistor or Electronic would pick up used ones for about $100, recase them for another $25, and sell them for about $389.50. These were so seldom satisfactory that their purchasers were forever trying to replace them with aids that worked. An eighty-one-year-old woman in Des Moines paid $359.50 for a hearing aid. By the time she was eighty-four, she had invested a total of $2,573.19 in her duel with deafness, but she still hadn't got a device that worked. She saved herself an additional $300 by stopping payment on a check in that amount after being warned against misrepresentations by a neighbor, who had begun by expressing curiosity at the frequency of sales calls from hearing-aid men along their street. Even if that octogenarian hadn't stopped payment, she would have got off easier than an eighty-seven-year-old widow living nearby, who was so charmed by the attentiveness of a hearing-aid peddler that in less than six months she wrote out seventeen checks totalling $7,174, in return for which she received such poor equipment that she could barely hear his fervent "Thank you's." A much younger woman—she was only seventy-six when she was first tested—spent much of her time and $2,221.22 of her money in the next eighteen months trying to improve her hearing, and instead of being angry after all that trouble and expense, she wrote to one of the men who had bamboozled her, "You have tried so very hard to fit me with proper hearing aids and have been so very kind to me. I want to cooperate in every way."

Some schemes are more richly imaginative than others. It was by chance another Iowan, a man named Samuel Cole Fulkerson, who hit upon the notion of broadening the medical-fraud market. Most medical frauds are directed at people who are sick. But at any given time in the United States, even ceding to the sick category all the hypochondriacs, there are apt to be more people who are healthy than who are not. Fulkerson's fancy was simple and beautiful. He would, for a fee that was peanuts compared to the average medical bill, cater to *healthy* people and *prevent* them from getting sick. He did this through three organizations with the high-sounding names of National Scientific Laboratories, Professional Foods, and Nutritional Research Associates, the last being, in Fulkerson's own description, a "non-profit corporation for basic deficiency research." It was not nonprofit for him. Over thirteen years, he was rewarded for his imaginativeness with millions of dollars, which he cheerfully shared with hundreds of salesmen and at least a thousand medical practitioners. Most of them were chiropractors and osteopaths, but a few were M.D.s with flexible ethics.

Born in 1891, Fulkerson had a routine Iowa upbringing, and then joined his father in the animal-feed business. They were wiped out in the Depression, an experience that may have given the younger Fulkerson an aversion to letting nature take its course. In 1940, he became a vitamin salesman, and the following year, judging the field to have a real potential, he founded Professional Foods, which distributed vitamins and other food supplements. The company did not set the world on fire, or even ignite Iowa, but it was doing moderately well when, at the end of 1949, Fulkerson took a trip to California and was badly injured in an automobile accident. While recuperating in Los Angeles, he met a man named John A. Restifo, who would sometimes claim to be an M.D. and sometimes to have a Ph.D. in chemistry, though there is no evidence that he ever even went to college. Restifo ran a pathological laboratory that occasionally did work for the Hollywood Presbyterian Hospital; it was a small operation, consisting of himself and one assistant, Robert B. Holmes.

Fulkerson and Restifo found they had one thing in common—a desire to expand their limited horizons. But how? It was then that Fulkerson got his inspiration about treating the healthy, and soon Restifo and he had charted the organizational steps that would be taken. A client, with or without a doctor's recommendation, would send a urine sample to National Scientific Laboratories. The Laboratories (Restifo and Holmes) would analyze the sample and come up with some dire-sounding report—"hormonal imbalance" or "impaired body chemistry" or whatever. Nutritional Research Associates (Fulkerson and an associated osteopath, Carl R. Nelson) would analyze the urinalysis report and would prescribe appropriate vitamins for the deficiencies indicated. Professional Foods (Fulkerson and his salesmen in the field) would sell the vitamins, but not as a rule directly to their consumers. The vitamins woud be transmitted largely through practitioners, who would benefit from both ends of the cycle: Of a thirty-dollar charge for each urinalysis and dosage prescription, the recommending practitioner would get half; and he would also get half the retail price on all the vitamins he sold.

Fulkerson began advertising extensively in osteopathic and chiropractic journals. Much of his copy, as well as the text of other promotional literature he got up, was prepared by a man who Fulkerson thought had the right touch; he was mainly a writer of Western stories for pulp magazines. In some of the literature, it was asserted that recent research at the Hollywood Presbyterian Hospital had demonstrated the value of hormone urinalysis in anticipating nutritional deficiencies, and in this connection Restifo's name was injected, with both an "M.D." and a "Ph.D." appended to it. Actually, Restifo's collaboration with Fulkerson had nothing to do with his work for the hospital.

The system worked beautifully for all involved. The victims received fat bottles of vitamin pills, each one a guarantee of good health. The practitioners not only received fifteen dollars a victim but also the markup money on pill sales that would otherwise have gone to drugstores. Restifo, until he began making Fulkerson's urinalyses, had never even flirted with prosperity. By 1958, however, the Internal Revenue Service took the position that he had underestimated his income between 1952 and 1957 in the amount of $207,909.49—nearly all of this coming from his thirteen-dollar cut of each thirty-dollar customer. (Fulkerson got only two dollars per urinalysis, but he could afford to be generous; the vitamins sustained him.) Restifo was indicted for tax evasion, skipped bail, and fled to Mexico. For a few months, Fulkerson had urine samples sent to him there, but it was a nuisance to operate across an international boundary.

Fortunately, Holmes, Restifo's lab assistant in Los Angeles, was still around, and in mid-1959 Fulkerson asked him to take over. Holmes, by then unemployed and looking for enough income to satisfy his own two principal desires—drinking Scotch and shooting pool—was delighted. He worked in Los Angeles for a bit and then, in the fall of 1959, shifted to Flagstaff, Arizona, where he installed National Scientific Laboratories in a one-room walk-up office, equipped with an out-of-date Polarograph machine. Holmes did ten thousand or so urinalyses a year, but they did not take especially long, and he had plenty of time left to patronize a combination saloon and billiard parlor that was only half a block away. He was so well known there that when someone went into the men's room, as soon as a toilet could be heard flushing, one of the other regulars would remark laughingly, "Hey, Holmes, there goes another thirteen dollars down the drain!"

As Holmes was becoming well known to the saloon customers, so was Fulkerson becoming known to various defenders of the public interest. His activities were logically of a sort that would make the Food and Drug Administration take notice; when one of its investigators came around for an informal chat, Fulkerson said that no less than 2,700 practitioners had referred patients to him for hormone assays. (This may not have been braggadocio; by the early 1960s, chiropractors were paying $175 fees for the privilege of attending seminars under Fulkerson's aegis; one Texas chiropractor much enamored of Fulkerson's method and equally enriched through it conducted more than a hundred classes touting the procedure.) Fulkerson also informed the F.D.A. that he had a Bachelor of Science degree from the University of California, which was untrue, and that a doctor reviewed all of Holmes's lab reports in Flagstaff, which was also a fib. These did have a name affixed to them, but it was merely the stamped signature of an eighty-five-year-old man, exact whereabouts unknown. Still, the F.D.A. had no proof that Fulkerson, Holmes, and Nelson were harming anybody by feeding them impurities; they merely seemed to be taking advantage of suckers, which might be heartless but was hardly homicidal.

In the fall of 1964, Jay L. McMullen, a producer at the Columbia Broadcasting System, gathering material for an exposé of mail-order medicine men on the Walter Cronkite television news show, wrote a letter of inquiry to Nutritional Research Associates at Cedar Rapids. McMullen did not specify his business; if he had, he might less precipitately have been visited by a Fulkerson salesman, who brought along a plastic bottle to mail a urine specimen in, some toluene preservative for the specimen, and a sheaf of literature. "Doctors used to discover illnesses *after* they showed up by use of stethoscopes, reflex tests, peering into the throats, etc.," one passage went. "Now they measure and study actions of controlling hormones in urine residues to get an early, more complete picture of what might be expected to happen. The entire chemical control of bodily functions lies in that portion of endocrine activity directed and mobilized by the steroid hormones."

McMullen had discussed his project with the New York City Department of Health, and now one of its physicians, Dr. Paul S. May, brewed some imitation urine out of demineralized distilled water, vegetable coloring, a drop of Lugol's iodine solution, and a dash of urea. There were no measurable hormones in this test solution, but by the time Holmes, Nelson, and Fulkerson had finished "analyzing" it, they had discovered fourteen of them, not to mention various androgens, ketosteroids, and corticoids in "low normal range," plus, as the final semantic chiller, "slightly low metabolic function with poor or improper conversion of the metabolites." Not a few people getting a report like that on their urine would gloomily expect next to get the last rites. McMullen had a larger batch of the same synthetic urine concocted. Two reputable laboratories analyzed the stuff, without being told what it was composed of, and concurred independently that there were no hormones in it. Ten more samples drawn from the batch were sent to Holmes's laboratory at Flagstaff, and they elicited ten different analyses, all different and all brimming with hormones.

Cronkite put McMullen's findings on the air late in June, 1965, and the Postal Inspection Service took it from there. The Service did not care whether or not anyone had been hurt by Fulkerson's vitamins; it did care that the mails were being used in connection with what had all the earmarks of misrepresentation. Inspector Charles Miller was assigned to the case, and he soon compiled some interesting research of his own. Whereas every single person, for instance, whose urine had been analyzed by the pill peddlers had been told he needed vitamins, according to Dr. Victor D. Herbert, a nutrition expert at the Harvard Medical School whom Miller consulted, less than 1 per cent of all Americans, whatever else might be wrong with them, suffered from vitamin deficiencies. It seemed beyond the law of probabilities that not a single patron of the three interlocking companies had got a clean bill of health. When, a few months afterward, Inspector Miller asked Fulkerson to explain this odd circumstance, the old Iowan blandly replied, "All specimens submitted came from sick people."

In gathering evidence, Miller went to unprecedented lengths; he poured his own urine into the cause. He sent one sample in under a fake male name and an identical sample under a fake female name; although there are hormonal differences in urine according to sex, they were not picked up. For a month, Miller, under a variety of aliases and through a variety of channels, bombarded Flagstaff with specimens—some of them his, some of them his confederates', some of them synthetic. The only consistency in reporting back on them was that all their producers—even in the case of the synthetic liquids—would be well advised to start taking vitamins, preferably those distributed by Professional Foods.

Miller even went to Flagstaff and asked Holmes to analyze some of the Inspector's urine on the spot. Holmes, shaken by the confrontation, declined. But Miller had by then little further use for the Arizona chemist and his Polarograph. Since hormones are produced by endocrine glands, the Inspector had already consulted a number of eminent endocrinologists, and they had agreed to a man that nobody reputable used Polarographs to measure hormones, and that the whole business being conducted by Fulkerson was, from a professional medical point of view, poppycock. By mid-November, when Miller filed a report on his investigation, he was rather gentle toward the practitioners who had steered patients to the trio. "While competent laboratory technicians and informed medical authorities interviewed during this investigation declare the promotion to represent a hodgepodge of medical nonsense and fantasy," Miller wrote, "it would be difficult, it seems, to impute actual criminal knowledge and intent to all practitioners who have used it." No practitioners, accordingly, were indicted, but Fulkerson, Holmes, and Nelson were, and all three were convicted of mail fraud. So that particular promotion was brought to a halt, but not before $3 million had been spent because of it on urinalyses and another $8 million on vitamins—all told, not a terribly large sum, perhaps, as expenditures go in contemporary medical research, but in Postal Inspectors' eyes a very respectable sum indeed, amounting as it did to more than their entire annual budget for investigating frauds of all descriptions.

# 10. A Unique Process

Is it more important to be beautiful or rich? Judging from the way Americans behave, there would seem to be little doubt that the primary hope of a good many of them is to reach a state of grace of which one or the other adjectives is descriptive, and it may be that a majority of the citizenry would never consider themselves supremely happy until they could claim both exalted attributes. It is perhaps not a sexist remark to say that there are probably more women than men with such dual standards of perfection. Certainly the evidence is abundant that women will go to almost any lengths to preserve or improve their looks.

Over the years, accordingly, they have generously supported countless beauticians catering to their vanity and occasionally preying on their gullibility. Among the practitioners who have benefited from women's aversion to wrinkles, crow's-feet, blemishes, blotches, furrows, bags, moles, jowls, dewlaps, freckles, and overall facial deterioration, none had a more beguiling career than a smooth-complexioned facial rejuvenator named Cora Galenti, who for—by her reckoning—more than thirty years got up to three thousand dollars per capita for providing what she called "new faces for old" to hundreds and possibly thousands of customers, from whom she normally demanded cash in advance. Miss Galenti, a veteran of romance who was married at least six times to at least five husbands, once tallied her total of patrons at over three thousand and her gross income during a single highly remunerative rejuvenative year at over one million dollars. These figures, like most of the facts she gave out about herself, were probably imprecise, but she was undeniably successful, although she twice found it convenient to go bankrupt. The continuing demand for her services was all the more remarkable considering that for part of her career she was a fugitive from justice and that what she did to most of her clients was to anoint their faces with a solution that was about one hundred proof carbolic acid.

Carbolic acid, which is also known as phenol, is sometimes used by dermatologists in what they call chemosurgery. A cauterant like phenol can be effective, for instance, in getting rid of warts. But even with their training and knowledge, doctors employ the stuff reluctantly and cautiously. The acid is extremely toxic. Even when half diluted, phenol can inflict severe burns on human skin. When the burns heal, the seared flesh is apt to be smoother than it was before, but it is also apt to have lost its pigmentation. Neck skin is usually thinner than face skin; when phenol is applied to a person's neck, it often leaves weltlike scars called keloids. Moreover, the acid penetrates flesh and enters the bloodstream, working its way to the kidneys and bladder and causing them to malfunction. A 1954 report of some doctors attached to the office of the Chief Medical Examiner of New York City said: "The authors have seen two cases in which phenolic preparation was applied to the face as a cosmetic treatment for the removal of acne scars, and a few minutes after the application the victims suddenly collapsed and died. . . . Locally phenol causes a precipitation or coagulation of the cellular protein and deep penetration into the tissues followed by necrosis. . . . If the burns are extensive, shock, toxemia or septic infection may supervene and cause death." As far as is known, none of Cora Galenti's patients died as a direct aftermath of a treatment by her; one nightclub performer, though, her face ravaged, committed suicide not long after she had had a rejuvenation to make her look better and then had concluded she was unemployable. Most doctors believe that phenol, in any concentration, should be kept far away from human bodies and used instead where it is harmless and helpful—as a disinfectant for toilets, drains, and cesspools.

Some of the women who patronized various establishments run by Cora Galenti, who had no medical or scientific background and never had any formal cosmetological training, were vaguely aware that carbolic acid was an ingredient of the liquid she applied to their faces. Their foreknowledge did not markedly deter them from putting themselves, quite literally, in her hands. Miss Galenti, by all accounts, was charming, glib, and persuasive. She talked of kings and queens and movie stars who frequented her salons, and she was able to avoid having to publicly identify any of these dazzling personages by claiming a confidential relationship to them akin to that of a doctor to his patients. Just about the only time she came close to pinpointing an eminent client was in August, 1959, when she sent out a publicity release asserting that a place she then had in Hollywood had been honored earlier that year by a visit from "an aunt of the Queen of England," whom Miss Galenti had allegedly treated free and who, in grateful return, was supposed to have given the face-peeler two bronze sixteenth-century statues of Dante and Virgil and "an original Bouchet painting"—all three *objets d'art*, the release added, probably having come from Buckingham Palace.

Most of Miss Galenti's known clients—none of whom will be identified here by their real names—were nonroyal, plain-looking women, reasonably advanced in age, who'd been bewitched by the Queen's aunt's friend's avowal that she could make their faces look twenty or more years younger. In some cases, indeed, Miss Galenti appeared to do that. The faces on which she worked tended to swell after their acid baths, and the swelling diminished wrinkles. She assembled an impressive batch of "before" and "after" photographs of her customers. She did not ordinarily bother to explain, though, that the "before" pictures were taken under harsh lights, without makeup, and were unretouched, whereas the "after" pictures were given the same loving care that a portrait photographer bestows on a bride. Moreover, the effect of a Galenti treatment often wore off after a while, and the women involved ended up with their face lines back, and some of them with unsightly keloids to boot. Also, having lost their facial pigmentation, they were obliged to shun sunshine.

Whatever the physiological results of a Galenti face job may have been, a good many of her clients felt psychologically uplifted. A California doctor, who for a time gave her clients perfunctory physical exams and furnished her with prescriptions for pain-killing drugs, once declared in a to-whom-it-may-concern affidavit—which he furnished her before one of her customers won a malpractice suit against him—that he'd seen some fifty women who'd had the treatment and that "the transformation in some of the women was so great that even I failed to recognize them. . . . They had a new lease on life, new vigor. . . . The psychological impact of new beauty in a woman is so intense it must be seen to be appreciated." Sometimes the new beauty would seem to have been largely in the eyes of the beholder—looking into a mirror. One woman whose transformation left her disenchanted said afterward that "you believe you are prettier and younger just because while there you sort of develop a psychological impression due to the system established in the institution." The highest-paying Galenti customer on record, a Louisiana woman who happily shelled out $2,500 for a face job and the same amount again for a neck-and-shoulders job, professed to be highly pleased that Miss Galenti had removed her freckles. It was a puzzling tribute, inasmuch as Miss Galenti had sworn on oath that she *couldn't* remove freckles.

Along with a good many testimonial letters of dubious authenticity, Miss Galenti collected quite a few bona-fide expressions of confidence in her ministrations. Another woman who'd paid $2,500 for a face job wrote her that she was so delighted she wished she'd been charged double. Still another called Miss Galenti a "miracle-working angel." "My two precious daughters think that their mama is 'just the most' now," wrote one client. "They tell me bless their sweet hearts that we look like three sisters now." It was indicative of the mesmeric hold Miss Galenti had on some of the women who went to her that one customer who said she wanted to erect a statue in her honor said in the same letter that she was a trifle upset because her neck was swollen and achy, because the neck condition made her head sag toward her chest, because her face seemed uncommonly red, and because there was a worrisome red pitted spot between her eyes; and that another customer, who swore eternal gratitude and said she'd acquired a new husband "younger than I am in years, but not in looks or actions," felt constrained to add that her nose looked peculiar and that her eyelids, which had been disconcertingly puffy before Miss Galenti went to work on them, were puffing up again. There were also those women who could find no praise with which to mitigate their disappointment. "After coming home and resting for a day I finally went out to meet some people," one such woman wrote Miss Galenti, "and to my surprise all I got in response to my face is what a burn I got." Some of the graduates of Miss Galenti's rigorous epidermal course called her place the Snake Pit.

A few of Miss Galenti's customers learned about her by word of mouth or by private correspondence. Women who fancy out-of-the-ordinary beauty treatments like to keep one another *au courant:* This plastic surgeon has an exciting way of drawing the skin into the ears and operating there, so no scars will show; that one has a marvelous hairline technique, and so on. Miss Galenti, who in her own correspondence liked to append the term "Beauty Scientist" to her name, got a good many more of her clients by direct-mail solicitation. Once she had the name and address of a prospect, she would send a letter—often on pink or peach stationery and usually turned out on a typewriter with script-style type—that went something like a come-on she was using in the summer of 1961:

Dear Madam:

In reply to your inquiry in which you express the desire to erase the wrinkles and tell-tale signs of age bothering you through the Cora

Galenti Method of Facial Rejuvenation, let me assure you that it will be one of the most rewarding decisions you have ever made.

This is a unique process. Nothing in the world is quite as successful as this method. The Cora Galenti method of Facial Rejuvenation has been imitated, copied, but never equalled for the past thirty years. In *this* process, wrinkles are removed without question. The skin becomes almost like that of a young girl. Time will virtually seem to have moved backward for you. . . .

The process that its originator described as unique took about three weeks from beginning to end. The women who submitted to it were customarily given some kind of sedative first. Their hairlines and eyebrows were shaved, and their faces scrubbed. Then, using a cotton-tipped swab stick, the beauty scientist would apply what she called her magic formula, starting with the forehead and working her way through eyelids, nose, upper and lower lip, and chin. That would take about forty-five minutes. The cheeks and neck would be attended to at a second session. The touch of the liquid was fiery, but after the first dab a client could hardly refuse to go on. For the acid solution first turned the skin white, and then bright red, and if a woman called it quits, she'd be left with a two-tone face. The treated portions were covered with a mask of adhesive tape. After three or four days, this would be removed, and powder and cream applied to the skin, which by then would be red and swollen and exuding liquid. Miss Galenti's explanation for this last was that the pores were weeping; dermatologists contend contrarily that what was happening was that tissue fluid was erupting from damaged blood vessels. In any event, to soak up the seepage, or weepage, the women were supposed to spend about a week coating their faces with absorbent cornstarch powder. Meanwhile—Miss Galenti evidently being aware of the potential impact of phenol on the urinary tract and wanting to get her clients flushed out as quickly as possibly—the women would be liberally dosed with Epsom salts. Since for a while their faces were taped up and the only nourishment they could take was what they could ingest through straws, a good many of them lost weight during their treatment. This gave a dietary fillip to the Galenti process.

The magic formula was a brownish liquid that Miss Galenti kept in a tinfoil-wrapped glass bottle about the size of a man's thumb. When using the formula, she would further wrap the bottle in Kleenex saturated with camphor or turpentine, to kill the odor of the contents of the bottle. The origins of the formula are moot. Miss Galenti contributed no little to the uncertainty herself by maintaining at one time or another that she had five formulas and by giving wildly conflicting descriptions of what they were. One of her recurring stories was that the principal formula was more than 150 years old and was found quite accidentally, in Italy or Sicily, by her grandfather's uncle, a doctor or chemist. There was a laboratory explosion one day, this yarn went, and a few people were sprayed with a chemical, and after a while their skins became unexpectedly and miraculously youthful. The secret was imparted to Cora when she was eighteen, by a grandmother, but the girl never wrote the formula down. A son of Miss Galenti's by her first marriage wrote an account of the history of the formula in which the central figure was an Italian woman known as La Belle Pazza—"the Mad Beauty"—who died, in her eighties, looking younger than any of her eight children. According to this chronicle, it was the Mad Beauty's granddaughter—Cora's grandmother—who gave Cora the secret, when Cora was two, pressing into the child's hand a box containing, among other family treasures, "the foundation of the fulfillment of every aging person's dreams since the beginning of time." In this version, the formula *was* written down—inscribed, in fact, on parched vellum.

It has been more mundanely suggested that Cora Galenti got her formula from another face-peeler, who died in 1949 and whose handyman became Cora's third husband, bringing the formula with him as a sort of dowry. Whoever first brewed the liquid in question, Miss Galenti said on one occasion that it consisted of 35 per cent phenol, and unspecified amounts of glycerin, oil of cloves, and water. In August, 1954, she took out a products-liability insurance policy with Lloyd's of London. (She made and pushed her own cosmetics, a costly line, and she insisted that her clients take home a selection to apply to their new faces.) She sent Lloyd's a formula—it may or may not have had anything to do with rejuvenation—which mentioned pure grain alcohol, salicylic acid, glycerin, Croton acid, Lysol, distilled water, cornstarch, and "thyrnochloride." (She never paid any premiums on the policy, and Lloyd's canceled it two months after issuing it; apparently all she wanted was the physical policy, so she could show it to clients by way of establishing the respectability of her business associations.) During a raid in 1961 on an establishment over which she then presided in Nevada, a tinfoil-wrapped bottle was found whose contents were found by analysis to be 48 per cent phenol, 46 per cent water, and 6 per cent impurities. Miss Galenti contended that this liquid had been used to treat athlete's foot, but a jury that convicted her of mail fraud, in October, 1962, seemed more inclined to go along with the prosecution's contention that, whoever had first dreamed up the combination of ingredients, that particular bottle contained Miss Galenti's not-so-magic formula.

Miss Galenti, who was a naturalized American citizen most of her life but in the early 1960s, through a fortuitous marriage to a Mexican, acquired her latest husband's citizenship, was last known to be operating at Tijuana, in the Mexican province of Baja California, just across the United States border. She last stepped over the border, as far as anyone knows, in the fall of 1963. If she had made such a move and had been spotted and apprehended, she would at once have been imprisoned, having jumped bail and fled the country after a five-year prison sentence was imposed on her. The United States would have liked to have her extradited, and a good many government officials devoted a good deal of time to her case. "It is virtually impossible in the space of one letter," Nathaniel Kossack, Chief of the Fraud Section of the Justice Department, wrote to a State Department official in 1964, "to detail the enormity of the defendant's activities as a purported beauty specialist." But mail fraud is not covered in the extradition treaty between the

United States and Mexico, and unless the American authorities could establish—as they have failed to so far—that Miss Galenti's Mexican marriage was illegal and that she was therefore not a Mexican at all but an undesirable alien and should be deported on that ground, she was free to scoff at American laws. She was also free to accept American clients, and, Tijuana being only thirty minutes by air from Los Angeles and less than an hour's drive from San Diego, she got quite a few. That she did lent further weight to her well-deserved reputation as the phenolic phenomenon of our era.

The first person on whom Cora Galenti experimented was, according to her own recollection, herself. "I had a very bad arm that I was quite displeased with on account of I used to dress quite frequently in evening clothes," she said during her mail-fraud trial. Her grandmother helped her to mix the formula on that occasion, she said, and to "do the proceeding things." That was in Brooklyn, in 1916, when Cora, the oldest of three children of a liquor importer, was eighteen. She had left school four years earlier, and then, at seventeen, had married a man named Charles Palma, whom she divorced thirteen years later, after they'd had three children. (She had a second, brief, childless marriage in 1939.) As a young woman, Cora met a garment manufacturer who urged her to take up fashion designing, and this led her, in the thirties, to Hollywood, where she designed movie wardrobes and did a little face-peeling on the side. The first people she worked on other than herself were, again according to her recollection, two sisters who'd been employed on a motion picture lot as a nurse and a hairdresser and had been laid off because they looked old. With new Galenti faces they soon got their jobs back. Miss Galenti treated them, she said, for nothing. The few paying customers she had in those days were charged five hundred dollars. Dual vocations notwithstanding, she first declared herself bankrupt in 1948. Such attestations of poverty are not uncommon among face-peelers. They don't like to have liquid assets in their own names, because there is always the risk of these being seized if they lose damage suits brought against them by disgruntled customers. In one ten-year stretch, a dozen women sued Miss Galenti for a total of $1.9 million, and were awarded judgments totaling $186,000, but there is no evidence that any of them received a cent.

In the 1940s, at least two other face-peelers were active in Hollywood, an environment hospitable to the craft. It was one of these, named Antoinette LaGasse, whose trade secrets Miss Galenti acquired. Miss LaGasse had been operating in California for a long time, and at some point apparently did a carbolic-acid face job on Miss Galenti. In November, 1949, Miss LaGasse took ill. Previously, in large part to avoid having to satisfy judgments secured against her by some of her clients, she had put most of her assets into the name of a French-Canadian handyman who'd been around her place for years in one capacity or another. When his employer lay dying, it has been reported, she needed some money and asked him for it. He refused unless she'd give him her secret formula, so she did. (This bequest, when it became known, enraged still another beautician, who ran a new-faces-for-old clinic in Miami until a narcotics arrest took her out of circulation; the Florida woman was under the impression that in Miss LaGasse's will *she* was named heir to the formula.) The story went further that Miss LaGasse, piqued at the handyman's hard bargaining, actually gave him a formula that differed ever so slightly from her real one, so that any faces Miss Galenti might use it on wouldn't turn out as well as *her* faces. There may have been some substance to this last: The only woman who is known to have gone to both Hollywood beauticians for a face job subsequently told a California law-enforcement officer that the treatment was "a terrible thing to undergo at anyone's hands, but that the pain was worse with Galenti than it had been with LaGasse." In any event, within a few weeks after Miss LaGasse's death, Miss Galenti had married the handyman and obtained the LaGasse formula from him. Not long after that, complaining that his bride had also relieved him of all his money, he left her.

Miss Galenti's full-time professional debut was not overly auspicious. Early in 1950, she opened up shop at Sunset Boulevard, up and down which accommodating thoroughfare she was to occupy half a dozen different addresses. She had a black maid who wanted her skin lightened; the beautician took a trial dab at the maid's arm, and the skin turned darker. In August of that year, Miss Galenti was arrested for the first time, on the charge of practicing medicine without a license. She admitted having worked on seven faces and promised never to do it again. She got a suspended sentence of sixty days and was fined $120. The judge, adding his authority to her pledge, further ordered her to cease and desist from facial rejuvenation. One month later, a California paper ran an advertisement: "Guaranteed Results—Face and Neck Rejuvenation—Parisian Method—No Surgery—Call CR. 2928." No name or address was listed; the phone number, though, was Cora Galenti's. The "Parisian Method" presumably alluded to Antoinette LaGasse, whose real name, one of her face-peeling rivals long insisted, was Sarah Shaw.

Emboldened by the failure of any authorities to enforce the court's stricture against her shenanigans, Miss Galenti even began to court publicity. In the winter of 1954, a Hollywood writer turned out a feature story describing her as "a feminine Dorian Gray . . . whose secret of youth has nothing to do with face-peeling." The secret, the story said, had been known to and used by the women of the Galenti clan for over 150 years; Cora's grandmother had died at 104 looking under fifty; and Cora's mother, at eighty-four, looked forty-five. Cora herself, moreover, had "rejuvenated hundreds of Hollywood's most glittering personalities, restoring their beauty and in many instances their careers." (At the end of 1965, a California woman undergoing rejuvenation at the Tijuana establishment said in a telephone conversation with an acquaintance in the States that Miss Galenti had treated half of all movie stars. "*Half?*" was the incredulous response. "Well, 30 or 40 per cent, anyway," said the client.)

An astonishing number of doctors and osteopaths—perhaps

speculating that if they could figure out just what Cora Galenti was so profitably doing they could do it themselves, legally—have been disposed to ally themselves with her over the years, though just how high their professional standards have been is debatable. One California doctor who provided her with drugs and now and then stopped by to check a patient's general condition never went in for face-peeling himself but reaped modest fringe benefits from the abundant Galenti harvest; she paid the doctor one hundred dollars a client for his services. One day he found a woman in considerable pain. She said her face hurt something terrible and that when she'd asked Cora what she should do Cora had said to apply ice to it. The doctor advised the woman to try warm compresses, but beseeched her not to tell Cora he'd interfered. He sounded like the kind of Hollywood doctor Jean Hersholt would have declined to portray. Miss Galenti, for her part, had evidently concluded soon after the Dorian Gray plug was published that she couldn't be charged with unlawful practice of medicine if she could find a doctor who'd become an all-out collaborator. Hearing about one New York physician who'd expressed curiosity about her work, she headed east, taking with her, as a guinea pig, an elderly widow who was helping her sell cosmetics. The doctor joined the two of them in a New York hotel room. When he sniffed what Miss Galenti was putting on the other woman's face, he exclaimed in disgust, "That's carbolic acid!," and walked out. The widow ended up with some nasty neck keloids, which she sought to have erased by going to still another face-peeler, who for a while did all right for herself by letting it be known that she specialized in salvaging faces that Cora Galenti had ruined. This woman's technique was to dab more carbolic acid on the troubling spots—a technique not unlike treating third-degree burns with a blowtorch.

A turning point in the Galenti career came in the spring of 1956, when she met a young man who was finishing law school and was interested in doing some public-relations work on the side. For a 5 per cent share of her gross income, he undertook to handle her advertising and publicity. Soon he was on his way to New York, in which mecca of mass media, he assured her, he would undoubtedly be able to sell the editors of *Life* or *Look* on a piece about her artistry. He ended up by winning over the editors of *Confidential*, a magazine with an almost unrivaled reputation for scurrility and irresponsibility. The November, 1956, issue of *Confidential* carried an article entitled "The Miracle the Medicos Can't Explain." There were "before" and "after" photographs of a supposedly eighty-year-old actress who'd hoped Cora could enable her to play sixty-five-year-old roles and who'd ended up, after "her face was reborn," depicting forty-five-year-olds. There were captions like "Feared She Looked Too Old for Middle Aged [*sic*] Fiancee.". . ."After the Galenti Treatment is Now Happily Married to Former Fiancee's [*sic*] Son." (The ethics of this switch were not discussed, just the cosmetics.) There were paragraphs of text like "Skeptical doctors have watched every step of the process that completely erases 20, 30, sometimes even 40 years of sags and wrinkles . . . without scraping, without burning, without peeling, and without any kind of surgery! They have seen the starry-eyed new beings who emerge from the clinic three weeks later, their faces as smooth, as firm and as fresh as a child's. They know *what* it does. They know *how* it's done. But they don't know *why* it works. Cora Galenti doesn't want her discovery announced until the doctors have come up with a scientific explanation. But it may take some time before present studies are complete. . . ."

There was a good deal more: "By 'tailoring' the mask and controlling the application of the shrinking agent, Mme. Galenti is often able to remold certain features at the same time she eliminates double chins and sagging muscles. For example, it is possible to reduce the size of a nose which has become fleshy with age, or to soften the lines of the mouth. . . . In the newborn faces that Galenti creates, old acne scars, pockmarks, even freckles vanish along with every line and wrinkle." *Confidential* described Miss Galenti—who, there was reason to believe, might have paid the magazine for the puff—as "publicity-shunning," and it recounted several heart-tugging anecdotes about her work, among them: "A heartbroken wife begged Cora Galenti to help her recapture the interest of a husband who was spending all his time chasing other women. Presently he's thinking of taking the Galenti treatment himself, hoping it will let him get to first base with the wife who is now convinced he isn't young enough for her!" (Several men took the Galenti treatment. Some of them underwent special torment because their beards began sprouting through the cornstarch masks. One of them complained that after he'd declined to sign a check he'd brought along until he had a chance to observe the results, Cora had doped him and guided his hand in a signature while he was semiconscious.)

How agreeable for a confidence woman to be so shiningly portrayed in a journal of which confidentiality was the very core! "The article you published on my behalf," the subject wrote to the magazine's publisher, "has been of immeasurable value to me. The reporting was both honest and factual, thereby alleviating any problems that would have ensued had it been otherwise." She was proud to be able to report to him that the *Confidential* piece had been translated into Chinese. She herself soon had five thousand reprints made up, in English, in the form of a six-page promotional brochure in which she incorporated some new material and in which the publicity-shunning Mme. Galenti's name appeared thirty-four times. There was room also for several letters of commendation, some signed by names and the others ("in keeping with the highly confidential nature of our relations with our clients") by the phrases "Views new horizons in business career," "Happy Housewife," "A Husband's Love Reawakened," "Youth Regained," "A Socialite Reborn," and "Prominent Clergyman." There was a photograph of "The Cora Galenti Establishment" in Hollywood, a stucco-sided, tile-roofed, palm-fringed edifice that in other instances its proprietor liked to describe as "a fabulous Italian villa" and that she formally designated the Fountain of Youth; and there was a personal message from Cora Galenti herself to women over forty: "As beauty consultant to thousands of women over the past 20 years, the question most asked of me is this: 'Is it possible for me to erase these tell-tale age lines, revitalize sagging tissues and face muscles thereby regaining some of my youthful appearance and loveliness . . . *without surgery or harmful ingredients?*' My answer to each and every woman . . . and to you . . . is 'POSITIVELY YES!' "

The interesting thing about the *Confidential* article was not so much that the magazine ran it as that women believed it. Some women who in the fall of 1956 couldn't afford the $1,800 rejuvenation fee that the magazine cited (in Miss Galenti's reprints, she edited the ante and made it $2,500) saved their copies for four or five years, by which time they had also saved enough cash to spend three weeks at the Galenti establishment. (By then, *Confidential* had been publicly discredited and had gone out of business.) In 1961, for instance, Miss Galenti was pleased to welcome one *Confidential* devotee, a New York woman just over forty who was a professional entertainer and had a modest enough aspiration. All she wanted was to hear somebody say, "How youthful you look!" Cora thought she looked so good even before treatment that she asked if she could use the woman's picture promotionally. The client was horrified; she had read about Miss Galenti in *Confidential* and wanted their relationship kept strictly that. A month later, the woman would be writing Cora ruefully that she looked so odd she couldn't get a job. "My face is several different colors," she said. "It is quite spotted. This is most disturbing to me." There had been a further indignity. After paying her $2,500, the woman had loaned Miss Galenti $25. Cora had repaid her, by check, as the client was leaving for home, and the check had bounced. The client might have demurred at making the loan in the first place if she'd known that the borrower was fiscally undependable. While in California, Miss Galenti was thirty-three times taken to court by creditors, for nonpayment of bills. Once, to meet a payroll, she borrowed some money from her own accountant; a year afterward, she hadn't repaid that loan and hadn't paid her accounting bill, either.

Quite a few readers of *Confidential* didn't have to wait for months or years to fulfill their dreams. They had enough money on hand when the magazine came out, and they headed for California. As if Miss Galenti didn't have trouble enough already, what with having been arrested on a charge of forging a prescription for a thousand barbiturate pills, now she had to handle twenty women at a time. She couldn't accommodate them all at her establishment, and farmed some out to nearby motels. "She never had it so good until *Confidential*," one of these women wrote another afterward. One of the participants in this special kind of California gold rush did pause, on her way to the Fountain of Youth, long enough to write a letter of inquiry to the Los Angeles Better Business Bureau. After being informed that Miss Galenti's reputation left something to be desired, the woman went on out, anyway. Subsequently, dissatisfied, she was annoyed because the Bureau couldn't get her her money back. Several of the customers were themselves beauticians, hoping while there to stumble on the secret behind the miracle unfathomable to the medicos. One of these women, who'd been running her own establishment for twenty-five years, had a face that she found quite acceptable, except for a solitary mole. Miss Galenti removed the mole, but this client ended up with a neck and shoulders of different colors and a dead-white face, and after a while the mole grew back. Another beautician agreed to pay Miss Galenti five thousand dollars to be taught the unique process, but asked first to have a drop of the magic formula put on her arm. It felt so much stronger than the 33 per cent phenol solution she herself had been using that she had second thoughts about her apprenticeship and went home.

Not all the ladies came from afar. Mrs. Marian Jarvis ran a Sunset Boulevard restaurant just a few doors away from the Galenti place. Cora would sometimes stop by for a meal, and they became friends. One day in the spring of 1957, Miss Galenti told Mrs. Jarvis that she was going to give her a free treatment, because she was putting on a demonstration of her technique for a motion picture crew and needed a suitable subject. Mrs. Jarvis said no thank you;

she'd heard that the process involved carbolic acid. Not at all, said Cora. Mrs. Jarvis was won over. She was agreeably surprised, as the cameras began whirring, to find that the liquid being applied to her face didn't hurt a bit. She soon learned why. After the photographers left, Miss Galenti removed the adhesive tape from Mrs. Jarvis's face. She said she'd used plain water for the performance and would now give her a bona-fide treatment. That did hurt. Mrs. Jarvis's neck, by then ringed with keloids, continued to bother her after she went back to work at the restaurant. Cora came around one day and put chopped lettuce on the neck, saying that might help. Eventually, Mrs. Jarvis sued her, for $330,000. She was awarded $36,000, which she never collected. So adroit was Miss Galenti at influencing people, though, that when she chided Mrs. Jarvis later for having made such a fuss and having impaired her business, and urged the injured woman to say, if anybody else asked, that she'd burned herself in a kitchen stove flare-up, Mrs. Jarvis assented. Around that time, Cora got married again, to a man named Robert Smith, who helped her run her business and, apparently feeling that the Dorian Gray analogy was an inadequate characterization of his wife, dubbed her "the Sister Kenny of facial rejuvenation."

Cora Galenti was becoming increasingly self-assured. She invited a *Time* reporter and photographer to watch the start of one treatment. The subject was a woman in her early forties (age wrinkles, crow's-feet, one mole) whose husband, a California physician named Harry Hill, had been so impressed by what he'd heard about Miss Galenti (he'd been persuaded by her son that she could, among other things, cure skin cancers) that once his wife's treatment was over, if it turned out all right, he planned to submit a paper about the episode to the American Medical Association and to use his wife as Exhibit A. As for Mrs. Hill, she was excited about regaining half her life, Cora having predicted she'd come out looking twenty-one, and she planned to go into business with Miss Galenti, helping her peddle a line of cosmetics called Wings to Youth. On December 2, 1957, with her face still swathed in tape, Mrs. Hill wrote to a Washington, D.C., friend who worked for the Food and Drug Administration of the Department of Health, Education, and Welfare. The doctor's wife called Miss Galenti "a wonderful woman," mentioned her "outstanding results from basal cell carcinomas of the face," and urged the government man to have an analysis made of the cosmetics, the ingredients of which Miss Galenti sometimes liked to say consisted in part of oils from India and South America, clays from Italy, and herbs and essences from France and the Orient. (A subsequent analysis by a different federal agency revealed that the Galenti products consisted chiefly of such unromantic, domestically procurable substances as mineral oil, zinc oxide, lanolin, witch hazel, and aluminum sulfate.) On December 20, 1957, Miss Galenti, who from time to time had engaged in arm's-length correspondence with the Better Business Bureau, boldly invited the Bureau to inspect her premises. The Bureau sent over a representative. He brought along, uninvited and incognito, a special investigator of the California State Board of Medical Examiners. There were five women on the premises, under treatment. None of them had much to say. Miss Galenti said she didn't use phenol. Mrs. Hill might have spoken a few sharp words, because by then her ardor had cooled; for one thing, she had a literally stiff upper lip. But the day before, Miss Galenti had promised her a mink coat if she'd keep both lips sealed while the visitors were around; there were veiled threats of disfigurement, moreover, if the doctor's wife spoke up. Mrs. Hill kept quiet. After what must have been for her an uncommonly bleak and sobering Christmas, she left the place on December 26. Her doctor husband, whose behavior throughout can most mercifully be construed as incomprehensible, had by then decided to skip the paper for the A.M.A. Instead, he took his wife to a hospital, where she spent seventeen days and was diagnosed as suffering from pneumonia, bilateral pericarditis, malnutrition, and toxicity induced by chemical burns.

The following August, Mrs. Hill, who by then had already taken civil-court action against Miss Galenti, told the Board of Medical

Examiners that she wanted to lodge a formal complaint that could lead to criminal-court proceedings. The Board did some further investigating, interviewing a number of one-time clients who'd been embittered by their experiences. On October 24, the Board raided the Galenti premises and arrested the proprietor on three counts of violating the State Business and Professional Code. (The raid flushed still another doctor—this one a man from Manila whose wife had a birthmark she hoped to have removed. The doctor hoped to get the Philippine Islands franchise for the Galenti method.) Tried before a jury, Miss Galenti was found guilty. She was fined $1,800 and given a 180-day jail sentence, which was suspended. She was put on probation for three years and once again forbidden to engage in facial rejuvenation. How lightly she regarded such admonitions was perhaps revealed by her having ordered—between her arrest and her trial—one thousand printed letters of solicitation to send to prospects. She paid her fine on December 16. Miffed at California for hounding her like that, she began thinking about new horizons. She came up with a new location and a new magazine. The place was Las Vegas, and the publication was *Harper's Bazaar.*

In February, 1960, Miss Galenti bought a new establishment, on the outskirts of Las Vegas, on which she conferred the alluring name Paradise Valley Fountain of Youth Ranch. She made cosmetics in a back bedroom. At times an exceedingly prudent businesswoman, she had a pay telephone installed; clients were required to use this for personal calls. While the place was being fitted out, she treated customers at motels. Business was brisk, for an ad that first ran in the January *Harper's Bazaar* had had gratifying results. One of that magazine's readers who arrived in Nevada expecting to check in at a posh health clinic was somewhat startled when Miss Galenti met her at the airport and escorted her to a motel, where she checked in both of them under the name of Smith. (At that time, of course, Miss Galenti *was* Mrs. Smith.) "Sounds like a mystery story plot, doesn't it?" the woman wrote her husband. "I guess all this hassle is because they made appointments for women to come to Las Vegas and then couldn't get into their new place right away. Embarrassing, isn't it? Ha, at these prices, it should be. If this letter sounds confusing, it's probably because I am confused."

Even more embarrassing for Miss Galenti was a probation report filed about her in California. The probation officer who'd been assigned to her case concluded that she was "clever, competent, and manipulative," and that nothing short of imprisonment could deter her from violating the court order not to engage in rejuvenation. A judge agreed, and when the face-peeler, commuting between her new and old haunts, went to California in February, she was picked up and lodged for thirty days in the Los Angeles City Jail. It was the only time she ever spent behind bars; one of her patients who'd been notably impressed by her cleverness and manipulativeness insists to this day that Cora didn't serve even that brief sentence but instead persuaded a double to take her place. At the Ranch, there was still further embarrassment for five women who were in mid-treatment when Miss Galenti was locked up. One of the five was a Mrs. Gallagher, whose looks were so far from being improved by her rejuvenation that her husband divorced her. When the magic formula had first been applied to her forehead, the pain had been so intense that she couldn't refrain from putting her hands to her face. That made Cora angry. She told her client to sit on her hands, and added that if she didn't her hands would be tied. After Miss Galenti had been in jail a week, Mrs. Gallagher and the other four customers allowed an assistant at the ranch to continue working on their half-done faces, but she botched the job; there was a marked difference in the color of the skin areas she treated and those Cora had treated. If for no other reason than to attain chromatic compatibility, the women went to Los Angeles, where, as soon as Miss Galenti was out of prison, she evened up their faces a bit, using the dining room table in a friend's home as a workbench.

After that, Miss Galenti made no known attempts to practice in California. The Better Business Bureau of Los Angeles was overjoyed. In 1953, it had been informed in writing by Cora that she did not engage in rejuvenation but was merely in the cosmetics business—a business that, she declared, with her customary casual attitude about dates, had been established forty-five years earlier by Antoinette LaGasse and that she had taken over in 1938. Now the Bureau, observing that in her *Harper's Bazaar* ad Miss Galenti was once again claiming to possess a beauty secret that had been in her family for over 150 years, devoted a good part of its weekly bulletin to her. "GALENTI MOVES REJUVENATING SCHEME TO LAS VEGAS," said a banner headline, and a subhead went, "45 Year Secret Ages 105 Years Since 1953." The text began, "The effrontery of Cora Galenti is something astounding to behold as the City Attorney's office as well as the Better Business Bureau can attest. It is more than possible that *Harper's Bazaar* will end up with the same feeling about her after having published her advertising in several issues of the magazine."

Early in 1960, the Postal Inspection Service began looking into Miss Galenti's activities. She did a good deal of mail-order business in cosmetics, the magazines she advertised in went through the mails, and she used the mails to solicit clients, to many of whom she would write, if asked, that her method was not painful and did not involve carbolic acid. None of the investigative or law-enforcement agencies that had been following her career could try to have her prosecuted simply for face-peeling. There was no legal justification for arresting Woman A just because Women B through Z were willing and indeed often eager to have A burn their faces. But using the mails for misrepresentation was something else again. Soon the Fraud Division of the Postal Inspection Service was in on the case, and toward the end of 1960 the pursuit of Miss Galenti was entrusted to Inspector Charles Miller, who has been dogging her elusive heels ever since.

In June, 1960, a New Haven, Connecticut, housewife, Mrs. Olive Bethel, who'd been impressed by the *Harper's Bazaar* ad, had sent Miss Galenti a one-thousand-dollar deposit on a face job she wanted done as soon as she could get time off from an office job.

She finally got to Las Vegas in November. Her neck didn't heal until the following March, and when it did it was scarred. There were scars on her nose and throat, too. She felt self-conscious about her appearance unless she was wearing high-necked dresses or scarves. At about the time she was being treated, the Postal Inspection Service had decided that neither Miss Galenti nor her mail-order cosmetics were all that she purported them to be, and it presented evidence to that effect to the General Counsel of the Postal Service, who invited her to stop by and discuss her business. When she failed to show up, a postal fraud order was issued against her. Mail sent to her, that meant, would be intercepted, stamped "Fraudulent," and returned, if there was a return address on it, to the sender.

On learning of the fraud order, Miss Galenti agreed to meet with postal officials, and at this change of attitude the order was rescinded. She had a talk with some Postal Inspectors in February, 1961. The upshot was that she promised to discontinue using the mails for business purposes and to submit any advertising copy that she contemplated having published to the Post Office for clearance. The Service was, for the time being, content; having won a seemingly sweeping victory over her, it magnanimously reimbursed her for $15.25 worth of cosmetics that it had ordered from her, C.O.D., at a dummy address. Not long afterward, though, without bothering to show her copy to even her local postman, she was advertising again, in Las Vegas publications that went through the mails. One ad announced that distributorships were available for a new product of hers (the lucky distributors, she predicted, would earn from fifty to a hundred thousand dollars a year), and another said, "Now . . . with the creams and lotions that are born by the regular rejuvenation work by Cora Galenti you can lift the veil of time." That ad was illustrated with an old photograph of Miss Galenti that had been prettily rejuvenated to match the text; a veil-like piece of lace had been superimposed over her right eye.

California had by now gladly washed its hands of her. Nevada had somehow got the impression she wasn't going to do rejuvenative work herself anymore but was going to teach her process to doctors who were authorized to fool around with human anatomy. Inspector Miller thought the time had come to start assembling some evidence that could be used to fortify a federal criminal charge against her—specifically, mail fraud. Soon Miss Galenti was involved in negotiations for face-peeling jobs on a "Mrs. Boone," ostensibly from Oregon, who was in fact Miller's secretary, and a "Mrs. Doncho," who was the wife of a Postmaster in a small New Mexico town. Cora was becoming cautious, though. In communicating with the two women, she wouldn't put anything incriminating in a letter; she made her pitches by telephone and telegraph.

In August, 1961, the Las Vegas office of the Better Business Bureau received a letter of complaint from Mrs. Bethel, the New Haven woman. After spending $2,500 and being so displeased with the results, she wrote, she had telephoned Cora, who had promised to fix her up if she'd come out to Las Vegas again, and what should she do? The Bureau showed the letter to the County Sheriff's office, which had had its own misgivings about the Galenti ranch for some time and was now moved to act. Miss Galenti was arrested on the charges of failing to file to do business, and practicing medicine without a license. Armed with a search warrant, the Sheriff's office also raided her ranch; it was this foray that yielded the thumb-sized bottle containing the 48 per cent phenol solution. Four women were at the ranch, in various stages of rejuvenative treatment. They were uncommunicative. Asked what she thought about all the goings-on, one of them said, "I would prefer not to say because I want her to finish my face so that it's all one color."

Miss Galenti was freed on bail, and at once she went to the Better Business Bureau, where she said tearfully that she was being persecuted—by, among others, the wife of a Las Vegas doctor who'd been hinting that the doctor was having an affair with Cora, whereas if anybody had been misbehaving it was the doctor's wife and Cora's husband. This assertion made the Bureau blink, but adultery hardly came within its province. (Cora and her fourth husband, actually, had been divorced just before her lachrymose visit to the Bureau; they remarried a month later.) Her trial was set for December 5, 1961, and was then postponed to the following February.

Inspector Miller had not been idle. During the raid on the Paradise Valley Fountain of Youth Ranch, the Sheriff's men, to their disappointment, hadn't found any business records of consequence. But from Better Business Bureau files and other sources, Miller had come up with 120 names and addresses of individuals who had probably gone to Miss Galenti for rejuvenation. He sent a questionnaire to each of the 120. He particularly wanted to know whether, if they'd been treated, they were satisfied. Thirteen of the addressees either had died or had moved and couldn't be traced. Fifty-eight either refused to answer or denied that they'd been treated. Of the remaining forty-nine, twelve owned up to being dissatisfied. Miller and other Postal Inspectors sought out the forty-nine, one of whom, a Midwest Inspector reported back, wouldn't talk to him even though parts of her face and neck were "splotchy as a pinto pony and ridged as a horned toad." Some people who not only were visibly scarred but were known to have filed damage suits against Miss Galenti wouldn't say a word against her. Presumably they were afraid of being called as witnesses at a trial and having to confess publicly what they'd done; their foolishness embarrassed them more than their complexions. One woman who refused to be interviewed in person and who in 1959 had sued Cora for $75,000 wrote to Miller in 1962, "I have been well pleased with the results and have had no after effects or complaints whatsoever from this treatment." Nor would one male customer give any useful information beyond saying that Miss Galenti had not improved his face any that he was aware of, even though he had a special grievance: He'd had the notion that she was a doctor when he sought her out, and had learned too late that the money he gave her was not a legitimate medical expense and was not tax-deductible.

While out on bail on the Nevada charge, Miss Galenti set up shop at a Saint George, Utah, motel, bringing that community a little unexpected business and hinting at much more. Her reunited husband told the local officials that she might well establish a rejuvenation clinic there and that they ought to think seriously about putting in an airstrip to handle the traffic the place would attract. One of the Utah clients was a thirty-six-year-old Oklahoma woman, Mrs. Mary Hastings, who'd sent Cora a thousand-dollar deposit in January, 1960. Subsequently hearing of Miss Galenti's brushes with the law, she'd asked for a refund. When she didn't get it, Mrs. Hastings decided not to waste the money she'd already spent and asked Miss Galenti if whatever it was she did would involve discomfort or scarring by acid. Cora told her her apprehensions were unwarranted. Mrs. Hastings then went to Las Vegas. She was taken aback to find out she'd have to go on to Saint George. She was treated there while sitting on a motel-room chair. The pain was so intense that she fainted. Afterward, she noticed that her face was spotty, so she submitted to a retouch, following which she bought three hundred dollars' worth of Galenti cosmetics to use at home. When Inspector Miller called on her in April, 1962, three months after her second treatment, her face was unnaturally red, and had some brown spots on it. Mrs. Hastings said, however, that some aggravating lines around her mouth had definitely diminished. But even while conveying as much as she did about her experience, she, too, was reticent; she thought she might someday want to have her whole body done, to match her face, and if that came to pass she didn't want Cora mad at her. Mrs. Hastings might not have said anything at all if she hadn't been a trifle mad at Cora; there were two young Hastings children, and their mother didn't dare go out into the sun to play with them.

Late in 1961, a number of conferences had been held in Washington among representatives of the Postal Inspection Service and the Departments of Justice and Health, Education, and Welfare. They were concerned about a rise in the rate of incidence of crimes involving medical quackery, and they wanted to take some action that might help deter quacks and deter other people from patronizing them. Inspector Miller had by then compiled a fairly comprehensive dossier on Miss Galenti, and although he still had a number of prospective witnesses to track down, he thought he had enough information on which to base a case against her. On January 5, 1962, he sent a long memorandum to the United States Attorney at Las Vegas, recounting most of what Miller knew about the woman and concluding: "It is believed that prompt and effective action must be taken to force this offender from further continuation of her fraudulent and dangerous practice in order that additional physical and emotional damage is not done to persons deceived into undergoing her treatment."

Miller got quick action. Six days later, at Carson City, a federal grand jury handed down a sealed indictment, charging Miss Galenti with four counts of mail fraud. One count said that at Las Vegas, on or about October 15, 1961, she had "caused a letter to be placed in an authorized depository," addressed to Mrs. Bethel of New Haven, "in furtherance of a scheme to defraud in connection with facial rejuvenation." Later that same day, Miller and two other Postal Inspectors, accompanied by a female United States Marshal, arrested Miss Galenti. She was let out on bail again, her bond being set at five thousand dollars, and within a fortnight, although Miller didn't know it at the time, she had applied for a passport.

The federal charge being more serious than the state one, prosecution of the latter was deferred pending the outcome of the mail-fraud case. While waiting for a trial date to be set, Miss Galenti, back in Las Vegas, went right on about her business. It was not altogether easy. A Minneapolis woman arrived in February for a treatment, wavered at the last minute, got in touch with the Better Business Bureau, and after being warned off, managed to stop payment on two one-thousand-dollar checks to Miss Galenti before they could be cashed. Seeking favorable publicity, Cora did an alleged rejuvenating job on her own face (no analysis was made of the liquids used in this demonstration) in the presence of a reporter and photographer for the Las Vegas *Sun*. The reporter, a woman, came through handsomely. "Cora Galenti appears to be a woman of integrity and honesty," she wrote, "who believes firmly in what she is doing."

The case went to trial in September, 1962, and Cora's attorney proposed that she be allowed to give a further demonstration of her treatment before the jury of nine men and three women. The presiding judge, however, thought such theatrics would be undignified, and would also be overly time-consuming, since the process would take three weeks from beginning to end. As it was, the trial lasted nearly two weeks. A dozen former clients testified against Miss Galenti and nearly as many for her. At one point, the defense attorney smeared some phenol on his arm, to convince the jury that it didn't hurt; the prosecutor swiftly put some on *his* arm, and winced. Miller and Inspector Frank Orr, not to be outdone, and not wishing to be uninformed if they were called to testify on the matter, went to a dermatologist and subjected themselves to two applications each, one of 100 per cent phenol and one of 50 per cent. "It didn't exactly burn," Miller recalled later. "It felt cold and funny. Then the skin turned white, and then it got red and sore." Nearly four years afterward, he still had two faint scars on his arm; no pigmentation. Miss Galenti took the stand herself, which she of course didn't have to and which may not have helped her much, since she got quite rattled under cross-examination and even forgot about one of her husbands. The jury deliberated for ten hours—it was later revealed that the three women members held out the longest—and ultimately found her guilty on two of the four counts in her indictment.

There was a twenty-six-day lull before sentence was pronounced. The judge was presumably aware, as was everybody in Nevada who read the local papers, that during that interval a woman was found dead in a Las Vegas motel, with a bright-red face. She was being rejuvenated by a former associate of Cora Galenti's, and the cause of death was the absorption of phenol into the bloodstream. During that same interval, Miss Galenti's son—

who on another occasion declared that his mother had been victimized because she had stopped paying blackmail to people who were out to destroy her—had a letter published in the Las Vegas *Review-Journal.* Miss Galenti had been railroaded by doctors, he wrote, adding that the Post Office Department was a front for the American Medical Association. "Christ is always crucified and only our grandchildren know and condemn the minds that lance His side," the son said. Some time later, in a more prolonged dissertation on Miss Galenti and her work, the son said she was to cosmetology what the atomic bomb was to physics, and he likened her personally to Madame Curie, Pasteur, and Alexander Graham Bell.

Miss Galenti was fined two thousand dollars, sentenced to five years in prison, and put on probation for another five years after that. Her lawyer begged for clemency. She was "in the twilight of her life," he said, was broke, and had a bankruptcy petition on file; if the sentence was mitigated, he went on, she "will never put any kind of a solution or formula, this I believe, on any person." It must have been with mixed feelings that he proprietor of the Paradise Valley Fountain of Youth Ranch sat and listened to a plea for her liberty based on the withered old argument that she was ancient enough to be her lawyer's mother. She appealed the verdict, was freed again on bail, and at once set about looking for new persons to put solutions or formulas on. Among the clients she approached, after consulting her files, was Inspector Miller's secretary, under her *nom de guerre* of Mrs. Boone. Miller was delighted to be in touch with the face-peeler. The day after her trial ended, he'd had a sobering note from Mrs. Florence Larson, the secretary in the Inspector's office in Las Vegas: "I'll bet you a double that she skips the country—Paris or Mexico?" Miller wanted to know where Miss Galenti was going, and it began to look like Mexico when, on January 16, 1963, "Mrs. Boone" got a telegram from Cora, who suggested that if she was interested in a treatment she come to San Diego. The secretary telephoned her the next day and professed hesitancy. Was some kind of acid treatment involved? "No, it is not so, no acid," said Miss Galenti. "Whatever years we take off, those years are gone forever, plus the fact that your complexion will be very beautiful." Well, would there be any pain? "There is some discomfort. You cannot expect to acquire a new face without some discomfort." Did it have to be San Diego? "Well, said Miss Galenti, the only alternatives were Los Angeles and the Bahamas. (Miller didn't take that seriously; he had never heard the Bahamas mentioned in connection with Miss Galenti's operations, and she was basically a Pacific Coast type.) The following day, Mrs. Boone called Miss Galenti again and said she'd go to San Diego. The women made a date to meet at the United Air Lines counter at the terminal there on January 26. Miss Galenti would be wearing "a very large pink coat," she said. "I had it made in Japan. It's a little different from anything bought in this country." Mrs. Boone said she'd have on a red coat, but she didn't keep the date. Two Postal Inspectors did, merely to see if Miss Galenti would materialize. She was there, all right, in a coat they described as pink-orange, and for the better part of two hours kept inquiring at the United desk for a woman in a red coat. The Postal Inspectors left her alone; they just wanted to confirm her whereabouts. Three days afterward, Miss Galenti sent another wire to Mrs. Boone. "I am worried about you," it said.

San Diego being as close as it is to Mexico, Miller was worried about Miss Galenti. He thought it might be wise to have her appeal bond revoked, and the Justice Department concurred. But nothing came of their joint concern before July, when her attorney argued on her behalf before the federal Court of Appeals in San Francisco. The conviction was affirmed. While the wheels of justice slowly turned—it wasn't until mid-September that a federal judge issued a warrant for her arrest as a fugitive—she had been moving fast. On August 21, it later developed, she'd gone to the Mexican consulate at San Diego, with her new passport, and obtained a tourist card good for six months. On the twenty-third, under her married name of Cora Smith, she'd flown to Mexico City, either taking with her or having shipped after her the mailing lists that had stood her in such good stead for so long and her dependable old script-type typewriter. In Mexico City, she found an obliging indigene named de Saras, and on November 18 she married him. (Just where and when she got a divorce from Smith, if she did, is still uncertain.) The following February 13, as the wife of a Mexican national, she applied for and was promptly granted Mexican citizenship.

In a sense, the Postal Inspection Service had long since completed its work on the case. It is primarily an investigating agency, and its inquiries had produced evidence of a crime that had led to prosecution, conviction, and sentencing. But what the Service had set out to stop—the abuse, at high prices, of American faces—was very likely still going on. So Inspector Miller and his colleagues wanted to find out exactly where Miss Galenti was; if they couldn't jail her, at least they could inhibit her use of the United States mails. Letters addressed to her in the United States could, under a fraud order, be stopped on our side of the border; mail from her, now that she was abroad, could be collected once it crossed the border and stamped "Supposed to contain matter prohibited importation." Toward the end of 1963, the Postal Inspection Service—which by that time had the F.B.I. and Miss Galenti's bail bondsman assisting in the search for her—found out, thanks to her having had a couple of long-distance chats with an old friend in Spokane, that she had settled in Tijuana. On January 2, 1964, Miller and Inspector Ken Fletcher from San Diego were at the Tijuana post office at the very moment that Cora Galenti stopped by to rent a box. She spotted Miller and fled; she was still a month shy of being a Mexican citizen. Later, Inspector Fletcher caught a glimpse of what he thought was her face peering out of a residential window. He had no right, on foreign soil, to do anything himself. What he could, and at once did, do was to phone the local Mexican immigration office, which said it would send an investigator of its own around right away. The Mexican investigator arrived an hour and a half later, looked at the outside of the building, looked at his watch, said it was time for his siesta, and departed.

Late in February, 1964, just eleven days after Miss Galenti was naturalized, she was sending letters to her United States mailing list advising one and all that she was back in business, in association with three Mexican doctors. One of her old customers who got this communication, which had a Tijuana address and phone number on it, nonetheless replied to Las Vegas: "Cora—You sent me the wrong kind of cleaning oil I know you have two kinds one with astringent in it and that is the kind you sent—so I am back in the hospital again. I am getting pretty dam sick of paying for things I can not use I have jars and jars of your dam creams I paid $25.20 for a piece for only to grease your shoes. Now rush me some of the other oil pronto or you are going to be in deep trouble. And I will not pay for it. I am dam sick of paying for things I can not use. This thing since I came home has cost me five thousand dollars and that is not hay and I can prove it."

Inspector Miller, on learning of the new address, had a fraud order issued to cover it as soon as he could. He had by then acquired a new secretary, who, under a new pseudonym, telephoned Cora and asked what the chances were of getting a treatment. The chances were very good; Miss Galenti said she could take the client on twenty-four hours' notice, in Tijuana. Miller, of course, wanted to get Cora onto United States soil, so his secretary pretended to be scared of Mexico. "You have to come here," said Miss Galenti. "It's only across the border." She said there'd be no bother; why, one could even bring one's fee in dollars—three thousand of them. "It's like America here," said Cora reassuringly. The secretary let the matter slide there, but a number of American women to whom Galenti sent letters unannotated—some of these she by now was having mailed for her from various California post offices—did make tracks for Cora's door. One Oregon woman, a Mrs. Stevens, had been on the Galenti mailing list for eight years. After Mrs. Stevens answered a letter from Tijuana, Cora telephoned her and urged her to come on down. The Oregon woman said she didn't have three thousand dollars, whereupon Cora asked if she had any jewelry and finally offered her a reduced rate—two thousand in cash plus a diamond ring that Mrs. Stevens thought was worth five hundred. Mrs. Stevens took off. At San Francisco, a strange woman bound for Los Angeles boarded her plane and took the seat next to hers. They fell to chatting, and Mrs. Stevens mentioned where she was going, and why. The stranger turned out to be Mrs. Hill, the doctor's wife who'd had the miserable Christmas in 1957. The conversation took a sudden new turn, and Mrs. Stevens cut short her trip at Los Angeles and went home.

In November, 1964, Miss Galenti sent a circular letter to the proprietors of beauty shops throughout the United States, inviting them to send her customers and promising them commissions. That Christmas, by means of a courier who went to a California post office with a sackful of holiday mail, Cora remembered all her acquaintances with a handsome greeting card—*"Pas en la Tierra,"* it said, in timely emulation of Pope John XXIII—illustrated with pictures of three magi and two Galenti patients, these last appearing in both "before" and "after" shots. On the back of the card was printed, "The CORA GALENTI Fountain of Youth, Inc., has been duly licensed and is legally authorized to do business in the State of Baja California." By the start of 1965, she was calling the establishment Clinicas Galenti. The clinic sent out an announcement about Cora Galenti in March of that year, written in the third person and signed "C. G. de Saras," her new married name. Her spelling had never been exemplary—the one word that most confidence men and women take pains to get right she would often write "sincerly"—and a key passage in this mailing went: "Prevented from continuing her work in the United States, and obstructed by the Post Office Department because she advertised the treatment as painless, when actually it was proved that plucking ones eye browns [*sic*] is painful, she will continue her wounderful [*sic*] rejuvenation from Tijuana, Mexico."

## 11. The Preacher

It is a tricky business to deal with religious charlatans. After all, since it is supposed to be difficult, if not impossible, for man to comprehend God's inscrutable ways, why should His spokesmen on earth be held accountable for their actions like ordinary mortals? All in all, most Postal Inspectors, being demonstrably human, would just as soon set out after their own mother as after anyone with a real or fancied affiliation with the Almighty. Moreover, inasmuch as strict cost accounting is sometimes considered infra dig in the world of the spirit, it is sometimes hard to establish in court the difference between a crook and crusader. They often sound much the same. In terms of man-hour effectiveness, it is sometimes simply uneconomic to chase churchmen.

One of the more outlandish individuals ever to have flourished in the tolerant environment of Southern California, for instance, was a man who in his heyday presided over something called the Kingdom of Yahweh, which he incorporated as a "religious association to support public worship." It principally supported him—to the tune of about $100,000 a year. The King of Yahweh's money came largely from correspondents who found the solicitations he mailed them irresistible. There are many Americans who complain that much of the mail they get is junk and who throw it away unread. But nobody knows how many others there are who feel ignored by society and who welcome anything that may be stuffed in their mailbox, even when it is unimpeachably junky. The people who relish such mail are not all small children, either, though some would seem to be well into second childhood—lonely, addled folk who derive great comfort from the attentions of pen pals.

Such a pal, to thousands, as well as their spiritual mentor, was the King of Yahweh, and he was a singular member of the epistolary species, because while treating of the mundane present he also beguiled his correspondents with purported glimpses into the past and peeks into the future. His principal stock in trade was the dissemination of "reincarnation revelations"; for a mere twenty-five dollars, he would tell you who you used to be. It was a solace to many of his followers to be able to reflect that, however drab their present external appearance might be, they had in better bygone times worn the trappings of a thirteenth-century nun or an eighteenth-century pirate. It heartened them, moreover, to receive this news from an expert who had already disclosed, by his own acknowledgment, Joseph Stalin's earlier existence as Nebuchadnezzar, Harry Truman's as King Darius, Huey Long's as Napoleon, the Duke of Windsor's as Richard the Lion-Hearted, Madame Chiang Kai-shek's as Cleopatra, and Winston Churchill's as Marie Antoinette. For a couple of prominent twentieth-century figures, the King had *two* prior incarnations: Franklin D. Roosevelt had been both King Saul and Belshazzar, and Adolf Hitler both Jonah and William the Conqueror.

The King arrogated unto himself an actual relationship to Thomas Jefferson, Jefferson Davis, and the actor Joseph Jefferson, and while he offered no compelling authentication of his lineage, this did not appear to bother his disciples, who would presumably have long since stopped reading his communications had they not shared one common trait: They believed *anything* he said. They even believed his forthright admission that his character, though lofty, was not without flaw; he confessed to a hopeless addiction to malted milk. They also believed that he was an ordained minister, and they did not seem to care, if they knew, that he had been married at least four times (he was forty years older than the fourth wife), had spent seventeen months in a federal prison for taking a stolen car across a state line, had spent another twenty-three months in jail for violating the terms of his parole, and spent a good deal of their money betting at dog tracks. When in the course of abnormal events Inspectors Charles Miller and Martin I. Dworkis began looking into his activities, it was easy enough to find him, at the betting windows, but hard to find many people who were willing to testify against him; one old woman the Inspectors approached was concerned solely that, after a decade or so of tithing on her Reverend's behalf, some unexpected medical expenses had obliged her to fall behind on her payments.

After three years of investigation, however, the Inspectors were able to round up enough dupes to get the King of Yahweh indicted on seventeen counts of mail fraud, which resulted in his conviction. But the clergy, no matter how comical, is hard to contain. The King's own bizarre behavior proved to be his saving grace; for when he appealed the verdict, his conviction was set aside on the ground that "the spectacle presented to the jury—of a sixty-seven-year-old eccentric purporting to have psychic powers and his attractive twenty-seven-year-old wife betting contributors' funds at the dog races—was so highly prejudicial that we cannot conclude that a fair trial was had." Not long before that, in one of his circular letters, the old man had likened himself to Joshua at Jericho, but as far as the Postal Inspectors were concerned the analogy proved inexact; for no matter how weakened the walls of the Kingdom of Yahweh might have become, they had failed to tumble down.

Of all the rascals who bilk their fellow men, religious charlatans may indeed be the worst, because, among other wicked devices, they use blasphemy to fleece the uncommonly devout. They are wolves who top off their sheeps' clothing with clerical collars. Among observers acquainted with their depredations but unimpressed by their protestations, they are informally known as "schlockministers." Some of them, passing themselves off as superpatriots, are further accoutered in the flag. Some claim to be faith healers, and for a suitable remittance will send their disciples "prayer cloths," scraps of material allegedly invested with curative powers. The schlockministers have flourished, and continue to flourish, in spite of periodic disavowals of them by reputable religious bodies—for example, the 1961 denunciation by the United Lutheran Church of those who "make a spectacle of human misery and exploit the hopes and fears, the frustrations and disappointments of the desperate, the disturbed, and the credulous."

Some faith healers have taken money from suckers on the ground that they could cure them of whatever ailed them and at the same time have sold their mailing lists—often thousands of names at a clip—to the no less scurrilous proprietors of quack medical clinics. These crooks are usually hard to catch and convict, sheathed as they are in their shenanigans by the reluctance of law-enforcement officials to tangle with men and women who are self-proclaimed surrogates of God. Now and then, one of them gets his comeuppance. There was John Richard Brinkley, for instance, the celebrated goat-gland entrepreneur, who had to shift his business to Mexico in the 1930s after he was thrown out of Kansas. There was Allen Clark Johnson, a stomach-lump specialist; he directed his followers to "touch the place on the stomach where it hurt with 13¢ and send the coins along with $6 and he would be able to do something." There was Roy W. DeWelles, who ran the Fremont Christian Clinic in Los Angeles; he would charge patients a thousand dollars for a treatment called a Detoxacolon, which consisted of nothing more than a simple enema apparatus tricked out with flashing lights. The schlockministers' techniques vary, but they all have one thing in common: Much as they vouchsafe their love of God, they love Mammon more, and they will descend to any nefarious lengths for it.

One of the most remarkable, most persistent, and most unregenerate of the bunch was a black-haired, pasty-faced man named Jessup—sometimes Jack Charles, sometimes Charles Edward—who, using radio broadcasts, direct-mail solicitations, and revival meetings, harvested some ten million dollars over twenty-eight years until in 1969, at the age of fifty-three, he was finally consigned to a federal prison. The judge who put him there, on pronouncing sentence, could not resist a small apposite pun: "Instead of praying for the multitude, he preyed on the multitude." Jessup's preying consisted in no small part of imaginative and impassioned recapitulations of his praying. He professed, for one thing, to enjoy an extraordinarily cozy relationship to God, with whom he would from time to time have intimate man-to-Man chats. He would babble to his flock by air that he had recently "sat and talked with God in the presence of a Heavenly choir," or would burble by letter, "I shall never, never, never forget that holy hour when the Lord met me, and He laid His Healing Hands upon my body! . . . Then the Lord spoke to me, saying, 'My Son, lift up your voice as a trumpet, and tell my people to work while it is day, for the night cometh! I will put my words in your mouth, and many shall believe and turn from their sinful ways.' "

Jessup also professed to be an ordained minister and made liberal use of the title "Reverend." It was understandably difficult for the Postal Inspectors who finally unfrocked him to tap his pipeline to Heaven, but they could and did look into his ministerial credentials. These were nonexistent. At the age of fourteen he had had some connection with a small fundamentalist sect in Mississippi called the Assembly of God Church, but it had never ordained him and had dropped him entirely from its rolls when he was nineteen, for questionable moral behavior. Ten years later, Jessup came into, and would sometimes display, a Doctor of Theology degree from something called the Temple Hall College and Seminary, but this was merely a fly-by-night, now defunct, Chicago diploma mill run by a confidence man whose own credentials consisted chiefly of two prison sentences for fraud.

Despite his utter lack of accreditation, such was the effect of Jessup's voice and of his prose that even after he pleaded nolo contendere (no contest) to a mail-fraud indictment and went to jail, a number of his victims continued to send him regular contributions, which for so long had enabled him to maintain a gracious life style, involving expensive automobiles, gambling for high stakes, and the upkeep of a couple of speedboats and a private seaplane. Jessup's disciples were in a few instances not even disillusioned by the disclosures that, in addition to obtaining their money on false pretenses, he was a fancier of the illegal sport of cockfighting and was also, for a man of his purported holiness, a rather aggressive womanizer. In the course of his singular career, he had acquired four wives, and had been adjudged the loser in a lawsuit filed against him by an outraged mother who'd been beaten up by a pack of Jessups after the evangelist had failed to make good on the promise of still another marriage—this one to the complainant's teen-age daughter, whom the dashing "Reverend" had seduced when she was fifteen.

Jessup was a scion of one of those nomadic tribes of evangelists —some of them honest—who range the rural South, whence many of his victims hailed. (Many of those cited in the indictments against him came from small towns like Newellton, Louisiana; Saluda, North Carolina; and Maysville, Missouri.) His father was an itinerant preacher, known as Brother Jessup, who worked the Mississippi River valley. Four of Brother Jessup's seven sons, including Jack-Charles-Edward, frequently performed as a teen-age vocal quartet at revivals, billed as the Jessup Brothers. They stuck together, occasionally running their own revivals, until sometime late in the 1940s, when Jack-Charles-Edward, who had already achieved evangelical primacy among them and was billing himself as the "Southwest's Greatest Boy Evangelist," went off on his own. He later asserted that he had paid two of his brothers $100,000 for 2,000 chairs they'd used at tent meetings. Maybe he had; he could certainly afford it. It was another of his recollections of his youth that when he was thirteen, after a month-long fast, Jesus had materialized in midair in his bedroom at 4 A.M. one morning. While about the same age, he had begun breeding gamecocks.

Precocious in all the spheres of activity that interested him, Jessup was married twice before he was twenty-one. He met both wives at gatherings of the Assembly of God Church. The first was seventeen and her husband eighteen when Brother Jessup married them in 1934. The newlyweds hit the revival trail for two months, at which point the bride concluded that her husband was unlikely ever to be a homebody and she returned, permanently, to her parents. Jessup divorced her in January, 1936, at Davenport, Iowa, falsely swearing in his petition that he had been a resident for twelve months, when in fact he'd been around only one month to conduct a revival meeting. He had been married as Charles Jessup but, possibly to avoid embarrassing local publicity, called himself "C. E. Jessup" in court. That same day he went over to Monmouth, Illinois, and with one of his younger brothers, then eighteen himself, officiating, got remarried. The new Mrs. Jessup soon became aware that her husband's probity was questionable, but she didn't believe in divorce and didn't even protest when a young woman singer tagged along on what was ostensibly their honeymoon.

In November, 1936, Jessup's wife bore him a son, his only child. The family at once took to the hustings again, accompanied by two hangers-on. The mother, still not fully recovered from childbirth, found herself cooking for five—Jessup allowed her a dollar a day for food for everybody—and doing all the laundry, which, in view of the paterfamilias' trade, included fourteen white shirts a week. By January, 1937, the routine became intolerable for Mrs. Jessup, and the couple separated. Jessup got a divorce a couple of years later in Memphis, this time swearing he'd been a resident Tennessean since 1929. His ex-wife later remarried, and her new husband adopted her son, to whose support his father, as the boy was growing up, contributed exactly ten dollars.

After his second divorce, Jessup settled down for a spell at Fort Worth, Texas, renting office space above a drugstore and incorporating himself as the Fellowship Revival Association. In 1941, the Bureau of Internal Revenue somewhat charitably granted the outfit tax-exempt status. Meanwhile, Jessup got married again. The third Mrs. Jessup, who was to become a valued business associate, was an Oklahoma City girl named Rose Viola Oden. She was eighteen when they met at a revival meeting in her home state, where she was singing and he was urging the faithful to cast away their crutches, with which he liked to surround himself in publicity photographs. Perhaps again to still doubts among his followers as to his matrimonial responsibility, he got married this time—over the strong protests of the bride's father, who had done some research into the evangelist's past—under the name of Jack C. Jessup. He would later contend in one of his autobiographical tracts, "I've been accused of being married many times. . . . I want to say I've never had but one living wife." It was true that he'd never taken more than one under the same name.

Around 1940, Jessup turned to the radio. He bought time for recorded inspirational messages and accompanying solicitations over stations in North Carolina, Tennessee, Oklahoma, and Missouri; but he was principally heard by means of the facilities of a number of outlets in Mexico, which were beyond the jurisdiction of the Federal Communications Commission and over which schlockministers could say with impunity just about everything that came into their inventive heads. One of them did a brisk business in advertising autographed photographs of John the Baptist. Another advertised pamphlets whose readers were supposed to be practically guaranteed highly paid jobs in Alaska; the Governor of that state soon afterward complained that northward-migrating Mexican radio aficionados were becoming a burden to Alaskan welfare agencies. Some of the Mexican stations had five times the maximum wattage allowed in the United States and could be heard in Canada; one in Monterrey to which Jessup was partial called itself the "friendly voice of North America," and one in Villa Acuña the "most powerful commercial operation in the entire world."

In 1947, Jessup moved his base of operations to Mississippi. By then, while regularly pleading poormouth on the air, he was bragging to close friends that his gross income ran to two thousand dollars a day. Certainly, he had accumulated enough capital to buy

—in the name of his Fellowship Revival Association—a $20,000 estate on the Gulf Coast, between Biloxi and Gulfport, for which he paid cash. Gulfport, whose postal services Jessup mainly patronized, had a population then of 33,000, and Jessup quickly achieved a kind of local celebrity: He was the biggest resident user of the mails. Before long, he was sending out 800,000 pieces of mail a year, with business-reply envelopes enclosed. He had two postage meters, and his monthly postal charges sometimes reached $20,000. His incoming mail averaged five hundred letters a day, most of them gratifyingly stuffed with money, and his correspondents were far-flung; a Post Office checkup revealed that over a single two-week stretch he received mail from thirty-eight states.

Eighty per cent of Jessup's victims were elderly women, in most instances women of limited education and practically no sophistication. Jessup would periodically put in a pitch for widows' mites; he knew his audience. He also asked for tithes; in the course of investigating his affairs, the Postal Inspection Service found one old Louisiana woman who had an annual income of $5,500 and over one twelve-month period had sent Jessup twenty-two checks adding up to precisely $550. Schlockministers are partial to prayer insurance, which they peddle to their flocks; the proprietor of the Cathedral of Compassion in Dallas called his insurance "God's Gold Book Plan." Jessup called his version "Lifetime Prayer Policies"; the premiums were not fixed, but the understanding was that if they were substantial enough, he would single out by name, in his daily prayers, for as long as he lived, each policyholder for as long as he or she lived. Jessup did not keep up his end of the bargain. This would have been arduous, inasmuch as he acquired nearly 20,000 prayer-policyholders. Rattling off one name a second would have taken close to six hours a day. So, perhaps not wishing to discriminate against any of this class of benefactors, he resolved the problem by ignoring all of them. In his never-ending pleas for support, he begged for plain contributions, love offerings, special gifts, office-equipment money, and "chair money"; although he supposedly had all those chairs he'd purchased from his brothers, he would tell his communicants that for a mere ten dollars they could enable him to obtain five more. In any case, Jessup would remind his followers that when they went to Heaven they couldn't take their money with them; an attractive alternative was to send it to him here on earth.

Still another fund-raising gimmick was the sale, for five dollars and up, of individual "prayer records." These were advertised as personal messages from him to God on behalf of the party concerned. In fact, there were only three kinds—one for a man, one for a woman, and one for a married couple—with the appropriate name or names dubbed in. Jessup was abetted in this lucrative sideline by a young man named Murphy Maddux, Jr., a musician who fell in with him around 1950, when Maddux was twenty-seven and not long discharged from the Navy. A decade later, Maddux moved some recording equipment he had into the Jessup establishment. A short man, nicknamed Pee Wee, Maddux for a time played the fiddle at Jessup's revival meetings. After he became a full-fledged member of the Jessup ménage, he sometimes moonlighted in a jazz combo at a local beer joint. Pee Wee was entrusted with taping his boss's radio spiels. At the peak of his radio career, Jessup was heard over seven stations for between fifteen and thirty minutes six days a week. He would tape a couple of weeks' worth of talk at a single session. When he accumulated a repertoire of a hundred and fifty messages, he began repeating them, on the probably sound premise that nobody would be able to remember whether he'd heard any particular one before.

Jessup had a high-pitched, nasal voice, and he could project it with such fervor that he sometimes seemed to be on the verge of breaking down from pure emotion. Some of his victims could hardly listen to such incantations as "The angel appeared to me in a dream and commissioned me to give myself to prayer" without reaching for their checkbooks or mortgaging their homes. A characteristic spiel by mail—this one framed entirely in capital letters—began, "DEAR CHRISTIAN FRIEND" and thundered: "THIS COULD BE THE MOST IMPORTANT LETTER YOU EVER RECEIVED!

WHAT YOU DO WHEN YOU HAVE FINISHED READING THIS LETTER COULD DETERMINE SOMEONE'S LIFE OR DEATH! IT COULD OPEN UP THE GATES TO HAPPINESS AND PROSPERITY, OR, GOD FORBID . . . IT COULD CLOSE THE DOOR OF HOPE FOREVER!" Jessup was prepared, the letter went on, to rebuke whatever the recipient wanted rebuked—the Devil, overweight, underweight, a bad temper, a wife's bad temper, or any one of almost a dozen other categories. "I WILL LAY MY HANDS UPON YOUR GIFT," he concluded. He always stood ready to lay his hands upon gifts.

Whatever medium Jessup happened to be using, he kept stressing his own sincerity, as if to allay any absurd doubts there might be about *that.* In one biographical tract about him, his father wrote, "He would actually go the whole length of death by the stake for what he believes!" By radio one time, Jessup *fils* delivered himself of what he called "a very special announcement": "You know, when I tell somebody on the radio or preach to you on the radio and tell you I'm going to do something, I do exactly what I say I'm going to do. . . . Friends, listen. I am honest, I am sincere, I'd rather have God take me out of this world than to be a miserable hypocrite or falsify or lie about religion."

In Gulfport, Jessup also became well known in banking circles. His deposits in a single Gulfport bank totaled $98,158.95 for 1959, $137,036.49 for 1960, and $174,624.27 for 1961. When he was on the road conducting revival meetings, two or three times a week he would instruct the bank to pick up suitcases at the Railway Express office; the bags were always stuffed with money, which the tellers would add up and credit to Jessup's account. He became comparatively inactive on the revival circuit in the late 1950s, but before then he was as busy there as a stinging bee. Especially memorable was a six-week meeting he put on in the fall of 1952 at Bowling Green, Kentucky, which attracted crowds so large—not a few of their members arriving by ambulance—that extra details of police had to be assigned to them. Jessup grossed $75,000 during that stay, which was good money in those days in any line of endeavor. He did a great deal of public laying-on of hands, and at the hotel where he rested up from his philanthropic exhortations he was suspected of further, private laying-on of hands. He was more or less run out of town when it appeared that there had been some energetic pawing of a perfectly healthy local housewife who had volunteered to do some secretarial work for his cause.

Revival meetings could be taxing, but Jessup tried to make the best of the inconveniences that he incurred. In Lexington, Kentucky, a couple of years after his summary departure from Bowling Green, a tent he was using blew down, and it got irreparably gashed by firemen poking around for people possibly buried beneath it. Jessup resourcefully saved the mangled canvas and stored it in a hangar where he kept his airplane. In subsequent months, whenever the women who helped process his mail had some time on their hands, he would have them snip the tent into one-inch squares and staple these to letters requesting funds for a new tent. The recipients were advised to keep their tent scraps in their Bibles. Jessup would also occasionally make mass distributions of his own prayer cloths—swatches of cheap cotton material that he bought by the bolt at the Gulfport J. C. Penney store. Once, he went so far as to propose sending to outstandingly generous contributors a bit of a page from his own Bible—the very selfsame, battered, tear-stained Bible, as he poignantly put it, that he planned to be buried with.

Money being, as this evil man's faithful followers scarcely had to be reminded, the root of all evil, it was what Jessup most liked them to confer upon him. But he was not averse, if some of them were short on cash, to barter his services. In return for his healing ministrations, he would sometimes accept jewelry, and in his commodious home he had a whole room filled with canned goods, which he made available, in lieu of salary, to one couple he employed to do odd jobs around the house. But money was preferable, and most of Jessup's scattered communicants managed to send it to him with such regularity that the president of his principal Gulfport bank estimated his net worth, in 1961, as somewhere around $3 million. The banker was unaware, though, that Jessup did not keep all his assets at home. He had at least one Swiss bank account. One time, he drove from Houston to Monterrey, Mexico, with Pee Wee Maddux. After they'd crossed the border, Jessup remarked offhandedly that he had some money in the back of the car, perhaps enough to buy a new Cadillac. A few miles farther on, he said that on further thought it was probably enough for three or four Cadillacs. At Monterrey, the two men registered at a motel. Jessup excused himself, went out to the car, and returned with its back seat, which he placed upside down on a bed. Instead of springs, it was stuffed with currency, enough to fill two good-sized suitcases. The next morning, Jessup and Maddux toted the bags to a Monterrey bank; the bug-eyed tellers who counted the contents came up with a figure of $55,000.

Jessup might never have come a cropper had not three United States government agencies got together in 1961, disturbed by recurring complaints that Americans were being hoodwinked by scoundrels using Mexican broadcasting facilities. The Federal Communications Commission, the Department of Justice, and the Post Office Department agreed among themselves that the F.C.C. would begin regularly to monitor and record some of the broadcasts; that the postal authorities would determine whether the broadcasters were violating the mail-fraud statutes; and that Justice would, if circumstances warranted, prosecute the most egregious offenders. Jessup's *modus operandi* quickly stirred the investigators' interest, and two veteran Postal Inspectors—Charles Miller, in Washington, and Oris R. Whitley, in Saint Louis—were assigned to his case. One aspect of his activities that they decided to look into right away was his establishment, earlier that year, of a Faith Hospital in downtown Gulfport, which, he said on the radio, was "the only Faith Hospital in the whole world where the prayer of faith is depended on to heal the sick." He told his listeners that "I don't believe that if you send your money to India, or Africa, or any heathen country that it would do as much good as we are doing over the radio and in Faith Hospital," which he declared had, among other innovations, a building-wide intercommunications system through which every patient could hear him pray for every other one.

Jessup had nothing against conventional hospitals. He used them for his family and himself. At the same time that his Faith Hospital was theoretically functioning, he checked in, for treatment of an aggravated ulcer, at the Ochner Clinic in New Orleans, where he wangled a 50 per cent discount by identifying himself as a Baptist minister. He did at least once confess the ulcer to his communicants, but he credited God with curing it in the course of a mountainside colloquy. As God had healed him, Jessup would preach, so could he, through God, heal others. Not only could he cure such general afflictions as poverty and nuclear warfare, but he was prepared to deal with specific ailments. "Do you know that a cancer fell off a lady's neck as I prayed for her and another one that was troubled with a terrific pain in her head, it was kind of a concussion, God has healed her!" he would broadcast. Among the ailments he had successfully treated, he ticked off blindness, tuberculosis, lameness, alcoholism, leukemia, rheumatism, deafness, dizzy spells, female trouble, heart trouble, tumors, infections, and poliomyelitis. One paralyzed boy did apparently give up his crutches for a while after Jessup's hands touched him; when he had to return to them, his parents blamed their own lack of faith for his retrogression. Jessup would occasionally circulate testimonials from his patients, which compensated in fervor for what they lacked in felicity—one, for instance, from a Louisiana woman who until he prayed for her had been at death's door: "The doctors had gave me up. I rote you. In three days I was up washing my dishes." Jessup was a somewhat less adept practitioner closer to home. One of his office workers was bitten on the hand by a squirrel she was feeding, but he did not rush to lay his healing hands upon her hurt one.

The Faith Hospital was inaugurated in February, 1961, when Jessup signed a five-year lease for the lobby and first two floors—each with twenty-six rooms—of a ramshackle hotel. He was to pay $350 a month rent for the first year and $400 a month after that.

He distributed photographs of the installation far and wide, with a sign reading "Faith Hospital" on the roof. The sign had been drawn in by an artist, who at the same time had brushed out a Budweiser beer sign that was visible in a ground-floor tavern window. Jessup also grandly announced that the board of directors of the hospital included an insurance executive and a bank officer. The insurance man was never apprised of his appointment and had never laid eyes on the building; the banker, one month before the hospital opened up, was implicated in a shortage at his bank and was later imprisoned for embezzlement. Jessup declared from the outset that no medicine would be provided at the hospital—merely bedside prayer. There would, however, be trained nurses, and private nurses, what was more. He did not mention the kitchen facilities, possibly because there were none; he arranged to provide meal tickets for his patients at a café down the street. As for the patients themselves, such were his powers of prayer, he asserted, that some who planned to stay a week went home completely cured the following day. One man who showed up with a stomach tumor did take a train home the day after Jessup stroked his swollen belly, but he died on the train. Then there was an old woman from Silsbee, Texas, with advanced arthritis, who chartered a funeral-home ambulance for the 340-mile trip to Gulfport. She told the driver she wouldn't need him for the return trip, since she'd be going back by bus. A week later, she summoned the ambulance to come fetch her. When she was interviewed, a few months later, by Inspector Whitley, she was completely crippled, but her faith in Jessup hadn't wavered. She couldn't have been a witness against him in any event, because, as Whitley's report on her laconically concluded, "She has since died."

Actually, the hospital was largely just another means of raising funds, and never housed more than a handful of patients. Four months after Jessup announced its opening, he was playing it down in his appeals for money; presumably, he felt he had milked that source for all it was worth. Prospective patients nonetheless kept applying for admittance—a dozen of them a day. They were put off by form letters informing them that the place was full. One man who sent the hospital a substantial contribution in the hope of getting his blind mother-in-law accepted was rewarded with slightly more than a form letter; he also got a piece of cloth to place on his mother-in-law's head as a "point of contact." When Miller and Whitley began checking up on the hospital, they learned that although people all over the country were familiar, through Jessup, with the marvels performed within its walls, the secretary of the Gulfcoast Counties Medical Association had never heard of it. Visiting the premises themselves, the two Postal Inspectors found no intercom, and only two people. One was an elderly widow who was supposed to be the resident nurse, but who had had no nurse's training whatever. She couldn't remember her maiden name. Her own initial point of contact with Jessup, she said, had been a letter she'd written him about an uncle of hers who'd suffered a stroke; she couldn't remember the uncle's name. She said the Lord had told her to go to Gulfport and offer Jessup her services. The only other information she had to convey was that Jessup thought 7 a lucky number—he was, after all, one of seven brothers—and that most of his patients, accordingly, were cured in either seven seconds, seven minutes, seven hours, seven weeks, seven months, or seven years. The only patient around was an eighty-seven-year-old man crippled with arthritis (it probably wouldn't have helped him much to be seventy-seven) who had been there for five months. In his room were a wheelchair, a pair of crutches, and ten bottles of assorted pills. The old man couldn't spell his own name. He said that all information about him would have to come from Jessup; the only information *about* Jessup he had to convey was that the good holy man had the power to cast out demons. So moribund was the hospital by the end of 1961 that the total number of meals catered to it by the neighborhood café had for several months, the Postal Inspectors learned, averaged just four a day—barely enough to sustain the addled old woman and the ailing old man.

To Postal Inspectors inured to all kinds of mischief, no facet of

Jessup's life proved more diverting, as they probed into his past, than his devotion to cockfighting. At one point he presided over a stable of 150 cocks, which he would pit on Sundays, there presumably being no need for fowl to respect the Sabbath. Every so often, Jessup would put in an appearance at Hot Springs, Arkansas, which was to cockfighting what Indianapolis is to auto racing; his entries sported the colors of the Magnolia Club, of Magnolia, Mississippi. One of Jessup's birds won the Hot Springs Derby in March, 1952, but the proprietor of the feathery flock had so little confidence in its combativeness that although he won $2,700 in prize money he ended up a loser, having dropped more than that in bets against himself. In cockfighting circles, Jessup was known as The Preacher. One breeder who had heard some of his unctuous broadcasts thought it odd that he should be in the pastime at all, and even odder that of the two kinds of people partial to it—the gentlemen fanciers and the riffraff—it was the riffraff with which Jessup always seemed to fraternize. The Preacher managed to combine his hobby with his work. At revival meetings, one of his favorite shills was a cockfighting crony, a convicted burglar on parole, who after being carried into a meeting on a stretcher, or after hobbling in on crutches, could with never-failing plausibility be counted on to jump up and prance around like a man whose debilitating demons had been indisputably put to rout.

Little of what Miller and Whitley learned about Jessup came from the man himself. They interviewed him a couple of times in January, 1962, but he was understandably uncommunicative. He was notably vague about his finances. He claimed that his total income was a $100-a-week salary from the Fellowship Revival Association. By normal organizational criteria the Association, like his hospital, was a rather loosely structured institution. Jessup was its president, but he professed at first not to know the names of its officers and directors. He may in this instance have been relatively truthful, inasmuch as there was a good deal of uncertainty about who they were or what they did. One shady minister who for a while was supposed to be a vice-president of the association and to have custody of some of its corporate records told the Postal Inspectors that he had unfortunately lost them all when a rope had snapped that was securing a trailer to the rear of his car. After the federal investigation of Jessup got under way, Jessup suddenly informed Pee Wee Maddux that *he* was a director of the F.R.A., and further persuaded a Dallas advertising man to compose some retroactive minutes of past annual directors' meetings. The Dallas man had a revivalist background himself; he had been business manager for a boy evangelist in the 1940s, and had been obliged to pay his client $10,000 following a lawsuit in which it was contended that whereas the manager had collected $67,000 at tent meetings, only $500 of that had ended up in the boy's bank account. Later, the Dallas man became a booking agent, arranging radio time on the Mexico stations for Jessup and other schlockministers; and he also was one of the organizers of a Dallas meeting in the spring of 1962 of something called the Full Gospel and Fundamental Ministers of America. It was a gathering of some twenty men, and high on the agenda was a discussion of an anti-Protestant conspiracy being mounted by President Kennedy and his Attorney General brother. The chief villains in this cabal, the radio agent revealed in a confidential memorandum he prepared for the meeting, were Postal Inspectors, whom he exaggeratedly and flatteringly credited with having investigated eighty-three fundamentalist ministers and obtained convictions of every single one.

Jessup's own labors in the special vineyard of the Lord he had elected to cultivate were, while rewarding, not particularly onerous, but he was good at simulating tribulation. One day in the fall of 1961, when he had a balance of $21,762.84 in his principal Gulfport bank account and when his radio time on Station XERF in Villa Acuña was paid for a couple of years in advance, his anguished voice could be heard on that outlet saying, "I'm in desperate financial need. My spirit is crushed. My heart is burdened. I am sad. I want you to know that the Devil has tried me more than I've ever been tried before." The next day, he bought six new IBM office typewriters. He had first-class office equipment: an automatic letter opener, an automatic envelope stuffer, and an Addressograph with some 75,000 nameplates to feed into it. An IBM man told the Postal Inspectors that it was the most sophisticated mail-processing plant between Mobile and New Orleans. Jessup's machines were operated by a staff of half a dozen or so women, closely supervised by his wife; the Faith Hospital might not have the intercom system credited to it, but Rose Jessup had one by means of which she could eavesdrop on the staff.

It was one of the main points in the Postal Inspectors' accusations against Jessup that whereas he kept inviting people to send personal requests for him to incorporate in his prayers, and to pay him for his trouble, he hardly ever looked at any of them. People would send him long, explicit accounts of *their* troubles, and for their pains (and some of them had truly dreadful pains) all they got was a form letter signed by one of the office workers. (Rose once complained that the young women were signing Jessup's name too neatly; men didn't write that well, she said. "Rose did not seem to have any religion at all," one of the office workers once remarked.) The plaintive letters themselves were often consigned, unread, to an incinerator. Rose opened all the mail herself, restuffing the accompanying contributions into a garbage can until her husband could get around to totting them up; the employees were warned that any attempt on their part to count, or even peek at, the proceeds would result in instant dismissal. Correspondents were graded in the files according to their generosity: "A" if they sent no money at all, "B" for less than five dollars, "C" for something between five and ten, and "D" for anything over that. Jessup would normally make a general solicitation once a month; anyone who remained in the unresponsive "A" category for four straight months had his Addressograph plate destroyed. The only other way of getting off Jessup's mailing list was to inquire about his multiple marriages; that was ground for immediate banishment. Unfortunately for his victims, too few of them knew about his background to hit inadvertently upon this means of escaping his clutches.

Jessup himself not only ignored the mail, but he was frequently not even on the premises. He preferred to go fishing in the Gulf of Mexico, and he was often to be found on an island ten miles out, where he affected to be fasting and praying but was more likely to be casting and trolling. Fishing was not only another hobby of his but also another business; he ran a small enterprise called Fish By Air, and would take sportsmen out to the island by seaplane. In the spring of 1968, after he had pleaded nolo contendere to mail fraud, he turned up in Saint Louis for a revival meeting and conned the fishing writer for the *Post-Dispatch,* who devoted a whole laudatory column to him, acclaiming him as a guide who could guarantee success. "And who would believe such a guarantee?" the writer said. "But one guide does make a promise of sure success. And as a rule, people believe him. After all, he's an ordained minister." The arrangement was that "Charley," as Jessup had persuaded the gullible writer to identify him, would give his customers their money back if he didn't provide a satisfactory catch; Charley was endowed in the story with the ability to spot schools of sea trout, redfish, or lemonfish from five hundred feet up, whereupon he would land his plane near his favorite island, whence his clients could wade out and haul in *their* prey. "I'd rather fish than do anything," said Charley, sticking the gaff into the writer to whom he had previously fed hook, line, and sinker. By that time, on a more mundane level of existence, Charley had divorced Rose, who had returned to Oklahoma City and obtained legitimate employment as a secretary in a manufacturing plant; and he was living with a Mexican woman thirty years his junior, whom he ultimately took as his fourth wife.

The most ambitious fasting-and-praying expeditions on which Jessup embarked were, appropriately, trips to the Holy Land, to defray which his supporters were asked to dig deeper than ever into their eroded pockets. He made three such pilgrimages between 1960 and 1964, each time taking along Pee Wee Maddux, as a combination luggage-bearer, photographer, and all-around factotum. The stated purpose of the first trip was to engage in a fourteen-day fast ("14" was twice the lucky "7") in the Garden of

Gethsemane, where Jesus had spent his last night alive in prayer beneath the olive trees. The Franciscan monks in charge of that shrine wouldn't let Jessup pitch a tent in the Garden itself, but had no objection to his setting up shop a short way off, behind the Church of the Agony. Maddux duly recorded on film a camel-saddle altar that Jessup stationed in front of his tent, but The Preacher's own word had to be taken for the exigencies of his stay: "I actually wallowed out two holes in the ground with my knees." But this was genuflection well spent, because "Now I can pray for the blind and they see, the lame and they walk, the deaf and they hear." Jessup's big moment, according to one of his accounts of the experience, came on his eleventh night out, when God and His Heavenly Host visited him and "for some seven minutes [there was the magic number again] I heard the angels of God singing above my tent. . . . This was the *most real experience of my entire life. . . . Everything that I now touch seems to have the Mighty Miracle working power of God flowing through it.*" An Arab newspaper called the *Jerusalem Times* ran a story about Jessup's mission, of which the subject later widely distributed reprints; he neglected to inform the recipients that he had paid to have it printed.

Jessup actually seems to have spent two nights and three days in the tent before checking into a hotel on Mount Scopus, in the Arab part of Jerusalem that was then governed by Jordan. On his return to the United States, he published a sixteen-page booklet reporting on the trip, illustrated with twenty-two photographs of himself, and unequivocally entitled "I Spent Fourteen Days and Nights in Fasting and Prayer in the Garden of Gethsemane." One of the pictures was of a "farewell dinner given to honor Brother Jessup at end of fourteen days fast"; the occasion was actually a Thanksgiving dinner that the hotel put on for all its American guests. This meal was served on November 24, just four days after Jessup pitched his tent; so on the day God supposedly materialized Jessup was more likely to have been suffering from too much turkey stuffing than from hunger pangs. Seven years later, in one of his mailing pieces, Jessup, probably then suffering less from remorse than from accusations of perfidy, inserted a "Notice of Correction Concerning Days Spent in Garden of Gethsemane"; he now said that while he had fasted for sixteen days at that time, only five had been in the Garden, and that the confusion in earlier brochures had been "do [*sic*] to human error."

Jessup was not especially popular in Jordan. For one thing, although the Franciscans tending the Garden made no charge for their assistance, he had been expected to make a donation to the gardeners who helped him erect his tent, and—*making* donations being not exactly his practice—had omitted this courtesy. Then the Jordanian police, perhaps sensing there was something fishy about him, searched his luggage and found Israeli literature in it; at that tindery time, this was pretext enough to deport him. By then he had ordered a thousand New Testaments with olive-wood covers, two bags of Gethsemane earth, and another bag of olive leaves. This amounted to a $2,500 purchase, and Jessup made a $500 down payment, promising to send along a check for the balance. He ultimately did, but only after some starchy correspondence with the seller's lawyer. For months afterward, Jessup would allude to his followers about this memorable excursion: "Yes, I spent two weeks under the little tent. . . . Before God Almighty, I speak the truth!"

Early in 1963, Jessup was back in Jerusalem, this time to commune with God over a suitcaseful of prayer slips that thousands of people had sent him, at his solicitation. He was going to pray "night and day" on the senders' behalf in the Holy Upper Room, the legendary scene of the Last Supper. "For two thousand years there has been no fasting and no prayer in the Upper Room," he reported in advance, while raising funds for the voyage. "This is the greatest mission of my life." The priest in charge of the chamber, to which visitors were routinely admitted from 8 A.M. to 5 P.M., thought Jessup was deranged when he came around asking to spend the night, and said he'd have to request permission from the Ministry of Religious Affairs. It is not known whether or not the American took that course. In any event, he only spent one and a half hours in the Upper Room, and never even bothered to unpack his prayer slips, which he later dumped—in a gesture ecologically as well as theologically disrespectful—into a well. Then he took off for Geneva to deposit ten thousand dollars in a bank. His own version of the episode, which did not mention the stop-off in Switzerland, was markedly different. He had been in the Room praying for the abolition of nuclear weapons, he declared, and he had said, " 'Oh God, give me a witness. Let me know that my prayers are answered.' . . . Immediately a mighty voice like thunder shook Mount Zion where I stood, and a man standing near me cried out, 'Surely this is a sign from Heaven!' "

The next year, the restless Jessup, with the subservient Maddux still in tow, was off again—this time to the island of Patmos, in the Aegean Sea, and specifically to the cave where Saint John is said to have written his portion of the New Testament. Jessup and Maddux did in this instance stay overnight inside the hallowed cavern, but only because they got accidentally locked in after official visiting hours. This time, Jessup had pledged to the senders of prayer slips (who had of course accompanied them with suitable remittances) that he would return each one with the exact time noted on it when he had intoned over it. But even though he had a whole night to fulfill this promise, again he merely touched an unopened bundle of slips, and then jettisoned the lot. The genesis of this journey was its most beguiling aspect. It seemed that Jesus had appeared before Jessup in a dream, "in the most beautiful golden glowing rainbow," and had led him to the end of the rainbow, which terminated at Patmos. Jessup had realized on awaking what that meant; it meant he had to go there with his eyes open for another chat with God; for those kind enough to finance the outing there would be a very special reward: a full-color artist's depiction of Jesus escorting Jessup along the spectral path.

Jessup may have gallivanted about so lightheartedly even after he knew he was under government surveillance out of a belief that he was in no real jeopardy; he was well aware how hard it is to put people out of business when they are assertedly in partnership with God. In the Deep South, especially, preachers' credentials are not scrupulously examined, and he had some fair political connections: After the investigation of him got under way, the Chief Postal Inspector's office was delicately asked about it by the office of a member of Congress from Mississippi. Inspectors Miller and Whitley, notwithstanding, plodded on obtaining evidence against him—in their view, a man who invited correspondents to send him specific requests and then didn't even bother to read his mail was beyond the pale—and in June, 1963, they submitted a detailed report on him to the United States Attorney at Jackson, Mississippi, who had jurisdiction over Gulfport and its environs. The case progressed slowly, and this distressed the Postal Inspectors, because they had good reason to suspect that if the case was delayed too long some of their witnesses might not be around. At a faith-healing session in Los Angeles in the fall of 1961, for instance, Jessup had besought one-thousand-dollar gifts from the audience. Among those who acquiesced was a ninety-two-year-old widow who was won over when he massaged the throat of a woman who'd ostensibly lost the power to speak and—wonder of wonders—the stilled voice had suddenly returned! The widow didn't have a thousand dollars but pledged it anyway, and when she told an eighty-year-old friend of hers about the miracle, the octogenarian borrowed a thousand dollars from an even much older sister and pressed it upon Jessup. Each old woman was duly rewarded with a Lifetime Prayer Policy and a tinted photo of her benefactor.

In November, 1964, inasmuch as many of Jessup's benefactors had mailed him funds from Tennessee, the Department of Justice transferred the Jessup file to the United States Attorney in Nashville, James F. Neal, who was more disposed to move ahead with it, and who acted so swiftly that within a week Jessup had been indicted by a grand jury and arrested. Freed on bond, he insisted he was being persecuted. He said that Nashville was a hotbed of

Church of Christ folk who were always out to calumnify men of the Gospel like himself, and that he wanted his case to be heard—as, after innumerable delays, it finally was—in Mississippi. Meanwhile, he continued to pursue his predatory vocation. He had sojourned in Mexico for a while after divorcing Rose, but by the start of 1964 had returned to Gulfport and was soon operating at full swing. He even had a new tête-à-tête with God to reveal, this one having occurred in the Sierra Madre. "I had to have a direct answer from God on several important decisions," he explained in one mailing, "and I can tell you that I have heard from Heaven!" By May, 1964, he was back on five radio stations. The case dragged on and on, until a federal judge in Biloxi, Mississippi, finally set a trial date for January 22, 1968—more than six years after the investigation had begun. In the 1964 indictment, Rose Jessup and Murphy Maddux had been cited as codefendants; now, two days before the trial date, Maddux asked for a severance (Rose ultimately got one, too) and made a voluntary statement to Miller and Whitley, in which a good many thitherto unknown details of Jessup's unorthodox behavior—the business of the car seat in Mexico stuffed with currency, for example—first became known to the Postal Inspectors. Jessup had wangled a further reprieve by switching lawyers, but after Maddux and Assistant U.S. Attorney Robert Travis, who'd been sent from his regular post in Fort Worth to prosecute the case, talked he must have been convinced that he didn't have a prayer in court, and on March 18, 1968, he pleaded nolo contendere.

It was not for another nine months after *that* that Jessup came up for sentencing. In the meantime, he had submitted a petition for clemency avowing his own repentance and accompanied by several character testimonials, one of these from a Biloxi pastor who observed that Jessup's ecumenical good will had been manifested by, among other humanitarian acts, lending chairs to Catholics without charge. The judge seemed unimpressed. He was more impressed by some exhibits he had before him. One was a photograph, taken the day of Jessup's arrest, of a large metal garbage can, with a one-by-four-inch slit in its lid, through which his mail proceeds were dropped en route to the bank. What most seemed to get the judge's dander up was a batch of stuff Jessup had unrepentantly mailed out after pleading nolo contendere, among them accounts of how he could cure gall bladders and kidney stones, and a November, 1968, recital of a nice little visit with God that was addressed to "My dearly beloved Christian Friend and Soul-Saving Partner." One could become a soul-saving partner, Jessup said in another letter, by remitting thirty dollars in six monthly installments: "God has given me this plan . . . a God-given nomination from Heaven, to be a silent soul-saving partner on earth." While the judge was reading some of this guff aloud, Jessup slumped to the floor; the judge had him propped up in a chair and went on reading. Then he sentenced Jessup to a fine of two thousand dollars, a year in prison, and five years' probation. Jessup actually spent slightly less than nine months behind bars. Before going off to serve his term, he symbolically terminated his lifelong career; he turned in his postage meters. He had informed the judge while beseeching leniency that if he was let off he would move to Arlington, Texas, where one of his brothers ran a small trailer-renting company, and start a new life as an automobile salesman. He might make a very good one.

# 12. No Grist from the Mills

There are more than two hundred thousand ministers, priests, and rabbis in the United States, and more than one million college and university students now receive a degree of one kind or another every year. Most of these men and women are perfectly entitled to the honorific titles and initials with which they sandwich their names (not to mention the more tangible perquisites, such as the reduced air fare, hotel, and hospital rates often granted to clergymen), but there are also quite a few individuals who don't deserve them and have acquired them, merely by paying cash, from mail-order diploma mills. Postal Inspectors, in the line of their peculiar duty, sometimes can be found in this latter group. Inspector Frank Orr, of Los Angeles, has been at least twice "ordained." In the course of one investigation of a self-proclaimed minister whose credentials had been supplied by a Los Angeles diploma mill called the International Evangelism Crusades, Orr applied to it himself and, with no effort other than the payment of a twenty-five-dollar fee, got the same accreditation as his quarry. Another time, for a mere twenty dollars, Orr was designated a Bishop of the Universal Life Church. This was an institution presided over by the Reverend Kirby J. Hensley, who worked out of Modesto, California, until the authorities of that usually accommodating state expressed too strenuous disapproval of his activities, at which point he simply transferred his base of operations to Phoenix, Arizona. Helnsley's business was so lucrative that others were understandably inspired to emulate it. For a while, Tampa, Florida, harbored a Universal Life Church of its own, until *its* proprietor, who had an unfinished jail term for bank robbery in his curriculum vitae, was enjoined by his parole officer to stop ordaining ministers. In nearby Fort Lauderdale, there was still another Universal Life Church peddling ordinations, this one run by a man who also claimed to be the head of a foundation to help deprived Americans. Its particular beneficiaries were supposed to be needy Indians, but some spectacularly underprivileged Seminoles who lived practically next door to him turned out on investigation never to have heard of him.

Some mail-order crooks operating on the shady fringes of the respectable world profess to be less interested in investing their victims with credentials than in finding them jobs. At any given time, the Postal Inspection Service has fifty or so such operations under scrutiny. It takes a certain special knack to make a go of it in this field, and some of its veterans are practically professionals. Two men who were convicted of mail fraud in connection with an outfit they set up in Fort Worth called Universal Motel Training had earlier sponsored fake training courses in heavy-equipment maintenance, business administration, jet engineering, and, of all things, law enforcement. (There briefly flourished in San Juan, Puerto Rico, something called the Instituto Internacional de Criminologia, Inc., which sold worthless correspondence courses to Spanish-speaking individuals aspiring to become private detectives.) The National School of Airline Training, in Milwaukee, not only falsely promised its students jobs as stewardesses but lured them into its clutches by also alluding to free vacations in Hawaii. More than a thousand high school graduates hoping to find themselves working on the railroad shelled out more than half a million dollars to the National Railroad Institute, a dubious concern that blossomed in Georgia and Tennessee. Another establishment that proved alluring to high school graduates, most of these in the

Southeast, was the Nationwide Training Service, of Danville, Virginia, a state which until 1971 did little policing of so-called educational institutions. Attracting its victims with newspaper and magazine ads containing provocative questions like "Who says you can't earn $15,000 a year without a college education?" the Service would sign them up for courses in computer programming or accident-insurance adjusting. Postal Inspectors found that over a four-year stretch more than a thousand ambitious young people had paid more than $300,000 to this outfit; they were unable, however, to find a single student anywhere who as a result of his enrollment in a training course it offered had landed a job. Then there was the Texas School of Practical Nursing, a Dallas enterprise that aimed its solicitations at people who for the most part had never come close to finishing high school—largely indigent and ignorant women. A typical victim was a laundress who felt that getting thirty dollars for a forty-hour week was an unrewarding way of life. In her case, the Dallas place did actually lead her to a job of sorts, but it was hardly a giant step forward; she ended up with an unskilled position in a run-down nursing home, where she was required to put in seventy-two hours a week and where she received $31.25. The School of Practical Nursing did much better. Over one decade, *its* income—earned largely by very skilled flimflam—amounted to ten million dollars.

Across the years, high school graduates have been faithful patrons also of diploma mills, which are delighted to confer degrees upon people without putting them to the trouble of taking any classes or reading any books. Bretton Woods University, ostensibly with a campus at Manchester, New Hampshire, was merrily run for a while by some rascals in Indiana who conducted their operation exclusively by mail and never bothered to set foot in New England once they'd established themselves there by means of a post office box and a forwarding address. Bretton Woods U. at least did provide its degree-holders with handsome certificates. A slightly different institution of non-higher learning, or non-institute of higher learning, surfaced in 1965 and might still be going but for the alertness of a bank teller at the Central Home Trust Company, in Elizabeth, New Jersey, Mrs. Helen Ricker. She got suspicious when two young men came in one day to open an account in the name of Marlowe University, at nearby Mount Holly. Mrs. Ricker was familiar with that area and had never heard that it boasted a university. She stalled the applicants, explaining that she was about to go on vacation, and that the necessary paper work would take too long to be finished up beforehand. By the time she got back, an investigation—turned over to the Postal Inspection Service as soon as it became evident that Marlowe functioned largely by mail—had reached a point where, when the would-be depositors next materialized, they were greeted, and arrested, by three Postal Inspectors. The two men had $6,000 on them, but this was a trifle compared with the $200,000 they had taken in from lazy students, at the going rates of $400 for a Bachelor's or Master's degree and $500 for a Ph.D.

The pair proved to be, of all unlikely things, Orthodox rabbis from Brooklyn—Bernard Fuchs, twenty-two, and Gershon Tannenbaum, twenty-three. They had been recruited by the founder of the university and, following his practice, had been advertising in English-language educational journals that were circulated all over the world and that were widely read in American consulates and libraries abroad. The ads touted an academic program said to be "equivalent to the usual resident university course except that the student can easily complete it in only a few months." People who wrote in were often further enticed by a brochure that listed the names of a totally fictitious Marlowe faculty and staff; should any inquiries be addressed to any of these folk, Fuchs and Tannenbaum stood ready to reply under the appropriate false name. Each student who applied for admission was required to send along a down payment of one hundred dollars; if a thesis he then submitted was deemed satisfactory, he had—as soon as he remitted the balance of his tuition—earned his degree. It was very difficult to write a thesis, of whatever length or rationality, that did not pass muster. Once a student paid up in full, he never heard from his distant alma mater. Marlowe, accordingly, was in a technical sense not precisely a diploma mill; for its graduates never even had the satisfaction of receiving from its proprietors the kind of elegant but spurious piece of paper that most mills furnish their myriad benefactors.

As long as there are willing customers, there will doubtless be such mills, grinding out the stuff that nourishes dreams. Until recently, there was one in Alabama that ground out divorces. Postal Inspectors have better reason than most of us to know how frayed can be the bonds of matrimony, and how knotty their dissolution. There is not an Inspector alive who does not have his favorite matrimonial predator. Perhaps it is the Illinois man who, though he had a wife and eleven children, spent a good deal of his time proposing marriage to other women—or at any rate those who seemed willing to pay for the dubious privilege; he got a year and a day in prison. Perhaps it is the Texan man (wife, one child) who got a three-year term; his sole means of support consisted of meeting other women through correspondence clubs, marrying them, and relieving them of whatever assets he could get his hands on. (His excuse generally was that he needed some quick cash to make a killing in oil or cattle.) Before returning to his full-time wife, who apparently voiced no objection to his chosen profession, he would beat up each of his new wives and, as he walked out of their bruised lives, threaten them with a *real* dose of violence if they ever sought to track him down. In his wake he left a disillusioned trail of erstwhile pen pals, all ruefully reflecting how much less mighty is the pen than the sword.

The case of the Alabama divorce mill was a sad, protracted episode that resulted from the understandable eagerness of that state, which usually comes out near the bottom of all the states in most measurable statistics—per capita income, dentists per 100,000, per cent of literacy and so on—to achieve a kind of primacy, or at least to make a run at Nevada. The trouble began back in 1945, when the Alabama legislature, aware that the quick-divorce business can be big business, amended the state code of laws, putting into the section that dealt with divorce the words: "When the defendant is a nonresident, the other party to the marriage must have been a bona fide resident of this state for one year next before the filing of the bill, which must be alleged in the bill and proved, provided, however, the provisions of this section shall not be of force and effect when the court has jurisdiction of both parties to the cause of action." The proviso was the key phrase; what it meant was that if a court—usually a circuit court —had proper jurisdiction of the man and woman involved, then neither of them had to be a bona fide resident after all. The way the system worked was that an Alabama lawyer would file the complaint of one party with a court, and along with it an answer and a waiver from the other party. The presiding circuit judge would then designate somebody to take some testimony from the aggrieved party, and when this was presented to him, he would examine it and make his decision. If he granted the divorce, the matter was then settled, and all that remained was for his decree to be filed by his Register in Chancery. The procedure sounded elaborate, but inasmuch as the legislature prescribed no timetable for the various steps in it, they could all be taken virtually simultaneously. It was enough for a husband or wife, after his spouse had signed a waiver, to turn up in Birmingham or Montgomery or wherever and go home the next day divorced. For sixteen years, to the glee of some attorneys and most hotelkeepers, Alabama, a much more convenient port of severance for the populous Northeast than either Nevada or Mexico, flourished as a divorce haven. But there were other, staider Alabama lawyers who didn't like the reputation the state was getting as a divorce mill, and their scruples prevailed. On October 31, 1961, the state's Supreme Court, with the enthusiastic backing of the state's Bar Association, decreed that thenceforth any lawyer would be subject to disbarment if he handled a divorce case when he had reason to believe that one or more of the parties involved was not a genuine resident.

Most Alabama lawyers at once washed their hands of the out-of-state divorce business, but the new turn of events did not sit well with some who had built up fat practices in handling practically nothing else. Notable among these attorneys were three in Birmingham, J. Robert Huie, Kermit C. Edwards, and John Ike Griffith. They had too good a thing going to give it up, so, Supreme Court or no Supreme Court, they decided to keep it going. To do this, they soon perceived, would require some connivance from the bench, and they quickly found it—Huie and Edwards in the person of Judge Bob Moore, Jr., of the 25th Judicial Circuit, which embraced Marion and Winston Counties; Griffith in the person of Judge Frank O. Whitten, Jr., of the 30th Judicial Circuit (Blount and Saint Clair Counties). What they were up to was not especially secret. Judge Moore was charged in 1964, for instance, with having granted five thousand divorces to nonresidents, but he escaped chastisement when his superiors in the judicial hierarchy decided that the Bar Association's rules of ethics for lawyers didn't apply to judges.

The three attorneys were not so lucky. Huie was disbarred in March, 1967. He had a ready line of retreat; he got Edwards to sign all pertinent documents for his clients. Edwards was in due course disbarred himself, but was allowed to continue the general practice of law after filing an affidavit in 1969 stating that he would take no further part in divorce litigation. Griffith was also disbarred, and in the spring of 1970, moreover, was found guilty, in the state's Circuit Court for Jefferson County, of practicing law without a license.

None of these irritating incidents slowed the lawyers down appreciably. The two judges in cahoots with them suggested that they could and would readily grant divorces on the basis of *pro se* petitions—documents, that was, signed only by the parties to the divorce themselves, and nowhere bearing the imprint of a disbarred lawyer's involvement. The out-of-state clients, needless to say, were never informed that the reason their Alabama lawyers didn't sign any papers was because legally they couldn't sign them.

So the mill ground on, and between 1967 and 1970 the three attorneys and two judges grossed some $2.5 million in some 5,000 divorce suits—many of these involving residents of New Jersey, where the business of getting a divorce is conventionally expensive and protracted. All 5,000 couples—the bulk of the others were from New York, Connecticut, Virginia, Massachusetts, and Ohio—ended up with highly suspect divorces.

The way the mill worked was simple enough. A distraught couple in, say, New Jersey would hear how comparatively easy it was to get divorced in Alabama, would check with a local lawyer or with a recently divorced person, and would be referred to one of the three Birmingham men, whose shaky legal status was not nationally known. (Griffith, for instance, long after his disbarment, went on using letterheads and calling cards with "Attorney at Law" on them; the reverse side of his cards cited "Twelve Things to Remember"—among these the value of time, the dignity of simplicity, the wisdom of economy, the virtue of patience, and the joy of originating.) In due course, the man in Alabama would forward to the supplicant in New Jersey a packet of papers: a bill of complaint for one party to make out, an answer and waiver for the other, and an agreement between both.

Once these were in order, one of the parties would proceed to Birmingham, to complete the painless process. The three "lawyers" were ready for them. Huie and Edwards, for instance, had in their office an inventory of blank divorce forms (they are known to have bought at least 11,000 of these between 1965 and 1970), along with court seals for Judge Moore's circuit, the seal of his Register in Chancery, and rubber stamps bearing the signatures of both the Judge and the Register. At the lawyer's office, the out-of-state visitor would quickly declaim to a secretary some ground or other for wishing to be divorced (this to conform with the provision of the law about testimony for a judge to scrutinize), would hand over $465, which was the going fee for arranging everything (Huie, Edwards, and Griffith could manage ten clients a day, when operating in high gear), and would then head home, ostensibly free. Within a day or two, the traveler would receive in the mail what appeared to be a certified copy, embellished with signatures and seals, of an authentically filed and recorded divorce decree. Not every Northern lawyer was taken in by this swift business. One attorney in New Jersey instructed a woman client that when she reached Birmingham she should personally accompany her Alabama lawyer to a courthouse and witness the filing of her decree. When, in April, 1969, she proposed this to Edwards, the solicitor got furious, grabbed her arm, and generally behaved in a manner that she took to be threatening and that was certainly not solicitous.

Edwards' reluctance to accommodate his client was understandable, inasmuch as filing decrees was a chore the principals in the divorce mill found tiresome. A couple of times a month, perhaps chiefly to prevent overcrowding of their premises, the lawyers would trundle a batch of divorce documents over to the judges' offices, where these would be stashed away informally and, in the great majority of instances, never formally filed at all. Meanwhile, the recipients of the divorces innocently went their way—remarrying, having children by these new unions, making property settlements, and getting themselves into all sorts of situations that could—and may yet—take countless aboveboard lawyers years to straighten out.

That the five principals in the scheme were aware that they were engaged in criminal business can, considering their knowledge and experience, hardly be doubted. Here they were representing to people, and using the mails to do it, that they could deliver divorce papers properly made out, recorded, stamped, sealed, filed, and whatever, when in fact they were transmitting documents that were, in the words of three federal judges who heard an appeal on the case, "as worthless as a blank sheet of paper." Surely the principals knew that according to Alabama law every judicial circuit is supposed to send the state's Bureau of Vital Statistics, once each month, a list of all the divorces granted within its bounds. Yet of 3,800 divorces supposedly issued in Winston

County—part of Judge Moore's bailiwick—between 1963 and 1970, only 420 ever reached the Bureau. This discrepancy came to light when out-of-state individuals who for one reason or another needed further proof of the termination of an old marriage would write, or have a lawyer write, to the Bureau of Vital Statistics, and would of course receive no satisfaction.

Both the Alabama Bar Association and the Birmingham Bar Association—especially the latter's Special Unauthorized Practice of Law Committee—began digging into the puzzling affair. The fact that Judges Moore and Whitten were involved in it made it all the more suspicious; one civic group had tried to persuade the State Attorney General to start impeachment proceedings against Whitten in 1967, and the following year the Alabama Bar Association had tried in vain to trim the sails of Moore. Everybody seemed to know what these fellows were up to, but how to stop them was something else again. At some point or other, somebody thought of the five men's use of the mails. The upshot was a conference among a federal judge in Montgomery, the state capital, officials of the Alabama Bar Association, and Postal Inspector Charles E. Davis, the ranking resident member of the Service. There were further talks in Washington between Chief Postal Inspector Cotter and Frank Bainbridge, Jr., chairman of Birmingham's Unauthorized Practice of Law Committee.

Postal Inspectors, unlike narcotics or gambling agents, do not often indulge in dramatic raids or swoops. On August 13, 1970, however, sixteen of them assembled in Alabama—numerically a modest-sized posse, but even so 1 per cent of all the Inspectors in the country. At nine-fifteen the following morning, their watches carefully synchronized, warrants in hand, and their ranks augmented by volunteers from the Birmingham Bar Association, they simultaneously invaded ten premises—the lawyers' offices, Judge Moore's home and office, and six courthouses, at Ashville, Double Springs, Haleyville, Hamilton, Oneonta, and Pell City. The Inspectors by then had lists of dozens of individuals who thought they had legitimate Alabama divorces; what they wanted to find out was how many of these divorces had been duly registered. They found just three—all of them, it developed, relating to individuals who had gone to the trouble of requesting copies of their decrees. In Judge Moore's office, the raiders came upon 2,756 decrees he had issued between May, 1966, and July, 1970, only eighty-one of which he had ever bothered to sign by hand, and none of which he had passed along for filing. The Inspectors had thirty names of individuals for whom Judge Whitten had officiated; none of their divorces had been filed. After Whitten and Moore were both summarily removed from office by the Governor, the judge who succeeded Whitten found 2,286 unrecorded divorce papers in a locked closet in his office.

The raid took place on a Friday, and was extensively covered in the local press. On Sunday, August 16, a Palisades Park, New Jersey, woman flew into Birmingham. She had a date the following morning at Griffith's office. She checked into a hotel, rested up after her flight, and then walked out to find a restaurant to dine in. As she looked idly through the glass front of a sidewalk vending machine for the Birmingham *Sun*, her eye was caught by the disconcerting headline "QUICK RAIDS UNCOVER GIGANTIC DIVORCE RACKET." She bought a paper and read it while she was trying to eat dinner, for which she suddenly had no appetite. She flew home the next morning. She had lost her round-trip air fare from Newark, but at least she still had the $465 she had brought along to give to Griffith. She ultimately got her divorce in New Jersey.

It is never easy to bring judges and lawyers to justice. After a grand jury indicted the five accomplices, the defendants argued that their difficulties really stemmed from a squabble within the legal professsion and that, besides—a weighty contention in Alabama, where states' rights are uncommonly cherished—the federal courts had no business impinging on the business of local courts. Judge Moore dismissed the charges against him, to the press, as a "complete fabrication of a bunch of lies," and added, "When you get in a contest with a bunch of skunks, you're at a loss for weapons, so I have nothing to say." Notwithstanding, after two jury trials—one for the Huie-Edwards-Moore cabal and the other for Griffith and Whitten—all five men were found guilty and given both prison sentences and fines, a minimum of three years and ten thousand dollars apiece.

There remained the ticklish question of what, if anything, to do about the unfortunate individuals who for all they knew, if their divorces were invalid, might have committed bigamy, or spawned illegitimate children. Some Alabamans, out of compassion for their fellow Americans, hoped their state legislature could pass a retroactive law to, as one Birmingham lawyer put it, "legitimize all those bastards in New Jersey." But the state constitution seemed to prohibit the legislature from granting divorces, and there seemed little value in superimposing a question of unconstitutionality on an already thoroughly mixed-up situation. (The situation was particularly complicated for a Jersey man and woman who, before their Alabama divorce, had both been township officials in their home state; thinking it was just a formality, they had both sworn in writing that they were residents of Alabama, and now they became aware that they weren't supposed to hold their Jersey jobs, whatever their marital status, unless they were domiciled *there*.) The Alabama legislature, however, could and did delete from the state code the tricky proviso that had made all the trouble possible in the first place.

No court anywhere has yet passed, though, on the validity of the Alabama divorces themselves. The judge at the original trial of Edwards, Huie, and Moore had instructed the jury "that if you find from the evidence that a divorce decree from the Circuit Court of Winston County, or of the 25th Judicial Circuit of Alabama, was not signed by the Judge of that court and did not in some other way reflect that it was the decision of the court and was not filed or enrolled in the records of that court, then you would be justified in finding that such a decree was not a valid divorce decree." The three judges who rejected the convicted defendants' appeal concurred. "We believe this instruction to be eminently correct," they declared. "It takes no more understanding of Alabama legal principles to determine that these pieces of paper were not decrees than it would take to determine that a horse is not a cow under Alabama law. It should go without saying that a private party may not grant a divorce in Alabama or any other State. Only judges, acting in their capacity as judges, may alter an individual's legal status. This is exactly what the evidence tended to show that Edwards and Huie, with the assistance of Judge Moore, attempted to do. There is no evidence reflected in the record that Judge Moore ever considered the petitions filed in his office, acted on them, made any sort of judicial determination, or in any other sense rendered a decree. Instead, the evidence establishes the contrary. All acts in regard to these purported decrees were made by the disbarred attorneys and their secretaries, who had no semblance of power to so act. In short, the evidence establishes that there was in fact no judgment, no decree, no rendition, and no judicial act whatsoever. The defendants' customers thus paid for a divorce and got nothing."

There may be a lot of honest lawyers in New Jersey and elsewhere who will get plenty in the years ahead from trying to unravel the domestic affairs of those who got nothing. And if—as seems not unlikely with more than ten thousand ex-marriage partners involved—a woman who thinks she got divorced in the 25th Judicial Circuit of Alabama should marry a man who thinks he got divorced in the 30th, the possible confusion may be too appalling to contemplate. It might in the long run simplify matters to legitimize bigamy.

# 13. The Ghouls of Greenwich

On June 6, 1964, Alexander Kish, a senior vice-president of the Bridgeport branch of the Connecticut National Bank, began going through his office mail. He was sorry to find in it a letter from a man named Frank J. Freccia, reporting the untimely death, on May 29, of Freccia's brother-in-law, Clyde A. Banks. To expedite the disposition of some unfinished business Banks had with the bank, Freccia had enclosed a death certificate. Kish remembered the deceased well. He had come around quite recently—on April 24, the banker determined by checking his files—to take out a modest loan. He had been accompanied by his wife Emily—his bride, really, for they had been married on March 26. During the April visit, Mrs. Banks had done most of the talking. Under her maiden name of C. Emily Freccia, she and her brother Frank had for some twenty years run a business in Greenwich, the Meadowbrook Realty Company, she explained, and now they were planning to expand. Specifically, they wanted to open an outlet in Bridgeport, with the bridegroom, Mr. Banks, as its manager. To that end, they needed roughly five thousand dollars, to cover office furnishings and miscellaneous start-up expenses. Now, the woman went on, she realized she was unknown in Bridgeport; accordingly, she proposed opening a five-thousand-dollar savings account in the Connecticut National, and she would put her passbook up as collateral. The loan application was swiftly approved; after all, having its own savings account as collateral represented the kind of in-house security that appeals to a bank. Oh, there was one more thing, Mrs. Banks had said: She wanted the loan covered by an insurance policy on her husband's life. Such an arrangement is fairly common practice in such transactions. The bank routinely got in touch with the Union Mutual Insurance Company, and a policy was written up to cover Banks's life until the loan, a three-year one payable in thirty-six monthly installments, would be fully liquidated.

Now, on June 6, Kish's thoughts were only fleetingly drawn to the death certificate; it was the kind of document that moves a thousandfold across bankers' desks, and his responsibility was merely to see that it got passed along to Union Mutual and that the insurance company in due course fulfilled *its* responsibility. Kish was about to consign the Freccia letter and its enclosure to his out basket when he chanced to take a harder look at the certificate. The cause of death was reported on it as Hodgkin's disease. Kish had heard that the illness was one that destroyed its sufferers slowly and visibly. Then how could this Banks, as close to cancerous death as he must have been, have walked into the bank in apparently good health and have taken out a loan, and have perished even before a single one of the thirty-six payments had come due? Kish mulled over this anomaly for a few days, talked to some of his associates about it, and finally got in touch with the nearest Postal Inspector, Robert W. DeLong.

More often than not, mail-fraud investigations are initiated after a number of complaints, all of which together point to a probable pattern of deception. Here was a case, unusually, that began with a single inquiry from an individual who hadn't even been personally victimized—a case that, before DeLong and his fellow Inspector, Frank A. McAvoy, had finished with it, struck them as so special that they referred to it in their last report, prepared for inclusion in the Service's quarterly internal bulletin, as "The Macabre Case of the Ghoulish Loan Sharks." (Just as most laymen are frustrated criminologists, so apparently are many Postal Inspectors frustrated authors.) For it did not take the Inspectors long to ascertain that the widow Banks—if, indeed, she was a widow—was a woman of singularly disagreeable deportment. One of the first things they learned that made them wonder about her character was that although she claimed to have married Banks less than a month before his sudden demise, she had not bothered to attend his funeral. She hadn't even sent flowers.

In more ways than that, Carmela Emily Freccia—or C. Emily Freccia, as the woman in the piece preferred to be known—was strikingly at variance with her environment. Greenwich, Connecticut, is, after all, one of the most genteel of the nation's affluent suburbs, and Emily Freccia, though hardly prototypical of the community, was no alien import to it. She had been born there, in 1916, had gone to secretarial school in the area, and as far as is known had, before she met Banks, never been married, though she had been arrested a few times—once for motor theft, once for forgery, and, as recently as October, 1963, for usury. But she had no convictions on her record. One reason may have been that when she came to trial on the loan-sharking charge, the witnesses who had been expected to testify against her suddenly changed their minds. Behind the front of Meadowbrook Realty, usury was her principal business, and she could be a tough businesswoman to deal with. Her collectors, or enforcers, were firm in their demands. One shopkeeper who had borrowed money from her, for instance—she generally charged 20 per cent interest a *week* on her loans—had an understanding with her that he would make his regular payments every Tuesday evening, at the close of his business; but her collectors, perhaps not wanting to stay up late, kept coming around earlier and earlier, to the anguish of the borrower. Another time, this same shopkeeper, who was in debt to Miss Freccia for five and a half years, put up two thousand dollars' worth of his wife's jewelry as security against a fifteen-hundred-dollar loan, but that wasn't enough; Miss Freccia also insisted on a second mortgage on his shop and on his cash register. Miss

Freccia's principal associate in this rigorous business, her brother Frank, had been born in Italy and was five years her senior. He had only one arrest on his record; at about the same time that his sister was picked up for usury, he was accused of illegally trapping woodpeckers. Inspectors McAvoy and DeLong did not concern themselves with this episode; many crimes can be related to the use, or misuse, of the mails, but snaring birds is not normally among them.

As soon as Kish expressed his puzzlement to the Inspectors, they began looking into Miss Freccia's affairs and Mr. Banks's involvement with them. The questionable bank loan might have been an isolated incident, of course; then again, it might not. It was not. Clyde Banks, it developed, had been exceedingly busy in the last anguished years of his life. Between August 31, 1962, and April 24, 1964, Banks—or someone purporting to be Banks—had borrowed a total of $73,999.96 from eleven banks in Connecticut and adjacent Westchester County in New York, nearly every time giving the same spiel about a new branch of Meadowbrook Realty, and every time with an insurance policy riding along with the loan. He had further purchased (on an installment basis, with the financing again underwritten by insurance on his ebbing life) a fleet of motor vehicles worth $50,228.64. What was most astonishing about it all was that on almost every day that Banks was supposed to be out on a borrowing or buying spree he was in fact in bed at a veterans' hospital at West Haven, Connecticut, where he was being treated, to the extent that any treatment was possible, for his fatal disease. The only vehicle in his name that he had ever sat behind the wheel of was a ramshackle 1957 Ford worth about $400.

Banks was not the sort of person who would have impressed a banker, or even a shopkeeper. Born in 1916, ten months younger than Emily, he was a native of Georgia. He had never got beyond the fourth grade in school, and he worked, when he worked at all, as a truck driver. He served in the Navy during the Second World War, and had a monthly pension of $77.67. He was single, but had been married three times, most recently to a practical nurse who had remarried after their divorce (or probable divorce; she got it in Winston County, Alabama, in November, 1962). Banks settled in Greenwich sometime before the spring of 1961, and got a job as a truck driver for a bakery. Needing some cash at one point, he approached the Freccias, who graciously loaned him $600, for which he was expected, without unreasonable delay, to return a thousand. They also sometimes let him park his Ford in a used-car lot they operated as a sideline, for which they charged him a storage fee.

Their interest in him quickened in the spring and summer of 1961. He complained then of a swelling in his groin, and they introduced him to their own doctor. Following some tests, including a biopsy, the grim diagnosis was revealed: Hodgkin's disease. Banks was not then yet divorced, and his wife came around to talk to the Freccias, who were recognized financial experts in their own way, about a matter of child support. When Mrs. Banks, based on her nursing background, said her husband was unlikely to live much longer, Emily Freccia proposed that she take out a large insurance policy on her husband's life, but the nurse said that would never work; in applying for *that* kind of policy, a man would surely have to take a physical examination, and his uninsurable condition would quickly be disclosed.

It seemed to the Freccias that *somebody* should benefit from the doomed man's passing. Why not them? So they hit upon the scheme of defrauding the banks and car dealers and insurance companies; in such transactions, insurance companies did not demand physical exams. Two men who had been involved in Emily's life and loan-sharking were pressed into service to help carry out the plan. One was Joseph A. Mastocciolo, or Joe Masto, who ran a taxi and school bus business across the Westchester County line, in Larchmont, New York. The other was Frank A. Doeberl, of Riverside, Connecticut, a suburb of Greenwich, who was an appliance salesman when he was honorably employed. Frank Doeberl had one unique asset for participation: He looked extraordinarily like Clyde Banks. Indeed, at a preliminary hearing just before the Freccias were indicted for mail fraud, one automobile salesman told Inspector McAvoy that he doubted he could be a good witness for the government because he had heard someone say that Banks was dead. Yes, said the Inspector; that, alas, was true. "Not the Clyde Banks I did business with," said the auto man. "He's sitting right over there." He pointed to Doeberl. Needless to say, the salesman turned out to be a very good witness indeed.

And so, with Banks getting frailer every day, and spending more and more of his time in the veterans' hospital, the conspirators went on assiduously taking his name in vain. By the time he was close to death, they had borrowed so much in his name that their total interest charges were running to about three thousand dollars a month. They could always defray these, naturally, by taking out more loans, but there was a limit to the number of banks and dealers in their region. So although Banks had been invaluable to them, he was getting to be a nuisance. When he was released from the hospital for a spell, and receiving injections as an outpatient to help alleviate his pain, he turned up one day for a scheduled shot and was told by the nurse who was supposed to administer it that she'd had a phone call from the hospital office telling her not to. It turned out later that no one in a position of authority had made any such call; the Postal Inspectors could only surmise that someone who wished to expedite Banks's departure had placed it.

There remained, though, one last potential drop of income to be squeezed out of the dying man's corpse—his estate, if any. So on March 26, at Fishkill, New York, a justice of the peace was glad to oblige Emily Freccia and Clyde Banks and proclaim them man and wife. The witnesses were Frank Freccia and Joseph Mastocciolo. The real Clyde Banks was not present on the scene. Inasmuch as Frank Doeberl was not a witness, he may have played another role, for which by then he had had much practice. Emily was not a successful widow; she was not aware that the V.A. does not recognize the rights of last-minute mates. Nor was she a doting wife. She continued to charge her "husband" for using her used-car lot. She had earlier persuaded him to have his pension checks sent to her office, and she would then endorse and cash them by forging his name. A few days before he died, Banks—who of course did not know that he was supposed to have a new wife—begged the Freccias through his ex-wife for his pension money, or, failing that, for at least a five-dollar advance against it, so he could buy some cigarettes at the hospital canteen. His request was ignored, and his ex-wife, who was at his bedside when he died and who ultimately attended to his funeral arrangements, gave him a few dollars. He was by then flat broke; not long before, in filling out a V.A. form, he had listed as his only and total assets his four-hundred-dollar car.

On the same day that he was itemizing that decrepit vehicle, he was also, on paper at least, the owner of a school bus, a pickup truck, a jeep with a snowplow, three Chevrolets, and five Cadillacs. Two of the Cadillacs and the school bus were in Larchmont, Mastocciolo territory. A son of Mastocciolo's was riding around in one rakish Chevrolet convertible, and a son of Frank Freccia's in another. Frank Doeberl had a robin's-egg-blue Cadillac convertible. There was still another car that belonged to a man who had nothing to do with the fraud; wanting to buy a new automobile, he had mentioned this to Emily Freccia, and she had said she would obtain it for him at a bargain price. The man had been paying her twenty dollars a week on it for some months—without ever getting a receipt—and was horrified when the Postal Inspectors advised him that he had no equity in it whatever, inasmuch as it was registered in the name of Clyde A. Banks.

Let not the women's liberationists believe that females are never judged by the same standards that apply to males. Sometimes, when they deserve more than males, they get more. After a federal jury found both Freccias guilty of mail fraud, the judge who sentenced them (at one point in the proceedings, he said that their acts were the most ruthless he'd ever heard of) gave Frank a four-year prison term and a fine of fifteen thousand dollars. Emily, befitting the member of the family who had always been its real driving force, got five years and twenty-five thousand.

# 14. The Franchise Hustlers

In the 1960s, to the delight of assorted purveyors of hamburgers, fried chicken, and other commodities apparently indispensable to the American way of life, there was a boom in franchises. Some of these ventures proved to be remarkably lucrative, and anything that involves money is certain to attract the attention of those Americans who specialize in making it illegally and those others at whose anguished cost they make it. Nobody knows, for instance, exactly how many individuals' fantasies of near-instant wealth were stirred by an advertisement that appeared in newspapers and magazines across the nation in the mid-sixties: "Exclusive Franchise: Amazing new liquid plastic coating used on all types of surfaces interior or exterior. Eliminates waxing when applied on Asphalt Tile, Vinyl, Linoleum, Vinyl Asbestos, Hard Wood and Furniture. Completely eliminates painting when applied to Wood, Metal, or Concrete surfaces. This finish is also recommended for boats and automobiles."

A Portland, Oregon, man read about the chance to cash in on this exciting new product in *Firm Foundation,* a religious magazine published in Austin, Texas. Anything appearing in a journal with so rock-solid a name and with a churchly orientation to boot was bound to elicit confidence. The Portland man got in touch with the sponsors of the ad, the Chem-Plastics and Paint Corporation, then in Saint Louis, and almost immediately a smooth-talking Chem-Plastics agent came around to see him. He was happy to be able to disclose to the Oregonian that nobody else had yet put in a bid to handle Pylon, as the paint was called, in his territory, and that for the trifling sum of $3,000 he could obtain exclusive rights to it not only in Portland itself but in eight adjacent counties. The paint would cost $6.00 a gallon wholesale and at the recommended retail price of $11.95 there would be a fat profit of $5.95 a gallon for the distributor, and if his business got so big that he had to hire salesmen to assist him, he could still count on $2.95 a gallon for himself from their achievements. The Portland man was shown a sheaf of testimonials from other dealers—he had no way of knowing, alas, that these were pure fabrications—attesting to their satisfaction and success: Here, just at random, was a chap in Michigan who in his very first year of operation was disposing of 1,500 gallons a month, for an annual gross profit of $108,000. Who would not wish to be cut in for a piece of that kind of action!

The amount of exclusive territory that a person could command, and its price, depended on the size of his initial orders from Chem-Plastics. Three thousand dollars was the fee for a 500-gallon-a-month outlet; a 1,000-gallon-a-month franchise went for $7,000. Whatever the dimensions of an approved area, the Chem-Plastics representative would assure his prospect, the parent company stood ready to furnish all sorts of helpful services. For a mere $144.25, it would provide 5,000 pieces of direct-mail promotion, not to mention an eye-catching assortment of window streamers, counter display cards, and brochures. Moreover, Chem-Plastics would mail postcards—these would cost $28.75 per thousand—to everybody listed in the classified telephone book within a given franchise area. Purchasers of this particular service, the Portland man was told, should make out their checks to "Postmaster." What the Oregonian and others like him could not know was that the men taking their money were using these last checks to buy stamps to expedite their plucking of additional pigeons.

As still another service provided by the parent company, prospects were told that Chem-Plastics would be sending around a man to help them get started, and would also furnish a detailed technical manual, which was reverently described as the "Bible." By the time a potential Pylon dealer had heard all of this, he could often hardly wait to sign up for a franchise, and in his eagerness he failed to reflect soberly on one mischievous little kicker in the standard contract, which obliged him to sell his entire initial shipment of paint within thirty days of closing the deal or to forfeit his franchise; this requirement would turn out to be hard to fulfill, inasmuch as the consignment sometimes didn't arrive until a few days before the deadline. The paint was real enough, but it had none of the magical qualities attributed to it; it was ordinary paint that Chem-Plastics bought for two dollars a gallon, thus assuring itself of a four-dollar-a-gallon profit over and beyond its franchise fees.

The dreams thus inspired in the Northwest had their counterparts across the country. A man in Denver saw the come-on advertisement in the *Post,* and after an inquiring phone call to Saint Louis, betook himself there, assured that his expenses would in due course be reimbursed. He elected to apply for a $7,000 franchise—most of Colorado, part of Wyoming, and an option on all of Utah—and a few days later a beaming Chem-Plastics official turned up in Denver to consummate the arrangements. The Denver man was impressed when his new business associate insisted on receiving the $7,000 in the form of a certified check. It is an old confidence-game trick for the betrayers to insist on proof of probity on the part of the betrayed.

At about the same time, a Boston man was happily shelling out $3,000 for a large chunk of New Hampshire and an option on some of the most desirable acreage in Vermont. All told, over a four-year period, at least three hundred people expended at least $1.5 million only to discover too late that they had painted themselves into a corner. There were six recipients of their generosity, principal among them a man named Harold E. Pritchard, who in earlier incarnations, as a used-car salesman, had been partial to such designations as Wild Man Pritchard and the Smiling Irishman. Pritchard had a real flair for malpractice. To coat his paint-franchise scheme with a veneer of respectability, he once circulated a Dun & Bradstreet report on his company, which stated, based on figures provided by Pritchard, that its net profits for one six-month period in 1964 had come to $78,052. But he took pains to delete from his version of the report a crucial Dun & Bradstreet caveat: "Under investigation; further report will follow." At the same time that Pritchard was proclaiming his profitability to Dun & Bradstreet, he was complaining to the Internal Revenue Service that the business was operating at a loss.

The good thing that Pritchard and his confreres had going for them began to turn sour thanks to a man who had quite literally got the runaround from them. He was an upstate New Yorker who will here be known, as there is no need to further embarrass the already hugely abashed, as Ernest Thompson. *He* had read about the available franchise early in 1964 in no less redoubtable a medium than the *Wall Street Journal,* which had no particular reason to question the motives of the advertisement Pritchard's group had inserted. Thompson had been invited to visit the paint company executives in a suite of offices they briefly maintained at Orlando, Florida, had been impressed by their spiel, and was delighted to learn that he was being seriously considered for New York, New Jersey, and Washington, D.C. Happening to return to Orlando not long afterward, he had been surprised to find the offices abandoned, but he pursued Pritchard and his accomplices by telephone, and finally tracked them down to Saint Louis. Then he hurried out there; rarely has a man exhibited such determination to get nothing for something.

In Missouri, Thompson was slightly put off because he couldn't get to visit the factory the Chem-Plastics Company supposedly operated (the excuse given him was that a change of facilities was under way), nor could he wangle a meeting with Pritchard, who always seemed to be tied up in an important conference. But the Smiling Irishman's unavailability merely reinforced Thompson's conviction that he was a businessman of consequence. And the New Yorker was further cheered by being introduced, ostensibly through long-distance telephone calls, to several Pylon dealers, in Houston, Los Angeles, and elsewhere, who rattled on enthusiastically about their franchises; he had no way of knowing that they were actually confederates of Pritchard sitting in the next room. All fired up, Thompson signed a contract, and was overjoyed when his new associates as a reward for his perseverance bestowed upon him southern Florida and the Virgin Islands. The best place from which to supervise such a far-flung enterprise, he concluded, would be Washington, D.C., so he hied himself there and made a down payment on a suite of offices.

In March, 1965, a sadly disillusioned Thompson hied himself further to the Better Business Bureau. It seemed that at a party, quite by accident, he had run into a man from Greenwich, Connecticut, and they had got to talking about their respective business ventures, and all of a sudden they discovered that they had something peculiar in common; each thought he was Chem-Plastics' representative in New York State. The Greenwich man, who also had Fairfield County, Connecticut, in his theoretical geographical pocket, ultimately squandered fifteen thousand dollars on his Pylon caper; hoping to recoup *something* from his debacle, he offered to sell Thompson several thousand gallons of paint. Thompson by then was trying to unload a similar inventory of his own.

Concurrently, disillusionment was setting in all over the country. The Portland, Oregon, man had seen another advertisement in a local paper: A salesman was wanted by a company called National Chem-Plastics, which was a corporate name Pritchard had switched to when he decided to switch his base of operations from Saint Louis to Las Vegas. The Portland man followed up on the ad, and was surprised to learn that there was another fellow in town peddling Pylon. The first Oregonian reproachfully called company headquarters in Las Vegas and was not completely mollified by its explanation that the second one was supposed to be a regional sales representative functioning on his behalf. Meanwhile, the fellow in Denver had dismayingly run into two other holders of exclusive rights in his territory, or their territory, or whosever territory it might turn out to be. And none of the three, they discovered on comparing notes on their troubling shared experience, had ever received the much-touted manual, the "Bible" that was supposed to be their guide to the land of milk and honey. There was good reason for this, the Postal Inspection Service would subsequently come to realize: Pritchard's Gospel was not only apocryphal; it did not exist.

A number of victims who expressed misgivings to the Better Business Bureau were advised to get in touch with the Inspection Service, which had a built-in interest in the case inasmuch as the mails had been used for, among other things, the transmittal of checks made out to "Postmaster" that were not used for the purposes their senders had been led to believe were intended. The investigation was turned over to Inspector John A. Schicker, of Saint Louis, and as he interviewed one sadder and wiser franchise holder after another, he compiled a touching catalogue of mischief. There was one man who, disgusted with the inferior quality of the paint Pritchard's people had shipped him, had sent it back, demanding a replacement, and on top of his other losses had accordingly had to foot a $133 freight bill. Schicker, after revelatory colloquies in Portland, Denver, and upstate New York, where Thompson told him of one breath-taking outing—a trip, no less, in a private airplane from Philadelphia to Syracuse, with a recently discharged Air Force pilot in Pritchard's employ at the controls—finished his investigation at the start of 1966, and as a result Pritchard and five of his accomplices were indicted for mail fraud. Ultimately all six were convicted, and they received sentences ranging from thirty months in prison and a $500 fine to, in Pritchard's case, ten years and $5,000. Furthermore, the cost of the trial was calculated at $12,231, and each of the defendants was ordered to pay one-sixth of that amount. They had to meet this obligation in hard cash, a circumstance that may have given some of their victims a small measure of satisfaction, for they, after they had trekked to Saint Louis or Las Vegas and had requested the promised reimbursement of their travel expenses, had, when they received anything at all, been recompensed merely in the form of additional quantities of the paint they had begun to wish they'd never heard of in the first place.

Most of the paint-franchise losers were middle-class Americans who were simply trying to move a rung or two up the slippery economic ladder, and who instead of scaling new heights tumbled crashingly to earth. Another fraudulent franchise operation was aimed, with startling accuracy, at a much similar group—at carpenters, plumbers, and ready-mix-concrete dealers, more than five hundred of whom, with singular unanimity of foolishness, succumbed to the blandishments of five honey-voiced men who convinced them they were going to prosper through exclusive franchises to build and sell swimming pools. It was a swindle of epic proportions, for a swimming pool is just about the largest tangible object ever used as a flimflam, and the spectacular success of its perpetrators demonstrated, if nothing else, the possibility that a close relationship exists between a hole in the ground and a hole in the head.

Operating variously under the business names of Bermuda Pools, Town and Country Pools, and—this one was pure genius—the Cinderella Pool Corporation, the five men managed to gross a million or so dollars from victims in five states without ever going to the trouble themselves of actually constructing a single pool. This case was unraveled by Postal Inspector Doyle C. Marshall, based in Denver, and he first got into it when a complaint was lodged in May, 1963, by two Oklahoma plumbers, each of whom had been told that his fortunate attainment of an exclusive franchise would enrich him by something like forty thousand dollars a year—a figure that sounded good even to plumbers. They were not the only two victims, Inspector Marshall would presently discover, whose supposedly exclusive territories overlapped. There were four other victims, for instance, each of whom thought he had a stranglehold on the entire southern half of Idaho.

The mastermind of this novel scheme was one Clair C. Wagner, for a time a schoolteacher and after that an itinerant home-improvement salesman until he aspired to higher things. With the help of four congenial assistants who were adept at playing interchangeable roles—vice-president in charge of dealerships, head of the engineering department, regional sales manager, or whatever title came handily to mind—he would telephone contractors listed in various classified directories. He was about to license a swimming pool dealer in the victim's neighborhood, Wagner would say, and he was looking for somebody with the right background who could dig pool foundations. There would be a lot of such work, for surveys just conducted for Bermuda Pools (or Cinderella Pools or whatever) had revealed a slew of customers, and a staff of salesmen was at that moment hustling about rounding up even more. Would the contractor be interested in coming to Denver—all expenses paid, naturally—to discuss the matter? There would be as his reward for taking the trouble, incidentally, if the parties concerned could come to an understanding, one absolutely free pool kit, so he could build a model pool; and at the time of installation the Denver company would be happy to send one of its engineers around to supervise the details. If all went well, there would of course be a slight deposit required from the contractor, merely as an instance of good faith. Criminals persistently demand good faith from their patsies.

Everyone knows how special a symbol the swimming pool has become of the increasing affluence and leisure time of the American middle class. Without any further checking, people telephoned by Wagner and his henchmen flocked by the dozens to Denver. There they were warmly received and, in a seemingly casual way, taken to look at the gaudy swimming pool at the Celebrity Sports Center, which the visitors were permitted to infer had been built by their hosts, though in fact they had had nothing to do with it. Discussions would get under way, and as a rule a hitch would quickly develop: Bermuda Pools wanted a firm estimate to cover each and every excavation. The visitors would demur, explaining that no one in his right mind could do that; you never did know in advance what site problems there might be, with slopes and underground rock and so forth and so on. The promoters of the scheme would then shrug and say all that was of little account; the *real* money in swimming pools accrued to the dealers who marketed them—$498 net profit for the 12 × 24 foot size, $785 for the 12 × 27, $1,315 for the 20 × 40, and for the most popular of four standard varieties, the 16 × 34, an even $1,000 for each and every pool installed. At this intelligence, the visitor would more often than not start wondering, and then asking, whether there was an opening for a dealership in his territory. Why be just a contractor? Why not also be the dealer himself?

The fish had cleanly taken the bait. His hosts would reply that that was a capital idea, but they were very much afraid that particular dealership had already been allotted. There would be a flurry of fake telephone calls to the vice-president in charge of Montana franchises. Had the deal pending for that territory gone through? Oh. Well, how far in the works was it? Had the richly illustrated brochures and irresistible advertising copy already been got up with somebody else's name on it? Ah, not yet! Well, then, there was this chap right in the office, splendid fellow, hotshot prospect, and couldn't they bend the rules a bit and swing the franchise over to him? They could? Congratulations! Handshakes all around, and a drink or two at the nearest bar.

Dazed by his luck, the victim would like as not accede passively to what he was next told: that he would have to start right in on his display pool—its basic ingredients would naturally be furnished him at no cost—even if it was in the dead of winter, but that he would in time benefit from his quickness, because it was company policy to let each dealer have his display pool for his own use after he'd shown it to customers for two years. Then, as a franchise agreement was being hastily drawn up, the new dealer would be told that of course some show-of-faith money would be expected from him. The sum was not fixed. Sometimes the pool sharks would ask for twelve thousand dollars, sometimes for less, but whatever they asked they explained that the funds advanced would ultimately be returned in the form of a five-hundred-dollar discount on each completed pool. Investigating the case, Inspector Marshall found that in one instance Wagner, perhaps desperate for ready cash, had let the acquirer of a new franchise off for a mere one hundred dollars.

The delighted apprentice dabbler in exclusivity would rush home, more often than not, and at once start tearing up his own back yard, or, if he didn't have one large enough, would prevail on a neighbor or relative to lend him a piece of land. His own regular business might suffer a bit while the digging was going on, but what did that matter? The important thing was to get the display pool finished so that Wagner's salesmen and advertising representatives, who he had the impression were legion, could start beating the bushes to sell its counterparts. As soon as the excavation, footings, wall construction, and basic plumbing were ready, he was to notify the Denver office, which would send him its standard display kit—a vinyl liner, rubber copings for the pool edges, a filtering system, a ladder, a diving board, and necessary couplings. These were not cheap—they cost Wagner about $500 a set—but when they arrived, they were accompanied by C.O.D. charges of from $2,240 to $2,990.

Surely there was some mistake. The puzzled dealer would grab the phone, call Denver, and remind Wagner's office that the pool kit was supposed to be free. Oh, no, he would be told; he must have misunderstood. If he got argumentative, as he more often than not did, he would be assured that although he was mistaken, the company would make him a special concession and credit him with 10 per cent of the C.O.D. charges on each of the first ten pools he sold. What could the poor man do? He already had a considerable investment in his hole in the ground. And what was an extra couple of thousand against an almost sure annual income twenty times that great? So most of the contractors paid the C.O.D.

charges. Those who still refused to were told crushingly that they had thereby forfeited their franchises. As Inspector Marshall put it in one of his reports, "Numerous dealers have holes in their yards but no pools because they would not pay anything to get the display pool kits."

Those dealers who accepted their kits then waited for the engineer who was supposed to come around and help put them together, but who never seemed to materialize. Nor did the salesmen who were supposed to be hot on his heels. Usually the dealers finished off their pools as well as they could by themselves. None of them ever sold a single pool to anyone else, since they could not mention the parent company without losing their temper. It did not take Inspector Marshall long, after listening to some of their impassioned laments, to amass enough evidence to have Wagner and his associates indicted for mail fraud, and they were subsequently convicted and jailed. As for the dealers, most of them had inadvertently moved up the social scale a notch or so. They had each acquired a swimming pool, albeit often a terribly expensive one, and every time they plunged into it, if they could bring themselves to, they could reflect, if they cared to, that they had truly taken a bath.

# 15. A Big Bump

The basic concept of insurance is that it is supposed to protect people against loss of life and property, or against injury and damage. But it has also been used, like practically every other invention of man, to turn a dishonest dollar. A professional banjo player whose musical pickings were slim managed to moonlight quite rewardingly by staging fake falls in supermarkets. He would profess to slip on a banana peel or gob of melted ice cream and would lie on the floor howling and demanding to be taken to a hospital, and would ultimately, more often than not, accept a settlement from an insurance company in lieu of a protracted wrangle over the cause of his convincing tumbles. Ultimately he came a cropper, in a nonphysical way, when he aroused suspicion by enacting his chosen role twice in a single day, at 2 P.M. in a Frederick, Maryland, store, and then at 7:50 that same evening on the premises of a Danville, Pennsylvania, establishment.

There have been numerous instances of people setting up phony insurance companies to bilk their fellow citizens. A popular procedure is to sell coverage, at appealingly low rates, to automobilists who are such proven bad risks that orthodox companies won't have anything to do with them. The sellers can afford their bargain rates because their insurance is nonexistent; whatever premiums they collect constitute a net profit. An even more common practice in a land where mischief abounds is the conning of legitimate insurance companies into paying claims on perfectly bona-fide policies, but for spurious reasons. A clever Alabama man would rent cars, change their identification numbers, and "sell" them to a confederate, who would have them insured under the new numbers. Then the Alabaman would restore the original numbers and return the cars to the rental agencies; simultaneously, his confederate would report the cars stolen and collect on the losses from his insurers. At least sixteen insurance companies were defrauded between 1964 and 1972 by a ring of Chicago scalawags who would capitalize on real automobile accidents. They were able to do this because their numbers included five policemen assigned to traffic duty. At the scene of a crash, the cops would jot down the participants' names and turn them over to a lawyer; he would quickly send around an emissary (a white one for white people, a black one for blacks) who would urge them, even though they said they hadn't been hurt, to have themselves hospitalized. The lawyer would provide them with doctors and, on a contingency basis, would submit claims on their behalf to insurance companies. It was a profitable operation; each of the policemen involved was on a ten-thousand-dollar-a-year retainer.

Then there was a family in Pennsylvania whose twenty adult members worked practically full time pretending to be hurt in car accidents. They would buy hospitalization insurance galore; would then persuade an innocent doctor to have them hospitalized for this allegedly aching back or that supposedly whiplashed neck; and would next, using their own photostating equipment, send copies of their paid-up hospital bills to each insurer—perhaps as many as twenty claims for a single painless institutionalization. Over one industrious stretch, the family racked up ninety hospitalizations, filed nine hundred claims, and collected $180,000. Their racket ended abruptly when a couple of careless insurance companies, instead of remitting directly to the insured persons, reimbursed the same hospital for the same hospitalization, which brought about an investigation and several households' worth of convictions.

Variations on this roguish theme have been played, fortissimo, from coast to coast. Louisiana, for instance, is a state with motoring habits not significantly more atrocious than those of any other, but for a year and a half, not long ago, there were heard in areas of it such rending of metal and shattering of glass and groaning of apparent victims as to make some of the population loath to take a Sunday drive. It was only after much howling on the part of insurance adjusters and much prowling on the part of Postal Inspectors that the cause of all this clatter came to light: It was an accident-insurance ring at work, whose 160 members included not only an unsurprising number of run-of-the-mill quick-buck artists but also, surprisingly, two dentists, seven doctors, and nine lawyers, all of whose professional ethics were conspicuously substandard.

An investigation of this ring, conducted largely by Postal Inspectors Charles Ellis, George Heaberg, and Augustus Statham, eventually revealed that during an eighteen-month period, starting in April, 1965, the group had staged a known thirty-six collisions, and had garnered $235,000 from twenty-six insurance companies, all of which would regret that they were not privy to the identity of each other's claimants. For in fourteen of the thirty-six accidents, either Kenneth DeMary or his brother Larry, a couple of Lake Charles ne'er-do-wells, was a participant. The crashes they put on generally involved just two cars, one of which they designated "the hitter" and the other "the target." The *sine qua non* for the hitter was that it have ample liability insurance, and the protagonists in these dramas sometimes used rented cars, knowing that these were always well covered. (Once they slipped up and used a vehicle whose liability insurance had lapsed just before it rammed into an old truck at a crossroads, shaking up half a dozen ready victims to no avail.) The target vehicle was often an older car with built-in scrapes and dents. One time, it was a 1961 Corvair, and when—Ralph Nader would no doubt have been amazed to hear it—a taxicab smashed into its rear at a stop sign, the two concerned drivers agreed, on examining the damage, that it wasn't severe enough to seem genuine. So they drove around the block and had a second collision. One very old car destined to be a target wouldn't even start at the time of its prearranged demolition, so the hitter vehicle towed it to the scene of the accident, disengaged itself, went around behind it, and gave it a resounding whack.

The more people involved in an accident, the more claims could be filed, and there were often half a dozen passengers in the two vehicles. These were mainly individuals eager to make a couple of hundred dollars for a few minutes' not excessively arduous work, and the DeMarys would recruit them at bars and nightclubs. Once, they spontaneously mustered a crew from the guests at a barbecue. When one man there remarked that his wife was pregnant, Larry DeMary urged him to get her into the act. But might that not be risky in view of her delicate condition? her husband wondered. Not at all, said Larry; he had used his own wife when *she* was pregnant. "If you brace yourself," he said, "it's no worse than hitting a big bump or something."

The top pay went to the driver of the hitter, who had to be skilled enough to mess up two vehicles and at the same time leave their occupants more or less intact. When one accomplished hitter-driver turned out to have an invalid operator's license, his sponsors hastily escorted him to the nearest motor vehicle bureau to get his credentials in order. Occasionally there were slip-ups. One of the doctors in the scheme, who normally just pretended to treat feigned injuries, did once actually have to remove a sliver of glass from a young woman's eye. The doctors were apprised of the accident schedule in advance, so that they could conveniently arrange to be at a hospital to welcome the ambulance they knew the "victims" in the crash would be summoning. (One time, waiting for an ambulance to arrive, a couple of the participants, concluding that they looked too healthy, slashed themselves with Coke bottles; meanwhile, the driver of the hitter vehicle was kicking out a windshield and the rest of that incident's cast of characters were lustily pounding away at fenders.) The so-called victims rarely had any difficulty getting admitted to hospitals, however raffish their backgrounds, because they asked to have their bills submitted to one of a number of attorneys of impeccable standing in the community.

The payoffs were sometimes impressively rewarding. One time a young woman drove her own car into the rear of her boyfriend's car. She had been cajoled into taking part out of pure affection, and as a result she received no payment other than to have the damage to her own vehicle repaired; but the four passengers in the target car, including both DeMarys, put on so convincing a show of agony that by the time all the claims were settled up one insurance company had paid out $13,125.51, including the cost of an upper plate for one passenger who didn't need it and the capping of a tooth for another who'd broken it when he was in elementary school. The lawyer supervising this accident felt constrained to reprimand its participants, too many of whom, he told them severely, had gone to the same dentist immediately afterward.

The lawyers handled most of the financial arrangements. Whoever the actors were in the clanging dramas, they would allot their share of the insurance proceeds to the attorneys, in advance, and would receive a flat fee of from one hundred to three hundred dollars on signing. (One regular hitter was fined seventy-five dollars by a lawyer for permitting a girl who was still a minor to ride in his car; after the "accident" in which she was involved, her father insisted on turning over her claim to his own lawyer, who was not in on the plot.) If there were six actors in one accident, they would generally be divided up as clients among two lawyers, who would instruct them which doctors would be treating whom. The lawyers tried to overlook nothing; on behalf of one "victim" they collected one hundred fifty dollars for the damage to a ten-dollar wristwatch. When Larry DeMary asked one of the attorneys how many faked accidents he thought he could safely take on, the lawyer answered, "Don't stop bringing them until I holler." He did suggest, though, that there had been a superfluity of rear-end collisions, and that it might be a good idea to vary the pattern by having a few of the hitter-drivers strike their targets broadside.

There was indeed a suspicious parallelism in some of the incidents, as the insurance companies and Postal Inspectors came to realize when they got to work on the case. A garage attendant who was involved in several rear-end crashes as a hitter claimed one time to have lost control of his vehicle because he had dropped a cigar on the floor and was bending to pick it up; another time his story was that he'd fleetingly taken his eyes off the road while lighting a cigarette. Still another time he had been a passenger in a target vehicle when another hitter-driver had dropped a cigarette. The skepticism of the investigators was further aroused by an accident in which the medical report filed by one of the scheming doctors had enumerated all sorts of injuries to a woman victim, but had said nothing about her jaw; yet at the same time a dentist had submitted a bill for $585 for work he'd supposedly had to do on her because of her misadventure. (There was a $25 entry on the dentist's bill for a "narrative report" he had sent to the lawyer representing her.) The dentists and doctors and lawyers, all things considered, came out substantially ahead of the people who actually figured in the crashes. One couple for whose ostensible injuries an insurance company paid out $2,123.43 got $374.01 for their troubles; another pair got $406.40 out of $2,396.89; another a mere $90 out of $957.90. Still, for the actors, as well as for the professional men, it was a steady source of extra income, and the actors had no overhead expenses. At worst, they had a few bruises, and these were far from crippling: When the investigators tracked down a pair of nightclub performers whose lawyer had been reimbursed for all sorts of horrendous injuries to them, they found that the young woman concerned was capable of putting on a thoroughly uninhibited go-go dance.

Only a handful of the actors themselves were among the two dozen men and women who were ultimately indicted; they were after all merely bit performers in a large-scale production. One hitter-driver who was obliged to stand trial was excused for what all parties concerned agreed was legitimate cause; while the court proceedings were in progress he was a passenger in an airplane that crashed and he was genuinely hurt. Four of the lawyers and two of the doctors were finally convicted of mail fraud, which no doubt hurt them, too.

# 16. What Made Sammy Run?

Among all the hunted criminals who have taken refuge in the accommodating ranks of the French Foreign Legion, there can have been few who seemed less cut out for such an adventurous destiny than Samuel Norman Savitt, a mild-mannered accountant from Rochester, New York. Savitt was a 4-F during the Second World War, but notwithstanding, in 1950, at the fairly advanced military age of thirty-one, he found himself toting a submachine gun through months of nasty fighting in the swamps of Indochina. The Legion was traditionally the haven of swashbuckling desperadoes wanted for murder, rape, or other sensational crimes. Savitt, a pudgy, strictly urban type, who looked about as swashbuckling as a Pekingese, was being sought during his nearly two years of service in the celebrated corps for misdeeds no more savage or spectacular than forgery, mail fraud, violation of Securities and Exchange Commission regulations, and income tax evasion. In refutation of the popularly held theory that once a wrongdoer joined the Foreign Legion, the law never caught up with him, Savitt found himself serving a three-year term in the Federal Penitentiary at Lewisburg, Pennsylvania, after having meekly pleaded guilty to several such nonviolent charges. From the sweltering barracks of Sidi-bel-Abbès to the rain-drenched cafés of Hanoi, there must have been considerable bewilderment.

Both the rise and the fall of Savitt, who had long been called Sammy by his acquaintances, were swift and audacious, and both, inevitably, prompted people who knew him or knew about him to wonder what made Sammy run. Savitt, a well-read and resolutely self-analytical man, sometimes resorted to this literary allusion himself. A psychiatrist who was asked the question, and had looked into the behavior of the subject of it, expressed the opinion that Savitt's illegal and elusive actions were motivated by overpowering ambition and uncontrollable impulses. Savitt, everyone agreed, wanted to be a big shot. As the head of the Savitt Audit Company and the American Audit & Tax Service, he was, before he got in trouble, one of Rochester's busiest and best-paid accountants, with hundreds of clients, a legitimate net income of around twenty thousand a year, and a suite of offices decorated like a movie set, with eye-catching imitation-leather furniture, splendid accessories, and a plentifully stocked bar. Still, he felt that he didn't have enough money to be as big a shot as he wanted to be. He once said that the kind of remark he loved to hear was, "There's Sammy Savitt. He can lose five hundred dollars at cards and it doesn't bother him at all." Savitt was a familiar figure in Rochester's gambling hideouts (he once won a restaurant in a gin rummy game), at two nearby trotting tracks, and in such far-flung recreational centers as Havana and Acapulco, where games of chance were then agreeably abundant. "Doesn't it make you elated to lose?" he asked a friend one time.

Having insufficient money of his own to live in the stylish manner that beguiled him, Savitt adopted a course not unusual in such circumstances. He took to spending money that other people had entrusted to his care. Nobody knows how much he appropriated and ran through in his attempt to assert himself. His wildly jumbled office records provided imprecise evidence. Some of the law-enforcement agencies that pored over them put the total sum at more than a hundred thousand dollars. Others believed fifty thousand would be closer. Savitt himself, once he was in jail and stood little immediate chance of being a big shot again, maintained that both estimates were absurdly inflated, and that his embezzlements, while real enough, were trifling. It grieved him to be thought of as a big-shot crook.

On December 19, 1949, eight weeks before Savitt enlisted in the Foreign Legion, he put in his final appearance at his Rochester office, where, in addition to doing auditing and accounting work, he conducted an investment-advisory service. He stayed there only briefly. His secretary was not surprised at his hasty departure, for a few of his clients had been inquiring about one seeming delinquency or another in his handling of their affairs, and it annoyed him to be bothered by such pests. The next day, the secretary received a telegram from him from New York City, informing her that he was there on a business trip. She returned to the office the following day and every working day thereafter for three weeks, awaiting instructions from her boss. Then, since Savitt had talked some of going on an extended trip, and since he had made no provision for paying her salary in his absence, she gave up her vigil. A day or two later, the landlord of the premises, who had a good deal of back rent due from his tenant, padlocked the office doors. They were reopened long enough to permit another disillusioned creditor—a furniture company, from which Savitt had bought most of his fancy business trappings, on the installment plan—to haul away a load of couches, chairs, and lamps. Savitt, who disliked paying outright for anything, had also bought on time a brand-new, custom-built Packard, and this was reclaimed by a finance company the following June, having finally been located in a Rochester garage, where he had left it, without specifying when he would pick it up, on the day he vanished. One of his last transactions that December 19 was the purchase of over a hundred dollars' worth of merchandise from a Rochester clothing store, which he paid for with two personal checks. Both bounced.

Savitt, a glib, clever, and personable young man who stood five feet seven inches, weighed around a hundred and seventy, and had black hair, brown eyes, a prominent nose, and a double chin, was born on December 2, 1919, in Estonia. His name was Savatsky then; he changed it in 1943. His parents—industrious, thrifty, middle-class Jews—brought him to the United States in 1923, heading straight for Rochester, where a brother of his father's had already settled. Sammy's father, who became naturalized in 1928, thus conferring citizenship upon his son, got a job in a shoe-manufacturing plant in Rochester. The boy did well in school, and was an honor student in an extension course in accounting given in Rochester by Niagara University, which awarded him the degree of Bachelor of Business Administration in 1942. He helped pay for his education by working at various odd jobs. (After he had got into the big money, by one means and another, it amused him to return to a cigar store where he had once been an errand boy and complain that it did not carry a brand of expensive cigar he had come to favor.) He was a sharp dresser, a smooth talker, and, beneath this façade, tense and insecure. He suffered chronically from a nervous stomach, and because of it he was rejected for the draft as a psychoneurotic. In 1946, he went to a psychiatrist, who diagnosed his troubles as anxiety and a sense of inferiority. Savitt started in on an analysis, but he abandoned it after a few sessions.

Even before Savitt got his degree from Niagara, he had begun making money by helping people with their income tax returns. He became a full-time accountant in the fall of 1942. Withholding, an unfathomable procedure to many taxpayers, was introduced a few months later, and Savitt was able to take lucrative advantage of the fact that a great many people who had never before required help in preparing their returns were now avid for it. He is believed to have made thirteen thousand dollars during one three-month stretch in that addled era. Also toward the end of 1942, he married a Rochester girl and set up housekeeping. A few years later, when the urge to squander money gripped him, he squandered a lot of it on other women, and in 1949 his wife divorced him for adultery. She moved to California and remarried. The Savitts had one child, a girl, who was brought up in Rochester by her maternal grandparents.

As Savitt began accumulating money, he invested it in the stock market, and his resources multiplied. Most stocks went up during the war, but Savitt's went up so speedily that a number of his friends and relatives and business associates asked him to apply his skill—he was not inclined to keep his triumphs to himself—to their funds. Savitt was glad to be of service, and early in 1947 he registered with the S.E.C. as an investment adviser. His clients were mostly people of moderate means—the proprietor of a Greek lunch counter, for example, a trio of brothers who ran a small printshop, a dealer in ladies' secondhand shoes, and a seventy-five-year-old widow, who was stone deaf and never asked Savitt any questions about his stewardship of her money because she couldn't hear the answers. "Leave everything in my hands," Savitt would jovially tell those of his clients who did ask. He persuaded them to compensate him for his efforts on a commission basis that gave him from 10 to 20 per cent of whatever capital gains he produced for them—an arrangement that was specifically declared illegal by the Federal Investment Advisers Act of 1940. In a few instances, involving clients who were relatively hard up, Savitt gallantly waived any remuneration. In a few other instances, he arrogated to himself as much as 100 per cent of the capital gains. He never assumed responsibility for any percentage of capital losses.

"Keeping the client uninformed was the cornerstone of Savitt's operations," the S.E.C. noted after it had looked into them. Savitt's clients had such confidence in him and in his supposedly magic touch that they didn't seek to be informed very often. Opening an account with the Rochester branch of Bache & Co., he left instructions there that all communications relating to his clients' investments, as well as all checks representing sales of securities, were to be mailed to them in his care, at his office. Without consulting his clients, Savitt would buy and sell securities in their name. Sometimes he would sell in their name and then buy in his own with the proceeds, or he would close out a client's account entirely and, when the brokerage house sent along a credit-balance check made out to the client, would appropriate that. He distributed enough money among his amazingly gullible clientele to keep everybody at ease, and he distributed the lion's share to himself. After a while, he got careless in his manipulations; he forged one client's name on three checks in three ways, all of them misspellings.

Meanwhile, Savitt was continuing to run his accounting and auditing business, and to run it in a similarly unorthodox fashion. Most accountants, when they prepare a tax return for an individual, submit it, completely typed out, to the taxpayer, who signs his name and makes out a check for the designated amount to the Collector of Internal Revenue, or, latterly, the Internal Revenue Service. Savitt often followed a different routine. When a client came in with the necessary facts and figures, Savitt would compute his tax on the proper form and then have the client sign an identical blank form, explaining that the data would be copied onto it later. Savitt would further instruct the client to make out a check payable to him personally for the amount owed the government. His excuse for this curious procedure was that at tax-filing time his office had a raft of returns to mail to the Bureau of Internal Revenue at the end of every day, and that it simplified things for Savitt and for the Bureau if he sent along one large check covering them all. After the client left, Savitt would redo the man's return, reducing his indebtedness to the government and pocketing the difference. When Savitt's affairs came under scrutiny, several of his clients were surprised to discover that to obtain rewarding deductions he had credited them with costly surgical operations for grave disorders they had never suffered from, at hospitals they had never set foot in. By endowing one sixty-seven-year-old man, whose parents had been dead for twenty years, with a dependent mother, Savitt shaved the man's tax from $83.58 to $29.39, earning himself a fast $54.19 by the resurrection.

Sometimes Savitt was even more forthright in fleecing his clients. After collecting their taxes, he would omit to file any return at all for them. He also adopted this course in his own case. He declared a small income for 1946, but for each of the following three years he didn't file a return, possibly because he knew that failure to file was a misdemeanor, whereas fraudulent filing was a felony. After the collapse of all his enterprises, it was estimated by more conventional accountants that he owed the government around thirty-three thousand dollars for the three-year period—twenty thousand in unpaid taxes and the remainder in penalties. Since Savitt ended up flat broke, the prospect of the government's ever collecting from him was dim. Some of his clients were in a worse spot than he was. The government was sorry that Savitt bilked them, but it took the position that they had freely chosen him as their agent, and that the fact of his deceiving them did not relieve them of their tax obligations. Those for whom he neglected to file returns could have been compelled to pay their taxes twice—once to Savitt and once, with 6 per cent interest for tardiness, to the United States. In protesting that his crimes were exaggerated, Savitt was apt to remark that he was being made the patsy for a lot of tax evaders he never heard of. "Gee, everybody in Rochester who didn't pay his income tax now claims he gave the money to me," he lamented after his arrest.

The Bureau of Internal Revenue was not as credulous as many of Savitt's clients were. The Collector's office at Buffalo became aware, during its examination of various returns for 1947 and 1948, that there seemed to be recurrent irregularities in those originating in Savitt's office. What was more, a couple of checks that he sent to the Collector, drawn on his own account, proved to be insufficiently backed by funds. The Rochester office of the Bureau's Intelligence Division was notified, and early in 1949 the special agent in charge of it, Milton M. Offen, began making discreet inquiries into Savitt's operations. A few of Savitt's clients, after being interviewed, got upset and asked him what was going on. He told them benignly not to worry—that whatever confusion had arisen was undoubtedly the result of bureaucratic red tape and that he'd get everything straightened out. Apparently, his outward calm was infectious, and they were reassured. In any event, none of them ever tried to bring charges against him, and even after his arrest and conviction quite a few continued to feel friendly toward him. While he was awaiting sentence, after pleading guilty, a number of former clients, as well as his former father-in-law, asked the judge presiding over his case to be lenient.

As the Bureau's investigation was getting under way, so was one by the S.E.C. At about the same time, moreover, the District Attorney's office of Monroe County, of which Rochester is the seat, got interested in Savitt. This came about through his defrauding of a man named Lawrence Petty, who worked as an attendant in a Rochester parking lot. Petty had a refund coming to him—it amounted to $61.25—on his 1948 income tax, and he didn't want the money sent to his home, because the mailboxes of a couple of his neighbors had been rifled. He asked Savitt, who used the parking lot and audited its books, if the refund check could be mailed to his office. Savitt was willing. The check was issued on May 11, 1949, and was cashed at a Rochester bank on May 13, with the names of Petty and Savitt inscribed on its back—both written, it was subsequently determined by the questioned-documents analyst of the Post Office Department in Washington, by Savitt. Petty had no knowledge of all this, and he kept asking Savitt if the check had arrived. After a couple of months, Petty got in touch with the Bureau and demanded an explanation of the delay. Told that the check had been mailed to Savitt's office, he hounded Savitt about the matter more persistently than ever, but Savitt kept brushing him off. An assistant district attorney of Monroe County also patronized the parking lot where Petty worked, and the frustrated attendant finally appealed to him for help. As a favor to Petty, the D.A. obtained a photostat of the canceled check, with the two signatures on the back, and Savitt, confronted by this, paid up.

On November 14, 1949, Savitt was arrested on a charge by his own bank, quite incidental to any of his other peccadilloes, that he had refused to make restitution on three bad checks he had written and the bank had covered for him. It was the first official blot on his record. (He had been nabbed the year before in a routine raid on a horse parlor, but he hadn't been booked.) After spending one night in the county jail, he made good on the three checks, with the result that the case against him was dismissed. Still, the incident must have shaken his poise and convinced him that the jig was up, for it was only five weeks later that, after giving the clothing store one last pair of worthless checks, as a sort of farewell gesture to a way of life, he took abrupt leave of Rochester. By March, 1950, the Bureau of Internal Revenue had assembled quite a dossier on him, and felt that it was time some action was taken. However, the Bureau could accuse him of nothing except nonpayment of his own taxes; as far as it was concerned, his systematic defrauding of his clients was the clients' affair, and not the federal government's. But it was known that Savitt had been using the mails to carry out his deceptions, and accordingly, on March 17, 1950, Treasury Agent Offen paid a call on Charles Miller, then the Postal Inspector in Rochester, and discussed the matter with him. Miller agreed that Savitt had been using the mails to defraud, and took on the case. He was pretty much in charge of it from then on.

The first step seemed to be to find Savitt. His family was no help; they were convinced he must be dead. His secretary not only told Miller about the telegram he had sent her from New York but that he had talked a good deal about traveling abroad, and had had her reserve a stateroom for him on the *Queen Elizabeth* for the December 29 sailing. It developed that Savitt had applied for a passport at the county clerk's office in Rochester on December 19. It would have taken a week or two for it to be delivered to him, and, apparently not wanting to wait that long, on December 20 he had applied again in Washington, at the Passport Division of the State Department, under the name of Samuel Norman Savatsky, claiming that he was going to England and France for three months to visit relatives and that he would be sailing from New York on December 23, aboard the *Parthia.* He had been issued a passport on the spot. Miller ascertained that there had been no Savitt, or Savatsky, on the passenger list of either the *Elizabeth* or the *Parthia* on the dates in question. It turned out later that Savitt, using the name of Samuel Savatsky, had sailed from New York on December 23; he had booked passage on the *Noordam* to Le Havre but went on to Rotterdam, and doubled back from there to Paris.

On May 9, 1950, Miller obtained two warrants—one for Savitt's arrest and another authorizing a search of his office. Postal Inspectors and deputy United States marshals removed enough papers from the office to fill a mail truck. Among other interesting documents were about a dozen income tax returns, dating back as far as 1947, to which were stapled checks made out by Savitt's clients to the Collector of Internal Revenue. Savitt, it appeared, hadn't taken the trouble to forward these, possibly out of pique that the checks had been made out in such a way as to preclude his cashing them. On the basis of this and other evidence, two indictments for mail fraud and his other federal offenses were drawn up against him by the United States Attorney's office in Rochester. Concurrently, a Monroe County grand jury handed down two more indictments, both for second-degree grand larceny.

There was still no trace of Savitt. While Miller suspected he had left the country, it was possible that his contradictory maneuvers in the matter of passports and steamship sailings had been deliberately misleading. So Miller drew up a "Wanted" circular, and had 150,000 copies of it printed and distributed to Postmasters and accountants in this country. Fortunately for Miller, an up-to-date photograph of Savitt, and his fingerprints, were available, having been obtained by the police when he was arrested on the bad-check charge the previous November. "Savitt likes crowds and entertainment," the circular read. "He frequents race tracks, night clubs, and gambling establishments. He is extremely fond of female company and is a lavish spender. Talks largely of financial matters and is a fluent and convincing talker. Possibly has engaged in tax-auditing business since his disappearance from Rochester, N.Y. Allegedly speaks Spanish and is known to have vacationed in Mexico and Cuba."

The circulars went out on November 15, 1950, and almost at

once bore fruit in the form of an unexpected reaction from a certified public accountant in Oregon. In an angry letter to Miller, which carried a notation that copies were being sent to the Secretary of the Treasury, Senator Wayne Morse, of Oregon, and other public officials, the accountant denounced the federal government for hounding Savitt, whose only fault, according to the letter writer, was that he had tried to be an individualist in an age of intolerable controls. Whatever excesses Savitt might have been driven to, the accountant continued, were caused by high taxes. "This man has been permanently ruined by the income tax," he wrote, which struck Miller as a rather odd conclusion for one accountant to draw about another. "He had to face the grim reality that if the pure white flame of integrity glowed within him it would not heat his shaving water." The Oregon man furnished no information on Savitt's whereabouts.

A lot of other people, however, did furnish information on Savitt's whereabouts—all of it wrong. (The Inspection Service doesn't mind, of course, tracking down phony tips; like any investigating agency, it would rather get a flock of false leads than no leads at all.) For two years, Miller and other Postal Inspectors around the country ran down hypothetical Savitts. So did cooperating authorities in Mexico and Canada. A Savitt was apprehended hitchhiking in Texas. One was grabbed while dancing in a ballroom in Los Angeles, and another while sitting at a table in a nightclub in Washington, D.C. When *Life* printed a photograph of the audience at an open-air concert in the Hollywood Bowl, a sharp-eyed reader spotted Savitt in the group. He was seen, and heard, conducting evangelistic services in Memphis. He was held for questioning when found working on a ranch at Oroville, California. He was spotted rolling dice at the Golden Nugget in Las Vegas. (Las Vegas and Reno, between them, produced a Savitt a week.) The hottest tip came from Norfolk, Virginia, where a lady who had seen Savitt's photograph on a post-office bulletin board overheard a man talking to a woman in a saloon. He was telling his companion that he was an expert on income taxes, and was chivalrously offering to assist her with hers. The witness of this scene notified a Postal Inspector, who showed Savitt's picture to the bartender at the place. "Absolutely! That's the man!" cried the bartender. The next time the suspect turned up in the saloon, the bartender telephoned the Inspector, who rushed over, peered at the man, and was certain that he was Savitt. Sidling up next to him, the Inspector engaged him in casual conversation. After a while, the man voluntarily identified himself as an agent of the Bureau of Internal Revenue. Fine, thought the Inspector; we'll get Savitt for impersonating a federal official, on top of everything else. It turned out that the man was an Internal Revenue agent.

The first real break in the case came one day in the spring of 1952, when Miller received a letter from the American Board of Missions to the Jews, a group in New York that, among other activities, published a monthly magazine called *The Chosen People.* One of the organization's field workers, the letter stated, had stopped in at the New York office, where a member of the staff happened to mention a fellow named Norman Savitt, in whom the Board was deeply interested. Hesitantly, the field worker said he thought he had seen a "Wanted" circular for a man with that name, or one very much like it, in a post office in Des Moines. The Board of Missions had checked up, and now, in astonishment, it was writing to Miller. It knew a good deal about Savitt, the writer said, and his name was mentioned in its office nearly every day, for how often did an organization like that get the opportunity to engage in correspondence with a soldier who had fought with the French Foreign Legion in Indochina and had later become a sort of international, mail-order Lothario? And what correspondence! The Board enclosed several letters from Savitt. The earliest was dated September 17, 1950—two months before the circulars about him had gone out. "My dear Friends," it began, "I am an American Jew who is writing you because I feel the need to know Christ. For the past eight years I have been wandering in the sea of despair without any religion." Savitt explained that he had heard about the Board from a German businessman in Hanoi, and went on to furnish a brief and rather imaginative autobiography. He said that he had been a psychological adviser and lay analyst in civilian life, that his wife and two children had died, and that he had enlisted in the Legion to lose his individual identity—"to forget and to be forgotten." He continued: "What I was really doing was running away from the world. Here, where I face constant death in this treacherous guerrilla warfare, I find that it is not enough to fight *against* something. One must fight *for* something. I want to know more about the Lord." His ambition upon leaving the Legion, he declared, was to become a missionary among the lost Jews of the world—either in the Middle East or in Australia. He went on to say that he would like to receive *The Chosen People* regularly but didn't know how to go about subscribing, since he was paid in piasters.

Miller knew he had found his man, or at any rate had found his trail. The handwriting was unquestionably Savitt's, and the interest in religion was characteristic, for Miller had learned from Savitt's classmates at Niagara that as an undergraduate he had done considerable reading along theological lines and had been known to discourse eloquently on themes so relatively esoteric for an accounting student as the history and principles of Buddhism. The Board of Missions informed Miller that it had answered Savitt's letter promptly and had put him on the free-subscription list. He had written again soon afterward, this time giving a moving and colorful account of one of his combat experiences. With two bullets in one shoulder, he reported, he had fought for four days and nights without water, food, or sleep. He had been with a squad of twelve men, and the sergeant in command had been killed. Savitt had taken over, and almost at once they had run into an ambush from a machine gun concealed in a native house. In the nick of time, Savitt had shouted, *"À terre!"* Lying on the ground, with bullets streaming overhead, he had felt an urge to pray, and had begun reciting the Twenty-third Psalm. Intoning its words, he had risen slowly to his feet and walked unhurriedly toward the machine gun, miraculously impervious to its bullets. Calmly and deliberately, he had pulled the pin on two grenades and had thrown them into the house. Each had found its mark, the house had exploded, and he and his men were saved. For this heroism, he revealed, he had been promoted to sergeant *au feu* and awarded the Croix de Guerre. Actually, Savitt was made an acting sergeant at some time or other, but he never received the Croix de Guerre. (After his return from Indochina to the Legion's headquarters in Algeria, however, he ran into an American sailor from Buffalo and gave him a Croix de Guerre that he claimed to have earned. Savitt told the sailor that he had been a practicing lawyer in Buffalo, held degrees from both N.Y.U. and C.C.N.Y., had been an officer in the American Army during the Second World War, and had a French wife living in Marseilles.) Savitt was never hit by a bullet in Indochina; he admitted this to a student of his case who talked to him after his arrest. He also said that he had no recollection of ever telling anybody he had been shot. He added that the only wound he had got in action was a bayonet slash on the back of the head, incurred in hand-to-hand fighting. The recipient of this confidence had no opportunity to examine Savitt's scalp.

A little dazed, but enchanted, by Savitt's account of his exploits, the Board of Missions went on writing. So did Savitt. In a series of stimulating letters—at one time he was composing three a week—he disclosed that he was having a hard time reconciling the homicidal life he was leading with the injunction "Thou shalt not kill." While he was on guard duty one bitter cold night, he said, he had been on the point of lighting a cigarette when it occurred to him to ask the Lord if he should stop smoking. A voice had said, "Yes." Savitt had inquired, further, whether he should throw away all the cigarettes he had on him. "Yes," he had heard again. "Was it my sense of good and evil that answered me or was it really the Lord?" he wrote. Then he had asked the Lord if he should try to get released from the Legion. Once more came the "Yes"—this time, Savitt said, "like a shot out of a gun." He said that he had written to the American consul at Hanoi, trying to enlist his aid in getting a discharge, but that the Legion's censors had intercepted his letter, and he was going to ask the Lord what to do next. "No censor can stop Him," Savitt wrote. "I can no longer kill anyone."

Savitt kept the missionary group posted on his movements. By the spring of 1951, the Board told Miller, he had been invalided to France and had received a medical discharge. The Board had learned from one of its subscribers, a lady in Calgary, Alberta, that he had written to her upon seeing her name and address in *The Chosen People* and that after they had corresponded for a while, she had sent him money a couple of times. She had last heard from him in September, 1951, when he informed her that he was leaving the Legion to start a new life, and was going to conduct Bible classes in Paris. It appeared that Savitt had also corresponded with a number of other women whose names and addresses he had got from the same source. One of them was an impressionable lady in England, whom he had subsequently visited and promised to marry. While he was there, in December, 1951, she had baked a birthday cake for him, but he had suddenly disappeared, leaving lady, wedding, and uncut cake behind. In the light of what the lady in Calgary had disclosed, and after learning that the Paris branch of the Burroughs Adding Machine Company had been given the name of a Rochester firm as a reference for a job-seeking American accountant named Samuel Norman Savatsky, Miller decided to proceed on the assumption that Savitt was in or near Paris, if not necessarily teaching Bible classes. The French police were asked to look for him, and on September 1, 1952, they competently tracked him down in Paris and arrested him in bed. He put up no resistance, but in their enthusiasm they knocked out two of his teeth.

The chronology of Savitt's flight from justice was in due course fairly definitely established. Upon arriving in Paris from Rotterdam at the start of 1950, he had around twelve hundred dollars, which he rapidly spent. In doing so, he met a Belgian girl, to whom he later became engaged. Once his funds were exhausted, he went to Nice, and there, on February 16, he impulsively enlisted in the

Legion, signing the usual contract, which committed a recruit to five years' service. He joined up under the singularly thin disguise of "Norman Savitt." The Legion soon stopped taking people in without asking questions, for when its troops started fighting Communists in Indochina, it couldn't afford to admit just any old Russian or Hungarian or Bulgarian applicant, who might well be an intelligence officer assigned to infiltrate its ranks. Savitt was asked not only to identify himself but to explain why he wanted in. "I told them I was in trouble and was emotionally disturbed," he said afterward. "I told them joining the Legion might do me some good, and they said they hoped it would. They asked me if I had any fear of being killed, and I said no. Actually, after my four months of basic training in North Africa, I requested assignment to the Third Battalion of the Third Regiment, because it had been in battle somewhere or other almost continuously since 1945 and I wanted to be killed. I didn't succeed in that, either. I've failed in a lot of things in my life."

It was Savitt's opinion that during his stay in the Legion there were comparatively few desperate criminals among his comrades; he thought they were far outnumbered by stateless Europeans, who had enlisted because they knew that an honorable discharge from the organization would make them eligible for French citizenship. He ran into only three Legionnaires who he was convinced were Americans; half a dozen others claimed to be, but he believed they were German soldiers who had been captured in the Second World War and interned in prison camps in this country, where they assimilated enough knowledge of American ways to fool non-Americans. Most of his fellow soldiers were indisputably Germans. (For many years, Germans dominated the Legion's ranks, and German was more widely spoken in it than French. Savitt, who learned a little French and German in school, became fluent in both languages.) A number of the Germans serving with him were former Nazis, but, as a Jew, he had no particular run-ins with them, because the Legion forbade any debate on such controversial topics as race, religion, and politics. Any Legionnaire who was heard using a provocative word like "Hun" or "Kike" or "Polack" or "Frog" was liable to a six-month tour of duty in a Legion disciplinary camp, where the treatment was as rough as the old-timers of that thoroughly disciplined group could make it.

In July, 1950, his training in North Africa completed, Savitt was shipped to Indochina, where he was supposed to stay two years. That December, his battalion, twelve hundred strong, was stationed at Caobang, in Tonkin, where it occupied a fort a mile and a half from the Chinese border. The French came under heavy attack from the enemy, and the battalion was ordered to fight a rear-guard holding action to enable the members of other outposts to withdraw. In the battle, Savitt recalled later, all but sixty-two of the twelve hundred men in his outfit were lost; it took him and the other survivors fourteen days to sneak back to friendly lines through enemy-held territory. By then, he was a casualty, suffering both from malaria and from an ulcer in his delicate stomach. He was put in a military hospital at Hanoi, where he remained several months, and in June, 1951, along with other veterans of the retreat from Caobang, he was flown to Paris. He spent a few weeks in a military hospital there, and was then moved to North Africa. A medical board in Oran looked him over, judged him unfit for further combat duty, and declared him eligible for a medical discharge, with an annual pension of forty thousand francs—at the then rate of exchange, about a hundred dollars.

Savitt could have stayed in the Legion in a noncombat capacity, and if he had, in view of the comparatively tame nature of his crimes, the Legion would probably never have turned him over to any foreign government. Or, upon accepting his medical discharge, he could have assumed a brand-new identity and been absorbed into the life of the Continent. Instead, after his mustering out and his romantic fling in England, he applied for and got the Burroughs job in Paris, giving, with seeming indifference to being traced, the Rochester reference. By the time Miller heard about this, however, Savitt had left Burroughs and had become manager, as Samuel Norman Savitt, of an office of American International Underwriters, in a Paris suburb. He was still employed there when he was arrested.

The French police who arrested Savitt put him in the Prison de la Santé, an institution that was founded by Napoleon as a hospital but subsequently became a jail, and one not greatly concerned about the well-being of its inmates. Savitt spent six months there, and survived, he said, only because he had some money for extra food, which the guards sold to their more prosperous prisoners, advertising each day's specials over loudspeakers. Once he was in custody, the United States began extradition proceedings, and discovered only then that, of forty-six counts in the two federal indictments against him, just one, according to the extradition treaty signed between this country and France in 1909, covered an extraditable offense. That count related to the business of the check for $61.25 that Savitt filched from Lawrence Petty, the parking-lot attendant. Austin J. Donovan, the United States Attorney who drew up the two indictments, had thrown this into the first of them more or less for the hell of it. (Even though Savitt had reimbursed Petty when the Monroe County D.A. had initially got onto this matter, the federal government still had a case against him for forging a signature on a Treasury Department check.) Early in October, a French court was convened to decide whether Savitt should be extradited. Through the Legion, he obtained as his attorney Count René de Chambrun, a direct descendant of the Marquis de Lafayette, a son of a former commanding general of the Legion, and a son-in-law of the late Pierre Laval. During each session of the proceedings, an escort of honor of five Legionnaires —an officer and four noncoms—paraded into the courtroom to lend moral support to their erstwhile comrade-in-arms. But even this formidable claque failed to help. The court recommended to the Minister of Justice that Savitt be handed over to the United States for cashing Petty's tax-refund check, and the Minister of Justice recommended to the Prime Minister that a request, signed personally by the President and the Secretary of State of the United States, for the return of the allegedly fraudulent casher of

Petty's check, be granted. Early in March, 1953, Miller was sent to Paris on the liner *United States* to bring Savitt home. He found his quarry in chains. After he had received custody of Savitt and had satisfied himself that the prisoner wasn't going to try anything funny, Miller astonished Savitt's French guardians by not even handcuffing him. Just before Savitt was removed from the Prison de la Santé, the authorities there, following a custom of theirs, thrust an enormous loaf of bread upon him. Miller and Savitt lugged it with them to Le Havre, where, upon boarding the *United States* for the trip home, they agreed that there were enough provisions on board to feed captor and captive alike, and tossed the loaf over the side.

Savitt seemed relieved to have been caught. Forgoing a trial, he pleaded guilty as soon as possible to the single extraditable count of the first federal indictment against him, and he voluntarily pleaded guilty also to the entire second federal indictment, which dealt with income tax evasion and under which, since it contained no extraditable counts, he could not have been tried without his consent, according to international law, until thirty days after the completion of the disposition of the charge for which he had been extradited. There were still the two Monroe County indictments hanging over his head; but once Savitt was behind bars he seemed unperturbed by them and, indeed, quite at ease with himself and the world. "I was all mixed up," he told a visitor. "I knew I had to endure certain things to prove certain things. I had never had any hard knocks in my life. I needed a strong emotional shock. What I wanted to do was cut myself off from everything, and I achieved it. I've been in the one outfit in the world where I could cut myself off completely. I think that I've recaptured the faith I lost. I wanted to be killed, but I didn't make it. Now I'm not sure whether wanting to be killed like that is a normal or a neurotic impulse. I hope it's neurotic. But I'm not claiming psychoneurosis as a justification for anything I've done. I've known all along that I've done wrong, and it's bothered me. What happened to me was I got panicky, and I ran."

# 17. I Have Been Tooken

Speed is often a crucial element of fraud. Many perpetrators of shady schemes adhere to hit-and-run tactics, and many of their victims are motivated by an itch to get rich quick, or to share in some bargain opportunity that runs counter to the normally sluggish pace of life. A pair of clever operators in New York, for instance, flourished for fifteen years, until the Postal Inspection Service finally outfoxed them, by peddling a dazzling variety of products that were alleged to have marvelously accelerated properties—something called Green Plasma, which would turn a sere lawn verdant in sixty seconds; a "wonder rose" guaranteed to throw out a thousand fresh blooms a week; an ailanthus tree that "soars roof-high in only a few months' time"; and a skin cream that would take fourteen years off a woman's face in just five minutes. They were men finely attuned to the needs of a clock-watching world.

At one point or another during their versatile career, these two enterprising men also sold a talking-fish lure; a compound that made it unnecessary to change one's motor oil more than once a year, and an even more beguiling device by means of which one could run a car half on gas and half on air; a floor polisher that eliminated waxing forever; and a human hair stretch wig with a lifetime set. The fact that none of these products behaved the way they were supposed to was an inconvenience only to their purchasers—among whom were almost certainly some of the individuals who for five years gave a million dollars annually to the distributors of an automobile battery that was guaranteed to last for a decade without any water.

Over the years, wigs have proved to be a steady, profitable item for glib-voiced sellers of shoddy merchandise. (Can these swindlers be aware—as their victims probably aren't—that in Chinese the same ideograph can be used for "righteousness" and for "false hairpiece"?) Wigs are much in demand among the vain or the hopeful, they are easy to ship, and from a distance few people can tell the difference between a good one and a worthless one. They are cheap enough, moreover, so that few people are likely to raise much of a fuss if they're stuck with an unsatisfactory hairpiece. One of the most redoubtable wig vendors in recent history was a Philadelphia man whose arsenal of tricks did not include rapid-action fire: He stuck to one leisurely *modus operandi* for several years and prevailed upon nearly 100,000 ingenuous women, all of whom thought they were getting something for practically nothing, to send him around $1.5 million, in return for which they got practically nothing. He was Elliott Nathaniel Scott, a hard-working promoter from Philadelphia, who, when he appeared before a federal judge to be sentenced after a conviction on ten counts of mail fraud, declared, "I have always sought during my forty years on earth to be an imaginative, creative person in business." Scott professed to believe that the way he operated was the way the mainstream of American business operated, and to an extent that may have been true, though few small honest businessmen have been quite as successful.

Scott, a personable and persuasive black man who started off his career as an orthodox beauty culturist, was born in Florida and moved north in the 1940s, attending high school in Newark and finally settling in Philadelphia, where he opened a beauty salon in 1949. Acquiring a wife and four children, he must have felt he could not adequately support them by conventional means, so around 1962 he went into wigs. For a while he advertised in newspapers in at least eight states, soliciting agents who could furnish him with names of prospective customers; he would usually order the insertions by letter and then not bother to pay for them. The agents were to get a two- or three-dollar commission per sale, but he sometimes neglected to pay them. In the spring of 1966, dispensing with middlemen and relying instead for names on telephone directories, Scott became a postcard pusher. He had postcards printed up by the tens of thousands, and he mailed them at so unremitting a clip that he soon became the biggest single user of the mails in East Germantown, Pennsylvania, a Philadelphia suburb whose postal facilities he chiefly patronized.

No one knows how many women, sorting through their usually dreary daily mail, were brought up with a start on espying a card that began, "Dear Lucky Lady," and went on to say "You have just won an expensive free wig in our annual drawing." An unexpected prize! In a contest they hadn't even known they'd entered! Heavens to Betsy and God bless the fates that had smiled upon them! The card went on to say that the recipient had a free wig worth eighty-nine dollars awaiting her; she had won it in a drawing held by a social club—perhaps the Rich Beauty and Health Club, or the Phillips Social Club, or the Simpson Wig Styling Club, depending on Scott's mood of the moment—and there was this signature of a woman identified as the club secretary to attest to this stroke of good fortune.

All the winner had to do to acquire her prize was to present her postcard at the Philadelphia address on it, or, if she was an out-of-towner, as she was more likely to be, to remit, in advance, the required postage—$2.87, $2.89, $2.91, $2.94, or $2.96, again depending on how Scott's creative imagination was running at the moment. There would be a further trifling assessment of $1.50 for a plastic head form and of $7.50 or thereabouts for each of two stylings that the wearing of such an elegant wig would naturally entail. Each postcard had stamped on it, often in red, a number—Scott was partial to six digits—which was supposed to be the winner's lucky number, and which had supposedly been drawn by a former wig winner. Sometimes the new winner was urged to send in four names and addresses for the next drawing; Scott never wanted to run out of prospects. The postcards closed with a ringing "Congratulations!" Few recipients seem to have been put off by the implicit warning that the congratulations were qualified; the word was enclosed in parentheses. Scott could be careless with figures—every Lucky Lady in the same mailing had the same lucky number—but he was meticulous about words: For a time he said on his cards, "Kindly send for or pick up your wig within two weeks," but then, evidently concluding that the phrase needed improving, changed it to "Kindly pick up or send for your wig within two weeks." When people failed to obey these orders, he would sometimes mail them a "Last Notice" card, but so voluminous was his correspondence that he could hardly have been expected to keep everything straight; as a result, some individuals were puzzled to receive a last notice from him that actually was their first notice.

Scott engaged a shifting crew of young women to staff his premises. When a Lucky Lady called in, the employees were under instructions first to ask for her winning number, to pause ten seconds, as if to verify its accuracy, and then to exclaim, "Congratulations, you *are* the winner!" The delighted winner would then be told to send along her trifling payments or to stop by in person. People who did come around to the "social club" would be shown a wig, usually of impeccable quality, and would then, on due payment of their first styling fee, be handed a plastic envelope containing *their* wig. They were not allowed to examine it on the scene—"for sanitary reasons," they would be advised. The real reason, as they would soon perceive to their dismay, was that Scott's wigs were apt to fall apart at first touch. He sometimes proclaimed them to be fashioned of 100 per cent human hair from Italy, or from France, and he would sometimes proclaim their durability: "If your free wig wears out or is lost or stolen within three years from the date below you will receive another free wig of equal value. The only thing you pay for is the wig style." In fact, the wigs were machine made, usually of some synthetic fiber like Celanese acetate yarn, and Scott bought them wholesale at slightly under a dollar apiece, so his "styling charges" were almost entirely net profit. (He paid 45 cents each for his $1.50 plastic head forms.) The wigs were so fragile they couldn't be set even once. The choices of colors that Scott offered his Lucky Ladies sounded glamorous—jet black, golden honey blonde, natural platinum, medium auburn, and so forth—but according to one law-enforcement official who looked into Scott's machinations, the majority sent out were "an obnoxious shade of red." And some of them, as the crowning, crushing flaw, had built-in bald spots.

Scott was undoubtedly aware that few women—or men, for that matter—like to admit they've been duped, and that the majority of his victims would suffer in silence. But he failed to reflect that some women get maddest when the cause of their anger involves their personal appearance; they will stoically endure a bad piece of meat but raise the devil over a bad pair of shoes. So there was from the start of his postcard distribution a scattering of complaints—some of these from women who'd received an unwearable wig and others from ones who after following instructions and sending in their money had received no wig at all. Many newspapers around the country now have Action Line departments in which their readers can air their gripes, and Scott and his social clubs soon became a familiar figure in these columns. The one in the Philadelphia *Evening Bulletin,* called "Mr. Fixit," had run a warning against him in March, 1967, but notwithstanding had in the following six months received 264 further complaints, one of them from a woman who said that whereas genuine hair burned, Scott's ersatz stuff merely melted. Chambers of Commerce and Better Business Bureaus from coast to coast kept hearing about Scott's tacky wigs. The Bureau's branch in Toledo ordered one and displayed it in its office as a symbol of perfidy, but unfortunately most of the women who are taken in by postcards do not regularly visit Better Business Bureaus. The Bureau of Greater Philadelphia had such unkind things to say about Scott in its November, 1967, bulletin that he boldly brought action against it in the Court of Common Pleas; the case was dismissed. Meanwhile, he continued to send postcards, and the complaints also continued—to the Federal Trade Commission, to the Department of Justice, to a Senator from New Mexico and a Representative from Michigan, and to the White House. A widow with six children wrote anguishedly to President Lyndon Johnson, "I am not making up excuses for my dumbnest, but I have been tooken."

Naturally enough, a good number of inquiries were addressed to Scott himself. "Any complaints directed personally to me will be adjusted within 48 hours, as always," Scott once wrote to the national headquarters of the Better Business Bureau, identifying himself as "general manager in charge of purchasing." But it did not always work out that way in practice. When people wrote to his headquarters demanding a better wig or their money back, either their laments were ignored or they simply received some more printed postcards (with Scott identified on these as "Sponsor"), requesting them to answer questions like "Was wig received and sent back for styling? Was wig sent back for color exchange?" Complainants who turned up at his premises might be told through a closed door that the place was closed and to go away, or, if they managed to get in and started to make a fuss, might be physically ejected. Those who tried to attain satisfaction by telephone never seemed to be able to get connected with anybody in a position of authority, and if they persisted, whoever happened to be manning Scott's phone at the moment would say, "That's too bad," or "Looks like you've been stuck," or would merely hang up.

Sooner or later, in most schemes that involve the use of the mails, someone notifies the Postal Inspection Service, which is resignedly aware that it cannot do much about misleading advertising, "puffing," or hard selling, but which goes into brisk action when it is convinced that deliberate fraud is in the air. In this instance, an Inspector then investigating fraud cases in Philadelphia, Elbridge M. Hamm, Jr., had heard about Scott as early as

September, 1966, but it took him a couple of years to amass enough evidence to make prosecution seem possible. Investigating the busy wig man, Hamm discovered, for one thing, that Scott was using no less than thirty-three business aliases, among these Revonda's Wig Styling Club, Charles Wig Styling Company, Modern Wigs, Win a Wig, Philadelphia Discount Wigs, United Wig Company, and Free Wig Club. In interviewing complainants, Hamm listened to enough tales of woe to make his own hair curl. There was the woman who had taken one disgusted look at her prize wig and had given it to a neighbor's child to wear for Halloween. There were women who had been sufficiently mesmerized by Scott's prose to order extra-special-fancy wigs from him at prices up to $150, who had paid for them by borrowing from finance companies and pledging their furniture or household appliances as collateral; who, dissatisfied with their wigs and unable to get their money back from Scott, had refused to pay off their loans; and who had accordingly ended up with nothing to put on their heads and no couches or washing machines, either. Inquiring among bona-fide wig dealers, Hamm learned that wigs better than Scott's could be bought at five-and-ten-cent stores for five dollars, with a plastic head form thrown in; one dealer, after scrutinizing a wig Scott had sent out, said it wasn't sturdy enough for a Halloween costume. As the one branch of the Post Office Department was thus delving into Scott's affairs, another branch—the East Germantown post office—was able to report that these were going along very nicely: Over a six-month stretch, Scott had cashed $100,000 worth of money orders.

By October, 1967, Inspector Hamm had accumulated a fat dossier on Scott, including the names of hundreds of women who said they'd be eager to testify against him, one or two among them adding that they'd welcome a chance to clench their hands in *his* hair. The United States Attorney's office in Philadelphia persuaded a grand jury to indict him for mail fraud, and he was arrested on October 9. Out on bail, he went right on as before, until he was ordered to stand trial in February, 1968.

Poor Scott! He got an all-woman jury. His trial lasted for fourteen days, and he did his best in his own defense by putting on a dramatic courtroom display of styling a wig on a complacent model. But he was overwhelmed by a parade of vengeful witnesses, who testified that the wigs he'd sent them were far less evocative of human hair than of dog hair. One woman said they reminded her of dead string, whatever that was. Another said that when she opened a C.O.D. package containing the wig she'd so looked forward to, the sight of it moved her to instant tears, and she feared she'd have a heart attack. One of the things that hurt Scott's case was that the prosecution and the defense had jointly stipulated that four hundred victims could testify that they had never received wigs they'd paid for. It was conditional to this stipulation that the defense could have a copy of the names and addresses of these women. Later, when the defense was arguing that Scott was a reputable businessman who maintained orderly records, it presented in support of this contention what purported to be some of his shipping records over the years. But it was easy for the prosecution to establish that these had been hastily and retroactively made up: There had been nine inadvertent errors in Inspector Hamm's list of four hundred names, and the identical nine mistakes turned up on Scott's records; what was more, Hamm had three women on his roster who had moved subsequent to their negotiations with Scott; and yet the Scott roster included the later addresses, though the women concerned had never heard of their new residences when they were trafficking with him.

On March 13, 1968, the jury returned a guilty verdict. While awaiting sentence, Scott wrote the judge that what had happened to him was a bad dream, and that in any event his prosecution was unfair not only to him but to all minority-group businessmen; if anyone had been victimized it was he who had been, and principally because of his color. The judge was unswayed and sentenced him to a year and a day in prison to be followed by four years of probation. Pending execution of the sentence, Scott unabashedly pursued his proven course; out on bail again, he generated 5,000 more complaints and $160,000 more in income. When the judge was apprised of this, in January, 1969, he stated that he could understand a man's continuing to operate after an indictment; stubbornness could have been the cause. But continuing to do so after a *conviction* was something else again. The judge revoked Scott's bail, and he was soon sent to prison. Scott may not have been too surprised by this interruption of his remunerative career, for he had once confided to one of the wholesalers he dealt with, "I am going to make all the money I can before they put me in jail."

Released after serving his year and a day, he was back at the old stand before the end of his probationary period. In June, 1972, he signed an agreement with the Postal Service's General Counsel authorizing all mail addressed to his principal place of business to be returned to the senders marked "Out of business." Two months later, following dozens of new complaints against him, he was once again arrested by Inspectors for mail fraud. As one of the Inspectors who followed his unswerving career remarked, it is hard to keep a bad man down.

# 18. A License to Steal

Most charitable organizations, at one time or another, make use of the mails to help their worthy causes, and it is exceedingly difficult, if not impossible, for a recipient of their appeals to determine which of them are on the level and which suspect. What should parents do, for instance, in the case of a young child who, eager to receive any kind of mail in the postman's daily delivery, leaps into correspondence with, and often endows with his nickels or dimes, any organization willing to correspond with him? Should the parents explain to him the harsh realities of the fund-raising world, and take a chance of forever stifling his honorable impulses; or should they keep quiet and let him squander his allowance on charlatans for whom charity ends at home?

Taking advantage of the humanitarian leanings of Western civilization can be a very successful *mode d'être.* A decade or so ago, for instance, John Wayne let it be publicly known that he was no longer a sponsor of the National Foundation for Asthmatic Children; he had learned that of $1,247,490 not long before collected by the Foundation's full-time promoters, only $170,000 had ever reached any children. When this discrepancy between donations and disbursements first came to the actor's attention, he was no doubt surprised; when, considerably earlier, it came to the attention of the Postal Inspection Service, that agency was less surprised than pained. The two groups of malefactors that are generally the most difficult to put out of business are those that cloak themselves in the trappings of charity and of religion, and most Inspectors would much rather be assigned to a simple mailbox-rifling complaint than try to take out after charlatans oozing piety or philanthropy from every perceptible pore. In the case of the Asthmatic Children, any Inspector on the job in the early 1960s would have said to himself, Of course; what could you expect? For within the Service, for a decade or so before *that*, the Foundation had already become known as a Koolish charity—a charity, that was, which, although established to benefit mankind or some especially deserving portion thereof, had as a practical matter ended up by chiefly benefiting Abraham L. Koolish, his son David, and random family members and unrelated associates who from time to time shared in their robust gains.

The Koolishes came close to being the nonpareils of tainted fund raising. They operated on a heroic scale. Endearing themselves, for example, to the Sister Elizabeth Kenny Foundation in 1948, they exploited their intimacy with such vigor and finesse that between 1951 and 1960 they managed to siphon off for themselves $13 million out of $22 million that that Foundation received through direct-mail solicitations. There is no fixed fee for fund raising, but various attempts have been made to arrive at reasonable recompense for the middlemen between donors and donees. The state of Pennsylvania and the cities of Oakland and Los Angeles have decreed that no more than 15 or 16 per cent of the gross receipts of any campaign can properly be allocated to expenses; and this ratio, considering the ineptitude of many professional fund raisers, seems extremely generous. The Koolishes had no use for such inhibiting arithmetic. They took 59.5 per cent of all the money that the Kenny Foundation garnered through the mails. In the fall of 1959, they ran a "cold-shot" mailing for the Foundation—a mailing to names selected more or less at random. They sent out 12,207,182 letters of solicitation. If the Koolishes hadn't secretly warmed the roster with a million and a half names of people who had already contributed to the institution, the net proceeds—after the fund raisers' substantial deductions for themselves—would have come to $427,000 *less* than the cost of the mailing. Three years before that, when the Kenny Foundation received $1.5 million in a similar direct-mail campaign, the entire proceeds went to the Koolishes.

When pushed for an explanation of where all the money had gone to, the Koolishes would sometimes profess that it had not really gone to them but to such high-sounding activities as Therapist Training Operations, Medical Education and Training Programs, Public Education and Information Services, and Promotion and Development of Additional Treatment Facilities. Or, to make their percentage of the total take seem less outrageously steep, they would claim that the Foundation had received $500,000 in bequests as a result of a random third-class-mail request. (Actually, the Koolishes ended up with 25 per cent of *all* the money contributed to the Kenny Foundation—from bequests, house-to-house calls, unsolicited gifts of grateful patients, and so forth.) Until their downfall, the Koolishes had scant trouble with the board of directors of the Foundation, who were for the most part busy, civic-minded individuals with little time or taste for detailed study of financial statements; and who were in a few instances susceptible to flattery and to attentiveness, such as free tickets to World Series baseball games. Those few directors who asked for explanations were summarily eased off the board. This was not too difficult to accomplish, because the Koolishes, it turned out, were in cozy cahoots with two men named Marvin L. Kline and Fred Fadell, who were, respectively, the executive director of the Foundation and its chief public-relations man. With Kline's and Fadell's approval and connivance, the fund raisers would blandly charge the Foundation twenty dollars a thousand for a mailing list of 9,441,000 names, a couple of million or more of which were names of past Kenny contributors taken from the Foundation's own files.

Not only was the Foundation thus paying for its own information, but the Koolishes were on the side renting out its list of proven contributors to other charities, for fifty dollars a thousand. When in 1953 the Koolishes were first approached by the Asthmatic Foundation for a mailing to 1.5 million people, they had no difficulty accomplishing this mission; they merely used 1.5 million Kenny Foundation names that by then were in *their* files. Over one seven-year stretch, Kline and Fadell, while receiving salaries from the Kenny Foundation, also received between them $359,-200 in cash from the Koolishes. At a time, moreover, when standard interest rates ran around 6 per cent, the Koolishes were happy to lend Kline some money at 2 per cent, and they were not pressing in their demands for payment of either principal or interest. As lagniappe, the general public that thought its money was going to the Foundation was, through the kind offices of the Koolishes, bestowing on Kline a seven-piece set of matched luggage, and on Fadell a television set, an air-conditioner, a movie camera, and an electric organ. It was useful—nay, crucial—for the Koolishes to have cronies in the Foundation office, for Kline and Fadell were in a postion to reject one competitive bid for a certain mailing, at $27.94 a thousand, and to award it instead to the Koolishes at $69.50 a thousand. If the Foundation had accepted the lower offer, it could have saved $335,000. When to make things look good the two Kenny employees had to let some rival fund raisers demonstrate their capabilities, they would assign to them all but hopeless test areas, like ghetto sections of Cleveland or Saint Louis, where the response to solicitations was bound to be slim.

When the Koolishes were taken on by the Kenny Foundation, they were operating under the firm name of Empire Associates, and under that titular umbrella they were engaged also by many other philanthropic groups, among them the Gold Star Wives and War Orphans, the National Haven for the Blind, and Boys Town of the Desert. In 1955, the nature of the fund raising of still another Koolish client, the Disabled American Veterans, came under public scrutiny, and it developed in the course of this examination that Empire Associates, without telling the veterans' organization, had been using *its* cherished list of names to raise money for a flock of other clients. In the light of the publicity that ensued, the directors of the Kenny Foundation were much relieved to be informed by Kline and Fadell that they were no longer being represented by Empire Associates but by the New Century Corporation. What Kline and Fadell neglected to add was that this replacement outfit was simply the Koolishes in a new disguise.

The wool that the Koolishes were pulling over everybody's eyes began to unravel when people all over the country started getting tired of receiving junk mail, and authorities at various levels of national life—municipal, state, federal, and John Wayne—began delving into the shrouded field of fund raising. The Koolishes' own laziness contributed to their comeuppance. (On September 13, 1963, Abraham and David Koolish were each sentenced to ten years in prison, a $17,000 fine, and $16,000 worth of court costs. Four associates of theirs were also convicted.) Sometimes, when they had a huge mailing to send out for the Kenny Foundation—upwards of ten million pieces—they would simply take names out of telephone directories. Postmasters across the country began complaining to the Inspection Service about the undeliverability of Kenny Foundation mail that was pouring into their offices—35 per cent of it undeliverable in Portland, Oregon; 43 per cent in Allenton, Rhode Island; 50 per cent in Kelso, Washington; 58 per cent in Magadore, Ohio. Apparently the Koolishes had been using out-of-date phone books.

Not all the abuses in philanthropy involve national organizations, not all of them involve direct payments of cash, and not all are conducted on a scatter-shot basis. Some nefarious appeals are specifically geared to the needs of their recipients. In the case of companies that manufacture consumer goods, for instance, it has been demonstrated that their interest in charity can be heightened by fusing generosity with greed. Some wholesalers have recurrent trouble getting rid of merchandise that has been returned to them by jobbers or retailers because it is out of style, or slightly damaged, or falls short of standards of quality, or simply hasn't been selling. When they get this surplus stuff back, they can either write if off as a loss or sell it at salvage prices. Or, if they are lucky, they can give it away to an organization that has tax-exempt status and can take as a charitable deduction the full market value of the merchandise.

The fact that corporate gifts of products, while no doubt in most instances heartfelt, are sometimes prompted by practicality, and even by profit, is well known in the business circles where scruples are not known at all. The harassed Disabled American Veterans once made what seemed to be a nice arrangement with a Chicago entrepreneur named Harold G. Sager, who, conceivably because it had a more trustworthy ring, liked to do business as Colonel Harold S. McClintock, before he was convicted of mail fraud in 1967 and given a five-year probationary sentence. He would undertake to persuade corporations to donate products to the D.A.V., and the veterans' organization was to get 51 per cent of whatever he could dispose of it for. (The donors, naturally, would get a 100 per cent deduction.) What the D.A.V. did not realize was that the Colonel was selling everything at a ludicrously low price to an accomplice. The D.A.V. would thus get 51 per cent of precious little; Sager and the accomplice split the bulk of the proceeds from the final sales, and since some two million dollars' worth of goods was involved, they were handsomely rewarded for their efforts.

Much of this kind of philanthropy is perfectly aboveboard. In New York City, for instance, there has existed for some time the Medical and Surgical Relief Committee, Inc., which acts as an upright collector and forwarder of gifts from drug companies and surgical suppliers to hospitals and clinics in underdeveloped countries abroad. Drug companies, accordingly, are accustomed to being asked to perform good deeds with surplus wares, and in the spring of 1967, their executives to whom such requests are channeled had no reason to doubt the legitimacy of a letter that was sent to, among others, American Home Products, Wyeth Laboratories, Colgate-Palmolive, Merck Sharp & Dohme, and Pfizer. The communication was from the New York branch of the Social Security Foundation of the Philippines, and the letterhead bore the Philippine flag. On the left-hand side were the names of four directors (also tautologically identified as trustees) and three members of an advisory committee. The chairman of the board of directors was Robert A. Miguel, described as editor of the *Manila Times;* the first-named adviser was Bartolome A. Umayam, described as Consul General of the Philippines. Another adviser, unidentified, was Murray Roth, and the letter was signed "David Roth, Executive Director." The text of the communication gave every evidence of having been designed to be read by executives who didn't want to waste time. Following the salutation, it began, briskly, "No, we are not asking for money. But we do need your help. Help, incidentally, that offers your firm an interesting tax advantage." That was the first come-on. The letter went on to say that the Foundation had been started "under the auspices of President Marcos to bring improved health and educational facilities to underdeveloped regions of this staunchly anti-communist young nation." That, considering the presumed ideological orientation of most corporation executives, was the second come-on. So far, David Roth continued, the Social Security Foundation had been supported largely by one-peso-a-year donations from citizens of the Philippines, through whose magnanimity it had already been possible to put up two modern hospitals, five free clinics, and several food and clothing centers. What was needed now was merchandise—inventory overages, goods returned for credit, items that the addressee might be carrying at a loss, and so forth—and a deduction could of course be taken at market price. The Social Security Foundation, furthermore, would pay shipping expenses to the Philippines on all goods received. And there was yet another come-on: "Our board chairman, Mr. Robert A. Miguel, as editor of the Manila Times, the Philippines' largest newspaper, will graciously give recognition of all contributions made to the

New York Foundation in the Times."

Not everybody took the bait, and not everybody who nibbled at it swallowed it. After some exploratory negotiations with Roth, in the course of which he furnished the names of the three members of his medical staff in New York—a physician, a podiatrist, and a pharmacist, by his account—the Pfizer company wrote its representative in Tokyo that "we have checked this organization and they are bona fide in every respect," but nonetheless besought his views on the proposition. He replied that the pharmaceutical situation in Manila was a touchy one; fake drug items were being circulated there, and also some drugs that had been given as charity were finding their way to the market. He suggested that if the company wanted to make a contribution, it do so in the form of some of its products that were actually being processed in Manila. Pfizer dropped the matter. Merck made a token response to Roth's entreaty; it sent some Procasenol granules and a carton of Hypobeta-20, worth in all a mere $197.50. But there were more than a dozen other companies that did much better—or, as they may have later come to believe, much worse. The Ex-Lax people were good for $40,000 worth of merchandise. The Whitehall Laboratories sent in all more than $100,000 worth, including an $80,000 dose of Anacin. The reputable Medical and Surgical Relief Committee, which had no distribution outlet in the Philippines and was delighted to know that one was now available, turned over to Roth $200,000 worth of supplies it had collected.

The Colgate-Palmolive company started off as one of Roth's most avid benefactors, and ended up as one of his grimmest pursuers. It had more than a million bottles of surplus Respond hand lotion on its hands at the time it first heard from Roth, and he seemed an ideal conduit for its favorable disposition. If the company harbored any reservations about how so much hand lotion could conceivably be of use in the Philippines, Roth tried ingeniously to dispel them; he advised one Colgate man during the halcyon stage of their relationship that the Respond "would bring a great deal of comfort to many thousands of people, as well as to many hospital patients when it is used as a body lotion etc." Roth took one Colgate man to lunch at a midtown restaurant in New York and afterward, skipping his office—which was just as well, since he had no staff, medical or otherwise, and only rented desk space in a dowdy part of town—to a warehouse near the Hudson River, where he stored his goods until they could be shipped out. He had a space-available arrangement, he explained to the Colgate man, on all Philippine flag vessels. Colgate ended up by giving him about $500,000 worth of hand lotion, and in a letter of acknowledgment Roth sent the company on August 29, 1967 ("With many thanks again from the countless Philippine people your gifts will aid"), he suggested that he could also use dentifrices, tonics, shampoos, and talcs. He wondered, by the way, whether Colgate would mind if he sold some of its largess to help defray his inevitable operational costs. "Many donor companies," he explained, "have given the foundation permission to sell the donated products outside the continental United States, in markets which they themselves designate. This avoids any conflict with their own international division."

Before Colgate-Palmolive could digest and reply to that suggestion, it received some troubling intelligence from one of its international divisions. Even earlier, though then unknown to Colgate, the Medical and Surgical Relief Committee had begun to entertain doubts about Roth's bona fides. When it had given him its supplies in the first place, he had insisted on immediate delivery, on the ground that a ship was leaving for the Philippines in two days. Later, the Committee had heard that some of its wares were being sold, cut rate, on the open market in New York, and when it had sought a clarification from Roth, he had been devilish hard to reach; finally pinned down, he had denied everything and insisted that receipts would soon be forthcoming from the beneficiaries of the shipment in the Philippines, but that had been the last word from him. Not the last word, though. The Committee had written worriedly to the United States consul in Manila, and he had replied that there was no Social Security Foundation of the Philippines listed in the phone book there and that its existence was unknown to, among other Philippine agencies he had approached, the Social Security Commission, the Social Welfare Administration, the Bureau of Medical Services, and the Department of Health.

As for Colgate-Palmolive, its apprehensions were aroused by a cablegram from Stockholm on September 5. A large supply of Respond hand lotion, which should have brought forty cents a bottle in northern Europe, was being dumped there at seventeen cents a bottle, the Stockholm agent reported, and this could "seriously jeopardize existing Swedish franchise." Bewildered, Colgate's headquarters fired off an inquiring cable to its agent in Manila, and his response on September 11 was even more disquieting: "Social Security Foudation of Philippines unheard of and appears to be spurious group headed by unknowns. Registered with Securities and Exchange Commission but not registered with Social Welfare Administration as required by law before solicitations can be made. Names and addresses you have given as original incorporators with residential address in low and middle income areas. Miguel is not the editor of Manila Times. Group formed July 9, 1965 before Marcos elected. The one peso project also unheard of here. Lawyers making discreet inquiries. Would help if had names of hospitals and clinics. The individuals are not known by other businessmen. . . . The official you mentioned may be the same one eased out of former position due to serious anomalies."

On September 13, 1967, the Postal Inspection Service got a phone call from the general counsel of Colgate-Palmolive, inviting its attention to the puzzling affair. Under the direction of Inspector Walter S. Palmer, agents at once began looking into the Social Security Foundation. There was some confusion as to just who Roth was; he sometimes called himself Murray David Roth and sometimes David Murray Roth. At first, the Service compiled a dossier on a perfectly innocent and unrelated tax lawyer with a similar name, but it finally zeroed in on the right quarry. Roth was a pharmacist by trade, it turned out, who had been in trouble before. In 1965, he had been involved with a couple of outfits called Ethical Export and Import, Ltd., and City Wide Wholesalers, which sold physicians' samples and other drug products to stores and discount houses in New York and New Jersey; among the stuff they peddled were Miltown tablets manufactured in the Philippines and supposed to be sold there exclusively. Roth had also been connected with a committee that had solicited contributions of drugs to help the sick of Israel. The E. R. Squibb people had had an unhappy experience with *that* group; drugs that Squibb had thought were en route to Tel Aviv and Jerusalem had mysteriously turned up on the counters of cut-rate stores in Brooklyn and the Bronx.

In the fall of 1966, it developed, Roth had decided to strike out on his own, and had incorporated the New York Branch of the Social Security Foundation, "to solicit, collect, and otherwise raise money for charitable, philanthropic, eleemosynary, and benevolent purposes; to solicit, collect, and obtain donations of medical, pharmaceutical, and similar supplies and equipment for the use of the Social Security Foundation of the Philippines, etc." That lofty expression of intent had enabled him, on February 26, 1967, to obtain tax-exempt status from the Internal Revenue Service, and a salesman he used to peddle his drugs recalled to Inspector Palmer with what glee Roth had received his formal notification from the I.R.S. Waving it in the air, he had exclaimed, "Now I have a license to steal!" Palmer also paid an inquiring visit to the Philippine consulate in New York, but learned little there other than that its staff was horrified to hear that President Marcos had been associated with the dubious venture. More fruitful was a visit that a handful of Inspectors, armed with a search warrant, made to the warehouse where Roth stored his booty, none of it seemingly earmarked for shipment to Manila. Cached in the warehouse were thirty trailerloads of pharmaceutical products—35,000 cases of Respond among them—with a total retail value of about $2 million. Like Harold Sager, alias Colonel McClintock, of Chicago, Roth, it soon became known, had an accomplice to whom he sold his wares at dirt-cheap prices. Roth's accomplice, however, was an entity he had created himself, the South East Asia Trading Corporation. By the winter of 1968, there was enough evidence accumulated to have Roth indicted on mail-fraud charges, but before his scheduled trial in May the investigators felt they should nail down the case by getting some evidence and recruiting witnesses from the Philippines. So Inspector William J. O'Keefe, of the New York office, betook himself to Manila, where he learned, *inter alia,* that the only permit to solicit ever granted to the Social Security Foundation by the Social Welfare Administration was a limited one that had been applied for considerably after the investigation had begun back in the United States.

After Roth came to trial and was found guilty of four counts of mail fraud, he got off with a relatively light sentence—a year and a day in prison. The leniency accorded him was prompted by his pledge to his prosecutors that the drugs he had wangled out of the manufacturers would be turned over to the Jesuit Seminary and Mission Bureau in New York, and transmitted under its auspices to Manila. "It seems poetic justice," Inspector Palmer remarked in summarizing the case, "that this merchandise would finally be received in the Philippines." Heaven only knows—unless Heaven has shared its knowledge with its Jesuit liaison men—what was finally done with all that hand lotion.

# 19. It Takes Two to Make a Fraud

One might reasonably, and gloomily, infer from the preceding chapters that there are crooks who use the mails to defraud in just about every aspect of contemporary living—in business and finance, in philanthropy, in religion, in beautification, and in romance. Alas, that is quite true. It is no less true that there is a great deal of ongoing fraud that—much to the relief of the Postal Inspection Service—is not mail fraud. Misleading advertising, unscrupulous merchandising, spurious investment schemes, shady dealings in works of art—we hear of them almost every day. Happily, we are also hearing with increasing frequency about, and from, the deterrents our society now has against them: the Federal Trade Commission, the Pure Food and Drug Administration, the Securities and Exchange Commission, Ralph Nader, and a host of agencies on all levels of government set up to protect the consumer from himself.

With so many watchdogs prowling our national premises, how can so many crooks get away with so much? They can because you help them. The Department of Defense, unfortunately, has no Anti-Gullibility Division. It is very difficult to commit a fraud without a victim, and as long as people are greedy they will be gullible, and as long as they are gullible they can be assured that there are plenty of other people around willing and eager to exploit their gullibility, and immensely skilled in their techniques.

You are understandably vulnerable because, like most sensible persons, you are always looking for a bargain. Why not? But whereas you might laugh off the suggestion that you buy a brand-new Cadillac for one thousand dollars, on the logical ground that it would most probably be a stolen car, you might be far less prudent about spending smaller sums on items with no more substantial provenance.

How can you be your own watchdog? Well, whoever you are and wherever you live, you can try to remember to beware of Greeks bearing gifts, and also of Turks, Hungarians, Filipinos, Indonesians, Englishmen, Germans, Russians, Americans, and that terribly nice-looking man who professes a close acquaintance with the wealthy distant cousin you never quite knew you had. Smooth-talking strangers are rarely what they appear to be, and the fact that they have had something printed up seemingly to corroborate their assertions is by no means assurance of their respectability. Anybody can get a job printer to run up a letter or brochure. Anybody can advertise his wares and services.

Take, for example, the man who called himself, for the most part, Sri Dr. Abn Donahji—variously, the originator and sole proprietor of the Brmhayati Cosmic Law Foundation for Development of Body, Mind, and Soul; the operator of the Western Regional Headquarters (there were no others) of the Brmhayati Yogodic Society; a Marriage and Family Counselor specializing, according to an ad he placed in a classified telephone directory, in "Problem Clinic, National Association for Family Service, Continued Counselling, Individual and Group Therapy"; a cosmic healer; a clairvoyant; the patron of a Candle, Incense and Curio Shop whose hundred or so items included Come to Me Powder, Africa Bats' Heart, and Jinx Removing Salt; a psychic analyst; a stock market consultant; a Doctor of Spiritual Therapy on World and Personal Problems; a Doctor of Divinity; a Doctor of Philosophy; the publisher of the *Embracer News;* a sales representative for the Perma Placque Corporation; the pastor of the Church of

Divine Reliance; and, for short, The Prophet.

Would you trust a man like that? Perhaps not, but more than four thousand suckers all over the world did, enriching him by about fifty thousand dollars a year, until some Postal Inspectors revealed him to be a confidence man, originally from Des Moines, with the mundane name of Donald Wilson. Along with spiritual advice, he dealt in tangibles. He peddled "Yogi Psychic Bands," which he described as "a cosmic development order from the Valley of the Saints, India." There was a beginner, or Athama, variety, at eighteen dollars; an advanced, or Madhyama, variety, at thirty dollars; and a High Order, or Uttama, variety, at seventy-eight dollars. In fact, there was no detectable difference among any of the styles, all of which Wilson, who like most practitioners of his sort believed in high markups, bought from a Los Angeles wholesaler of plain copper bracelets for a dollar or two apiece.

Would you have bought one from Donahji? Maybe not. But hundreds of your fellow citizens did. Even so, he was a small-fry operator, and no doubt the majority of intelligent people would steer clear of him. Confidence men, however, operate on the well-founded assumption that not everybody is as smart as you are—and certainly not as smart as they are. The spiritual heir of Packy Lennon is around somewhere right now, you can be sure, and what he has going for him is that he is certain he can make you (or if not you, your neighbor) trust him implicitly. *Trust* him? You may decide that he is just about the most likable chap who ever crossed your lucky path, and once you have made that grievous mistake in judgment, he has got you where he wants you.

What can you do to avoid being mulcted, or simply embarrassed? For one thing, it wouldn't hurt to throw away all your second-class mail. For another, never invest in anything without first checking with someone you *know* to be trustworthy—a lawyer or broker of previous acquaintance or impeccable reputation. Your consultant may not be able to tell you whether a prospective investment is good or bad, but at least he can probably say if it's aboveboard. For still another, you might consider never giving any money to a stranger who appears at your door. There are perfectly bona-fide house-to-house salesmen of brushes and cosmetics, but for every one of them there is somebody else ringing a doorbell down the block and offering a sensational bargain in roof shingling or driveway paving.

What do you do if, in the words of the poor woman who bought an unsatisfactory wig, you think you have been tooken? Or if you have doubts about someone with whom you are on the verge of closing a deal? If you live in a large city, there may be a branch of the Better Business Bureau on hand, and if the person or organization you're suspicious of has been operating for any length of time, the Bureau will probably know about them and tell you what it knows. You will at least then be proceeding with your eyes open.

And you can always get in touch with the Postal Inspection Service. There is no part of the United States that some Inspector does not cover. If you can't readily find one, you can ask your local Postmaster. *He* will know where the nearest Inspector is; he may just have gone through an Inspection Service audit himself. You may be surprised to learn how much the Inspector already knows about the person you have doubts about.

Another good rule of thumb is to insist that anybody who wants to do business with you put what he has to say in writing and mail it to you. Anyone who is reluctant to use the mails probably has good reason for holding back: Whatever other charges he may be facing, he doesn't want to risk a mail-fraud indictment. Even so, as we have seen, an awful lot of criminals do use the mails. If they have been committing a fraud at your expense, and you want to help expedite their downfall, there is still one last thing to remember: Try to save all the mail they have sent you. Some detectives are gladdened by fingerprints, and others by bloodstains or spent bullets, but there is nothing that more warms the heart of a Postal Inspector preparing to submit a case for prosecution than a recognizably stamped and canceled envelope.

73 74 75 76 77 10 9 8 7 6 5 4 3 2 1